2 —

The Literary Use of
the Psychoanalytic Process

The Literary Use of the Psychoanalytic Process

MEREDITH ANNE SKURA

NEW HAVEN AND LONDON
YALE UNIVERSITY PRESS

Published with assistance from the foundation established in memory
of Philip Hamilton McMillan of the Class of 1894, Yale College.

Designed by John O. McCrillis and set in Baskerville type.
Printed in the United States of America by Edwards Brothers Inc.,
Ann Arbor, Mich.

Library of Congress Cataloging in Publication Data

Skura, Meredith Anne, 1944–
    The literary use of the psychoanalytic process.

    Includes index.
    1. Psychoanalysis and literature. 2. Criticism.
I. Title.
PN98.P75858   801'.92   80-23990
ISBN 0-300-02380-4
ISBN 0-300-03098-3 (pbk.)
10   9   8   7   6   5   4   3   2

Contents

Acknowledgments

I have tried to indicate as many specific debts as possible in the footnotes; the recent reexamination of "meaning" which stimulated this book, however, has stimulated much else, and I am indebted in many ways to a general climate of discussion about the complexities which I have here identified with the psychoanalytic process. To those whose influence has been of this more pervasive kind, I here give grateful if inadequate thanks. Apart from specifically intellectual debts I want especially to record my gratitude to the two people to whom my thinking in this book owes most, Jay Katz and Anne Few. The manuscript has also profited from the generously full and suggestive advice of Roy Schafer, Norman Holland, Margaret Ferguson, David Willbern, Rob Goble, and an unidentified reader at Yale Press, who have read it all. Others have read parts of it and helped me make the whole better: Henry Abelove, Harold Bloom, Geoffrey Hartman, Robert Litan, Arthur Marotti, Tom Morawetz, Martin Price, David Riggs, Elyse Snyder, Martin Wiener, and too many colleagues at Yale and at the Western New England Institute for Psychoanalysis for me to be able to identify them individually here. A grant from Yale in 1975–76 allowed me to begin work on the project. Lectures at Yale, at the Kanzer Seminar for Psychoanalysis and the Humanities, and at the California Institute of Technology gave me opportunities to try out portions of the manuscript. An earlier version of chapter 4 appeared in *The Literary Freud: Mechanisms of Defense and the Poetic Will*, Psychiatry and the Humanities, edited by Joseph Smith, volume 4 (New Haven: Yale University Press, 1980). Part of chapter 6 first appeared in *Boundary 2*, whose editor has kindly given permission to include the revised version here. Without the assistance of Roy Bird, along with Prudence Crewdson, Pamela Walker, and Elizabeth Alkaaoud, the manuscript would not have become a book. Finally I want to thank Marty for his patience—and everything else—during the process. And to end with the beginning, I want to thank my parents and to dedicate this book to my mother and the memory of my father.

1

Literature, Psychoanalysis, and the Psychoanalytic Process

Meaning is an affair of consciousness.
—E. D. Hirsch

What is related to consciousness only becomes comprehensible and explicable when the meaning behind it is plumbed.
—S. Ferenczi

Freud recommended that any young analyst include the study of literature as part of his training, and he himself drew on literary texts as illustration and inspiration for his "scientific" discipline. "The poets and philosophers discovered the unconscious before I did," he explained more than once.[1] Probably very few literary critics, however, would advise their young colleagues to make such direct use of psychoanalysis in their discipline. The poets may indeed share with the analysts a knowledge of the unconscious depths which the rest of us had avoided, but it is the poets' conscious control when they write which interests the critics. It is not clear what literary critics can learn from a field which is devoted, if not to the study of unconscious illness, as we once thought, at least to the study of the unconscious, which is the lowest common denominator of the mind—a field devoted to every-

---

1. For a list of Freud's (finally contradictory) references to what the poets discovered, see Norman Holland, *Psychoanalysis and Shakespeare* (New York: McGraw-Hill, 1964), pp. 1–44, and Jack J. Spector, *The Aesthetics of Freud: A Study in Psychoanalysis and Art* (New York: McGraw-Hill, 1974), pp. 33–145.

thing that seems farthest from consciously shaped art. How can the study of our common primitive heritage reveal anything about works whose very identity lies in their uncommon escape from mundane responses to experience?

One answer, of course, is that everything we understand about the way we think is helpful in understanding the way literature works. Every new discrimination we learn to make in observing our own thoughts or our exchanges with one another, every new alternative we become aware of as we study the given of what we have actually thought or said, makes us better and more responsive readers. And we can learn not only from the best and subtlest uses but from all uses of language; as we come to appreciate the variety of discourse, we better appreciate its excellences.

The most accurate reply, however, is that psychoanalysis is not merely the discovery of the unconscious. It is not dedicated solely to disease or symptoms or primitive experiences, but offers instead a theory and a method for studying how the whole mind works—for understanding another human being as he tries to describe his world in words and to draw on all his resources, both conscious and unconscious, in doing so. In fact the very identification of a so-called unconscious as a thing or a separate part of the mind existing unknown to us is misleading. It is the product of a falsely neat dichotomy between our rational, acceptable thinking (supposedly all conscious) and our irrational, primitive, and repressed thinking (supposedly all unconscious). Freud discovered that we are unaware of much that goes on in our minds and that indeed some of it has been willfully cast out of awareness, so that it does not easily return to consciousness, nor is it easily recognized when it does. Nonetheless, the quality of consciousness is not to be automatically assigned to a particular part of the mind or to a particular kind of thinking or even to a particular kind of thought. Freud himself later discarded the dichotomy of conscious and unconscious as an identification of parts of the mind and limited it to describing whether or not we are consciously aware of a particular thought, whatever that thought might be.[2]

Even limited this way to its proper, descriptive function, however, the dichotomy has led to a good deal of fruitless debate about the relative value of conscious and unconscious meanings in applying psychoanalysis to literature. It has polarized critics and analysts, so that on the one hand the critic E. D. Hirsch declares that "meaning is an affair of consciousness,"[3] and on the other, Sandor Ferenczi argues that the conscious meaning can only be understood once we have plumbed the depths of the unconscious meaning.[4] I shall argue, however, that there is no single neatly definable meaning of which we are directly and all-encompassingly conscious in all it manifestations, nor is there any such thing as a meaning of which we are totally unconscious. There are, rather, different ways of being aware of things and different aspects of a text which compel a certain kind of awareness. Rather than looking only for unconscious or conscious meaning, the analyst describes a whole range of what has been called "modes of consciousness," or modes of representation.[5] Rather than simply discovering the unconscious, Freud discovered the variety of ways in which we become aware of ourselves and our world and the means by which we represent both.

2. Sigmund Freud, "The Unconscious" (1915e), in *Standard Edition of the Complete Psychological Works of Sigmund Freud* (hereafter *SE*), vol. 14 (London: The Hogarth Press, 1953), pp. 172–76.

3. E. D. Hirsch, *Validity in Interpretation* (New Haven: Yale University Press, 1967), p. 22.

4. Sandor Ferenczi, "The Psychoanalysis of Wit and the Comical," in *Further Contributions to the Theory and Technique of Psychoanalysis*, comp. John Rickman, trans. Jane Suttie et al., 2d ed. (London: Hogarth Press, 1950), p. 335.

5. George S. Klein, "The Several Grades of Memory," in *Perception, Motives and Personality* (New York: Alfred A. Knopf, 1970), p. 303. Klein distinguished "modes of conscious experience" to discriminate between different ways in which past experience can be activated: as recall, as fantasy, as intellectual reconstruction, and so forth.

THE PSYCHOANALYTIC PROCESS: MODELS FOR CRITICISM

The first purpose of my argument is to show that other connections exist between Freud and the poets besides the fact that they discovered the unconscious before he did, and to suggest that therefore other connections exist between psychoanalysis and literary criticism. I shall argue that the poets discovered *psychoanalysis* before Freud did, and that at its subtlest and most wide-ranging, this is what Freud's legacy has in common with his literary predecessors. It is not the mere presence or expression of primitive and unconsciously apprehended elements but the attempt to come to terms with them and to work them into the texture of conscious experience that makes the poets the predecessors of Freud.

There are of course different ways of coming to terms with these elements. Freud's theorizing and his metapsychological essays were one way, a way to which, perhaps inevitably, literary critics with their interest in written texts have been most often drawn as a source for their criticism or as a measure for what psychoanalysis can contribute to literature. My own emphasis is not on the *theory* but rather on the *process* of psychoanalysis; as such it differs fundamentally from these earlier applications which are not concerned with the real difference between theory and practice. The theory consists of abstractions from the raw data of experience and psychoanalytic observation, and while of course the raw data cannot be completely separated from the theoretical instruments used to approach them, still, as I shall argue, the difference is impressive and has to be taken into account. We can feel it immediately as we turn from Freud's metapsychological essays to his case histories—or from the case histories themselves, which are edited and organized, to the process notes which he jotted down during Rat Man's analysis. The theory, as Freud himself warned, is only the top of the pyramid;[6] it is the most expendable and most easily reshaped part of psychoanalysis; it is no more a reliable representative of the whole than that

6. Sigmund Freud, "On Narcissism: An Introduction" (1914), *SE* 14:77.

other tip of the iceberg, consciousness, is a reliable indicator of what goes on in the mind.

My emphasis on process draws attention to psychoanalysis as a method rather than as a body of knowledge, as a way of interpreting rather than as a specific product or interpretation. I am interested in psychoanalysis not so much for what it reveals about human nature, or even about the particular human being presently on the couch, but for the way in which it reveals anything at all. A sensitivity to the delicate changes in consciousness taking place moment by moment in the actual process of an analytic hour can lead to a renewed awareness of the possibilities of language and narrative—an awareness that will increase our range of discriminations rather than reduce them to a fixed pattern, as the theory tends to do. The dynamic movement of the process brings us closer to what goes on in literature than the theory, with its rigid hypostatizations, can ever come.

My second purpose in the argument that follows is to examine representative samples of the different kinds of psychoanalytic literary criticism and to suggest that all of them ultimately derive, whether explicitly or not, from different aspects of the psychoanalytic process. It is true that all attempts to actually reproduce the psychoanalytic process must be to some degree makeshift ones. As Anna Freud said, the analyst is "tied to his own laborious and slow method"[7]—to the room, the regular hours, the free association, and the exchange between analyst and patient; and he no more sees without it than the bacteriologist, deprived of his microscope, sees bacilli with his naked eye. The literary critic can deal with this problem, however, the way the bacteriologist would have to—the latter may not have his microscope, but if he has had enough experience with microscopes he can probably detect traces of bacteria even without one and can tell something about what they are doing. In fact, since all data in psycho-

7. Anna Freud, *Normality and Pathology in Childhood: Assessments of Development* (New York: International Universities Press, 1965), p. 12.

analysis come ultimately from the clinical situation, critics have had to deal with this problem whether they realize it or not, even if they themselves refer only to the theory. What they have done in talking about literature, I shall suggest, is to draw on examples of psychoanalytic exchanges in the clinical situation; they have used as models for their texts phenomena like dreams, which have been described and defined in theoretical formulas but which present another face when they appear in the analytic situation, where they have been subjected to the slow, laborious—and far more dynamic—scrutiny which Anna Freud describes.

Even a quick survey of all the models used reveals the surprisingly overlooked fact that there are so many of them. There are a wide variety of activities called psychoanalytic criticism, and one of my main points in selecting models is that we need to determine more exactly which tools psychoanalysis offers before we can either accept or reject any of them as ways of understanding literature. It is important to define the differences between the models because, if used properly, each model can be, within its limits, at best a provocative stimulant to reseeing a text and, even at worst, a helpful supplementary study of interest to literary criticism. If we fail to recognize the differences, however, and ask the models to do the wrong things, they will not only disappoint but also mislead.[8]

I have chosen five models: the case history; the fantasy; the dream; the rhetorical exchange between analyst and patient; and the entire psychoanalytic process, which draws on all the others and which I shall suggest is the most promising for lit-

---

8. The models are treated differently by analysts themselves, who ask different questions about them and use different language to describe them. Analysts usually talk about the dream, for example, in terms of Freud's older "topographical" point of view, which looks for a conflict between conscious and unconscious ideas. But they usually discuss the daydream in terms of Freud's later "structural" point of view, which looks for conflict among id, ego, and superego elements. See, e.g., Bertram D. Lewin, "Phobic Symptoms and Dream Interpretation," *Psychoanalytic Quarterly* 21 (1952): 295–322.

erary criticism at the present time. I have omitted from consideration all purely biographical studies of the author and all psychoanalyses of individual eccentric readers, and I have left out as well comparisons of Freud's philosophy about life and love to that of the poets—though some of these are already subsumed in the models I have mentioned. Roland Barthes and René Girard, for example, take Freud's pseudoanthropological myth of the primal hoard and use it as a point of reference to interpret analogous events in literary texts, much as Northrop Frye uses the quest myth.[9] But Barthes and Girard, I would argue, are practicing a particularly specialized sort of fantasy analysis, taking as their model only one out of the many universal fantasies analysts have described. Again, I will suggest that both the joke and the parapraxis, which Victor Rosen[10] and others have on occasion suggested as models for discourse, are elementary forms of the psychoanalytic process and have been treated as such since Freud.

To a degree, of course, all such categories are arbitrary, and these are no exceptions. The models overlap, and distinctions may seem serendipitous without further explanation.

9. Roland Barthes finds the myth structuring Racine's plays; see "Racinian Man," in *On Racine*, trans. Richard Howard (New York: Hill and Wang, 1964), pp. 8–10. See also René Girard, *Violence and the Sacred*, trans. Patrick Gregory (Baltimore: Johns Hopkins University Press, 1977).

10. On jokes, see Victor Rosen, "Variants of Comic Caricature and Their Relationship to Obsessive-Compulsive Phenomena," *Journal of the American Psychoanalytic Association* 11 (1963): 704–25. On parapraxes, see Jacques Lacan, *Ecrits* (Paris: Editions du Seuil, 1966), pp. 379–80, 390, 477; and Anthony Wilden's commentary in his translation of Lacan's *The Language of the Self: The Function of Language in Psychoanalysis* (Baltimore: Johns Hopkins University Press, 1968), pp. 243–44, as well as Wilden's "Freud, Signorelli and Lacan . . . ," *American Imago* 23 (1966): 332–66. See also Rosen, "Sign Phenomena and Their Relation to Unconscious Meaning," *International Journal of Psychoanalysis* 50 (1969): 197–207 ("Finding the meaning of a parapraxis is the paradigm of the process by which we arrive at most interpretations in the analytic process"). See also Jean G. Schimek, "The Parapraxis Specimen of Psychoanalysis," in *Psychoanalysis and Contemporary Science: An Annual of Integrative and Interdisciplinary Studies* 3 (New York: International Universities Press, 1974), pp. 210–30.

Does it matter whether we call a joke a sophisticated form of dream or an elementary kind of psychoanalytic insight? I think it does. I have selected these models not only because they happen to be used most often in literary criticism, but also because they define the different dimensions of the material being analyzed and the different approaches to interpretation which each has generated, both in the analytic situation and in literary criticism.

In part, the relationship among the models is a historical one; as taken up here, they roughly represent a chronological evolution in Freud's thinking. Though it is not possible to isolate and define exact states in Freud's thought, it is nevertheless clear that the first—and in some sense presiding—model for Freud's activity was the case of the hysteric, based on the whole person, or rather on the whole disturbed person. His first psychoanalytic studies, from the early 1890s, were analyses of people, not phenomena, published in *Studies on Hysteria* (1893–95). These naturally led Freud next to become interested in certain recurring phenomena from the cases, particularly in the role of daydreams and other fantasies in hysteria. His letters and papers during the 1890s return to the subject,[11] although his important recognition that *fantasies* about seduction, rather than actual memories, lay at the core of his patients' illnesses did not come until 1897. Meanwhile Freud had begun *The Interpretation of Dreams* (not published, however, until 1900), in which he worked out a theory of dreams that took for granted and built on his thinking about daydreams and fantasies.

The psychoanalytic process, unlike the case history, the fantasy, and the dream, was almost never chosen by Freud as a subject for investigation per se, but rather forced itself on his attention gradually and indirectly when he found that his

---

11. E.g., Freud's letters to Fliess on May 2, May 16, and May 25, 1897, the last including his "Draft M"; the famous letter to Fliess on September 21, 1897, in which he admitted doubts about the reality of the seduction scenes his patients had described; "Screen Memories" (1899), *SE* 3:301–22.

therapeutic procedure was not working. As first his interest in the process of analysis seemed merely pragmatic and tangential to his main goal, but it eventually took its place at the heart of psychoanalysis. In fact, the whole history of psychoanalysis may be seen as a record of modifications in Freud's technique. Psychoanalysis began, Freud said, only when he stopped trying to hypnotize his patients and asked them instead to talk. It evolved only as his attention became diverted more and more from the supposed goal of the process—recovering the repressed material—and focused more and more on the process of recovery itself. Scrutiny of the psychoanalytic process, however, did not receive full attention until after Freud's death.

I suspect that this chronological relationship is based on another one, however, and that the models developed in this order because they emerged from a gradual movement away from the search for what "really happened" in a patient's life. They depend on Freud's movement away from the referential to other aspects of a patient's discourse—in particular, to its intrapsychic function (in fantasies); to its mode of representation (in dreams); and to its rhetorical or interpsychic function (in the psychoanalytic exchange).

Freud was at first interested only in the referential aspect of what his patients were telling him. In other words, what was the patient's real life story, and how could it be explained? Freud's unique contribution was to insist on explaining one part of the story by another—today's symptom by yesterday's trauma—instead of evoking external physiological explanations as the traditional psychiatrist would have done in the 1890s. Nonetheless, his expectations were extraordinarily literal; a symptom was not so much a mental symbol as a souvenir of past experience—and one more like a photograph than a personal impression. When Freud discovered that Frau Cäcilie's neurotic facial pains developed because she felt that she had a "slap in the face," he did not stop searching until he found an actual memory of a real slap.

"Symbolism seems to be reduced to secondary importance," he said, "as is no doubt the general rule."[12]

When he talked about fantasies, however, Freud did see more than a literal mimetic representation of a real past event. He found that fantasies served a function in the psychic economy; they created a psychic reality which broke away from the reality principle in order to fulfill wishes or to allay fears. He found too that fantasies were often expressed in a kind of natural language of symbolism and exaggeration which corresponded to the newly discovered psychic reality.

Then, in his book on dreams, while still keeping the referential and functional aspects in mind, Freud turned to still another aspect of his patients' productions when he examined the dream's bizarre language and means of representation: the "dream-work." Dreams are even further than fantasies from a simple reference to a literal external world, because they defy not only the reality principle but also the ordinary means for representing reality. Unlike the fantasy, the dream is not even a picture of psychic reality, but only a cryptically coded version of it.

Next, in turning his attention to the psychoanalytic exchange in which the patient's story emerges, Freud was interested not only in its content, the way that content functioned in the patient's own psychic economy, and the strange way it may have been being represented, but also in the social or rhetorical effect of what was being said. He saw the narrated events as acts which did something to or had some effect on the listening analyst, rather than as representations of any external reality.

Freud thus moved away from the referential significance of what his patients said, and when the literary critic applies these first four models to literary texts he shows a corresponding movement away from the realistic surface—though not a final indifference to it. Before going on to describe the

    12. Freud, "Fraulein Elisbeth von R.," *Studies on Hysteria* (1893–95), *SE* 2:179.

last model, I want to distinguish my use of these four models from another sort of psychoanalytic interpretation familiar in some psychoanalytic biography and unmasking. In such an interpretation the analyst strips away the surface of *Hamlet* as we know it—just as Freud stripped away the surface of a dream to expose a previously unguessed-at latent or unconscious meaning behind the play (or "under" it). Instead, I am suggesting that we see the relation between manifest and latent meanings as a relation between two different ways of organizing or looking at the perfectly visible surface of a dream—or of *Hamlet*. The analyst is a connoisseur of strange relations, not between conscious and unconscious, but between different modes of consciousness which work both together and against each other in shaping each aspect of the material: what it refers to, how it functions psychically, how it is represented, and how it functions rhetorically in the context of the analytic hour.

Finally, taken together, these four models suggest a more encompassing one—the whole psychoanalytic process in which each has a role—and this is the last model I will consider. The intense but uncritical scrutiny of what is being said in the process provides a "laboratory of the humanities," as M. Masud Khan has called it, where we can study not only the dynamic play in each aspect of the material, but also the dynamic play among these aspects—so that the analyst finds, for example, that the patient's insistent *reference* to florid sexual experiences is being used to cover a less obvious *function* of his anecdotes as a means of avoiding talk about his bill.

The psychoanalytic process is a very special kind of laboratory, of course, one which changes what it studies by the way it studies it—and here I return to my suggestion that it was something like psychoanalysis, not the naked unconscious, which the poets discovered. The complex ways in which literary texts elaborate and call attention to the play of consciousness have no parallel in simpler phenomena like fantasies and dreams which turn up in the course of an analysis. But they do have a parallel in the way that these phenomena are handled in analysis—in the moments of integration and insight about them which characterize the psychoanalytic process. The process promises to provide a more subtle and more appropriate model, which considers art not as neurosis or symptom or dream but as the dynamic movement toward self-conscious wholeness that encompasses phenomena like these.

I should add here a note about the relation between the notions of text and interpretation in these models, since each of these terms has acquired more or less figurative force as it has been transferred to psychoanalysis from its original usage in literary criticism, and the resulting ambiguity is multiplied in an interdisciplinary study like this one. I have identified each of the models by naming the "text" it is associated with—the case history, the fantasy, the dream, the process of psychoanalysis. Within psychoanalysis itself, the first two models, the case history and the fantasy, were in fact historically defined in this way by the material being analyzed: a whole life in the first case and a special kind of fiction in the second. The two later models, however, have emerged in the psychoanalytic context at least as much from definitions of the method of interpretation as from definitions of what is being interpreted. Of course, both the dream and the psychoanalytic process can also be seen as referential texts like the case history and the fantasy, but each has in fact been discussed primarily in terms of the special methods needed for interpreting it. The title of Freud's *Interpretation of Dreams*, as he himself pointed out, makes clear his special emphasis on the act of interpretation rather than on the thing itself;[13] and in the last model, the psychoanalytic process, the interpretation and the thing interpreted are impossible to separate.

My aim in identifying the models by text rather than process was first of all to establish the model as a model for the literary text itself, and not for the act of interpretation. This is true even in the case of the rhetorical exchange model which parallels conflicting organizations of the text itself instead of

13. Freud, *The Interpretation of Dreams* (1900), *SE* 4:96, and *SE* 5:510–11.

serving as a model for a potential critic-analyst working on a text-patient. This confusion itself, between text and interpretation—between what is "in" the text and what is being imported from outside, or between what is the "text" and what is the "reader's response"—is very much related to changing concepts of interpretation in both literature and psychoanalysis which the psychoanalytic process is uniquely suited to explore.

PSYCHOANALYSIS: BACKGROUND OF THE MODELS

This book's emphasis on the fluidity and dynamic qualities of psychoanalysis should have become clear by now. Epitomized in Freud's own inconsistencies and most of all in the psychoanalytic process itself, psychoanalysis is a dynamic discipline, not a formulaic one, though it has often been reduced to formulas by both analyst and literary critic. I have already hinted that I find one source of this reductionism to be too heavy a dependence on psychoanalytic theory rather than practice, and I have implicitly contrasted the clinical use of these models with the theories about them. In each case an original formulaic theory about the model has been healthily modified by the actualities of the clinical situation, so that each model has evolved into something more responsive to the dynamics we see in practice, rather than remaining a static category. Even the psychoanalytic process itself was first described in a theoretical formula which limited it to cathartic recall, but it turned out to be much more alive and complicated. These changes have kept all the models alive and workable, and have been responsible for the fact that none of them has disappeared, even though interest has generally shifted toward the kind of interpretation implied by the later ones.

Nonetheless I come back momentarily to the topic of psychoanalytic theory because the very fact of the tension between theory and practice is important to psychoanalysis and to any applications of it. As Freud himself reminds us, psychoanalysis is simultaneously a therapy, a theory of the mind, and a method of investigation. The theory alone, the "meta-psychology," came to include five distinct "points of view," or ways of explaining experience: the dynamic (what is struggling for expression and what is repressing it?); the economic (what is the distribution of energy?); the genetic (which phases of childhood are playing roles?); and the adaptive.[14] None of these, Freud cautioned, is adequate in itself to explain the mind's "extraordinary intricacy."[15] Nor can they be reduced to one another, any more than Aristotle's four causes can be condensed. The play between these different aspects of psychoanalysis is one source of the difficulties in applying it to literature; but this play is also a source of strength in psychoanalysis, allowing it somewhat contradictorily to keep in touch with so many aspects of the contradictory human beings—and human stories—it studies. The relationship of these aspects is worth examining briefly here, though of course it cannot be fully explored, because it is a source of some of the confusion about what psychoanalysis is and how the psychoanalytic models can be used.

Even limiting consideration to Freud's own writings, as literary critics have tended recently to do, the variety of interpretations is indeed striking. We have had many Freuds. The Americans who were first revolted by Freud's interest in sex nonetheless soon came to see him as someone who might finally explain the mysteries of creativity.[16] Lionel Trilling

14. Freud discussed only the dynamic, topographical, and economic points of view. See *The Psychopathology of Everyday Life* (1901b), *SE* 6:258–59; and "The Unconscious" (1915e), *SE* 14:181, for Freud's references to the term itself. The genetic point of view was added by Heinz Hartman, Ernst Kris, and Rudolf Loewenstein, and the point of view of adaptation by David Rapaport and Merton Gill. See, e.g., their essay "The Points of View and Assumptions of Metapsychology," *International Journal of Psychoanalysis* 40 (1959): 153–62.

15. Freud, "Repression" (1915d), *SE* 14:157.

16. For Freud's early reception in America, see Claudia C. Morrison, "The American Reaction to Freud," in *Freud and the Critic: The Early Use of Depth Psychology in Literary Criticism* (Chapel Hill: University of North Carolina Press, 1968).

has described a liberal Freud,[17] and Philip Rieff, a moralist,[18] both during the period when American "ego psychologists" had begun to make him into a rigorous scientist.[19] The English built a new version of psychoanalysis from hints in Freud and discarded the rest, stressing preoedipal experience and "object relations" rather than instincts, as Freud had.[20] The most recent images of Freud have come from France: the religious Freud emerging from Paul Ricoeur's theological studies[21] or, more conspicuously, Jacques Lacan's semiotician Freud, whose main discovery, Lacan says, was the bar between signifier and signified,[22] and finally Jacques Derrida's philosopher Freud, whose real discovery was *différance*[23] —and the paradoxes of priority Derrida explores.

There has been an accompanying confusion about what Freudian analysis looks for in a text, from reductions to deconstructions, and again, the variety is striking. Freud has been invoked in the search for sex, or for instincts and wishes in general; for emotions, to counteract "anesthetic" criticism;

17. Lionel Trilling's two early and influential essays are the well-known "Art and Neurosis" (1945) and "Freud and Literature" (1940); the latter is still one of the best introductions to the subject. Both essays are included in Trilling's *The Liberal Imagination: Essays on Society and Literature* (1950; reprint ed., New York: Anchor Books, 1953).

18. Philip Rieff, *Freud: The Mind of the Moralist* (New York: Viking Press, 1959).

19. The "ego psychologists"—associated with Heinz Hartman, Ernst Kris, Rudolf Loewenstein, and others—tried to extend Freud's purely economic theory of the mind so that it could account for the ego's *un*conflicted activity, as well as for conflicts between the ego and the id. They have stimulated recent criticism from the French analytic school.

20. E.g., Melanie Klein, Michael Balint, W. R. D. Fairbairn, Paula Heimann, and Hanna Segal.

21. Especially Paul Ricoeur's *Freud and Philosophy: An Essay on Interpretation*, trans. Denis Savage (New Haven: Yale University Press, 1970).

22. Jacques Lacan, "L'Instance de la lettre," published in English as "The Insistence of the Letter in the Unconscious," trans. Jan Miehl, in *Structuralism*, Yale French Studies 36/37 (1966) : p. 136.

23. Jacques Derrida, "Freud and the Scene of Writing," trans. Jeffrey Mehlman, in *French Freud: Structural Studies in Psychoanalysis*, Yale French Studies 48 (1972): p. 87.

for some primitive, raw, irrational force, whether demonic or divine; and most recently, for linguistic complexities. Criticism of Freud has often been criticism of different things: the search for the oedipal complex which bored Stanley Edgar Hyman in 1949; for oral and anal impulses, of which, Geoffrey Hartman complained more recently, we have had enough; or for various forms of what Jacques Lacan has called "imaginary" interpretation and Frederick Crews has now rejected as "allegorizing of a particularly silly kind." ("Falstaff and Heathcliff are not the id," as W. J. Harvey said in an attempt to protect literature from psychoanalysts; "Mr. Knightly is not the superego.")[24]

Of course some of this confusion can be explained by indiscriminate or piecemeal borrowings from Freud. His writings encourage such rummaging. His formulations, even the titles of his essays, have taken on life of their own, not as psychoanalytic, but almost as poetic, touchstones: the "Oedipus complex," the "family romance," or "defense mechanisms" hardly sound Freudian any longer; we seem always to have talked about civilization and its discontents or about what lies beyond the pleasure principle. Freud's individual formulations were boldly simple ("Every dream is the fulfillment of a wish"), even epigrammatic ("We fall in love so as not to become ill"). The evidence of the whole canon, however, does not support the borrowing which its language lures us into.

Freud's statements are not a series of independent pronouncements. When they are isolated from their context, they lose their validity as "complex" words and phrases, to use William Empson's term. We cannot evoke "the return of the

---

24. Stanley Edgar Hyman, *The Armed Vision: A Study in the Methods of Modern Literary Criticism* (New York: Vintage Books, 1955), p. 160; Geoffrey Hartman, "I. A. Richards and the Dream of Communication," in *The Fate of Reading and Other Essays* (Chicago: University of Chicago Press, 1975), pp. 20–40; Frederick Crews, "Out of My System," in *Out of My System: Psychoanalysis, Ideology and Critical Method* (New York: Oxford University Press, 1975), p. 166; W. J. Harvey, "The Attack on Character," in *Character and the Novel* (Ithaca, N.Y.: Cornell University Press, 1965), p. 210.

repressed" or "the repression of repression" to explain behavior, any more than we can explain one of Shakespeare's clown scenes by invoking "comic relief." Instead we have to ask, "What *is* 'repression'—*here*? What does it mean in the previous paragraph?" His statements have to be understood in the context of his evolving definitions which, for example, transform "wish" into its opposite, even within the boundaries of a single essay (see chapter 4).

Nor can Freud's scattered and often contradictory statements be smoothly recombined out of context into new syllogisms to elaborate his theory. "If desire is primarily sex, and sex is originally and fundamentally incestuous, then . . . ," begins one literary critic in an attempt to demonstrate the reductiveness of Freud's supposed definition of desire in character.[25] But if anything is clear from the spirit of Freud's writing, it is that there are no such definitional necessities governing all behavior. Freud could discover odd truths in certain cases precisely because all behavior works according to its own logic, so that desire can be incestuous and yet, by virtue of the mind's strange twists, not seem so. Freud's statements are examples of the sort of probing we need to do, *not* of the absolute truths we will find in all cases. Were there such truths, no one would need analysis. If Freud teaches us anything, it is not that "desire is primarily sex," but that we never know what desire is, or what sex is—and that in fact there may be involutions in which, as Otto Fenichel found, the patient's sexual activity is a disguise for his fear of sex.[26]

All these confusions, however, are only symptoms of the real tension inherent in psychoanalysis itself, even when taken as a whole. Freud was simply not consistent, and there is no way around the fact that if we go back to Freud to support a theory of psychoanalysis, we will find only contradictory support. "Je ne suis pas un Freudiste," Freud is reported

25. Leo Bersani, *A Future for Astyanax: Character and Desire in Fiction* (Boston: Little, Brown, 1976), p. 42.

26. Otto Fenichel, *Problems of Psychoanalytic Technique*, trans. David Brunswick (New York: Psychoanalytic Quarterly, 1941), p. 59.

to have said in his last conversation with Theodore Reik, and indeed his statements were part of a continual reworking of certain problems rather than refinements of a constant position. "The best way of understanding psychoanalysis," he said in 1922, is "by tracing its origin and development,"[27] and that remains true today. Analysts still go back to his writings for instruction, not because they can find isolated directives and follow them literally, but rather because Freud's continually shifting formulations define constant underlying areas of concern. In fact, the earliest essays, long superseded as textbooks even by Freud's own later writing, are among the most instructive, because there he is struggling to define those concerns and to find a new language to use in discussing them.

So long as Freud was alive, psychoanalysis was unified in the sense that only what *he* did was called analysis; he simply discarded the rest. After Freud's death, the tension in his thought became increasingly apparent as researchers, both disciples and revisionists, developed their own versions of psychoanalysis. It is these different approaches to psychoanalysis which interest me here; I do not wish to take sides in any attempt to find the "other" Freud or the "real" Freud and restore him to himself by taking him away from someone else. I simply want to note that differences exist and have existed for some time, attracting little comment; though now they are more frequently the focus of both literary and psychoanalytic attention. In the midst of conflicting claims about psychoanalysis, we come closest to the truth by admitting that it is, at least at present, defined by conflicting descriptions.

The tension between theory and practice—or within theory itself—is only one of several lively tensions within psychoanalysis, and I want to mention a second and a third which must be taken into account before we can go on to apply psychoanalytic interpretive models to literature. The second is as per-

---

27. Sigmund Freud, "Two Encyclopedia Articles," Part A, "Psychoanalysis," *SE* 18:235.

manently a part of psychoanalysis as the tension between theory and process, and it is inherent in the very attempt to explain behavior and see its various aspects as functions of one another: this is the tension between two different ways of seeing the *logical status* of psychoanalytic statements. The third is just as central and even more germane to the actual practice of psychoanalytic interpretation, but it is perhaps easier to deal with because it concerns the *content* of psychoanalytic statements and promises to be resolvable as a psychoanalytic investigators learn more about the way the mind works. Both tensions raise the question at the heart of all psychoanalytic inquiry: What is the relation between our motives and the meaning of our experience?

The second tension, the debate about logical status, derives as usual from Freud. He was a scientist, and he saw experience from the outside, like a physicist observing the movements of particles, looking for the causes and effects of movement and describing them in external terms. But he also saw it from the inside and looked for the significance of even the most "meaningless" symptom to the person who was experiencing it: his concern for the patient's phenomenology revolutionized nineteenth-century psychiatry. Freud was trying to create a "scientific psychology,"[28] but his essays, as most readers have felt, more closely resemble those of a biographer, mythographer, historian, or philosopher.

This double vision generates inevitable conflict, and analysts after Freud have often found it useful to simplify matters by ignoring one or the other of his aims. The ego psychologists got caught up in a particularly limiting effort to be scientific; but recent semioticians have adopted a phenomenology which may be equally destructive to the original vital-

---

28. The proposed title for his early physiologically based attempt to explain mental behavior as neurologically determined was "Project for a Scientific Psychology" (1950a [1895])—a study which many now see as shaping the rest of his psychological theories, if only implicitly. See, e.g., Ernst Kris's introduction to Sigmund Freud, *The Origins of Psychoanalysis: Letters to Wilhelm Fliess* (New York: Basic Books, 1954).

ity of Freud's system. For it was Freud's unique promise to reconcile the two visions. He is known as the man who put sex at the center of life, but in fact he put dreams at the center—or rather, he made the two inseparable. The dream book is based on that single disconcerting assumption that we fulfill our wishes not by acting on them directly but by dreaming and by symbolic behavior. Freud's method promises, as Paul Ricoeur has said, to show how "the vicissitudes of instincts can be attained only in the vicissitudes of meaning"[29] and therefore how we may better understand the meanings we discern in the world and in literature by paying more attention to our motives. Or, to expand Ricoeur's statement in light of the whole metapsychology, Freud promised to link the sources and function of our experience with its meaning for us.

The tension between extrinsic and intrinsic explanation makes itself felt in Freud's terminology and in the problematic status of explanations phrased in his terms. The problem is apparent in Freud's borrowing from medicine to describe psychology—as in his description of "trauma." It is, however, most obvious in the vocabulary borrowed from physics to explain the mind's economy. One difficulty with this vocabulary is by now familiar enough—a result less of its being drawn from science than of its being drawn from a positivist science intended to describe concrete objects. The trouble, of course, is that mental experiences are not physical entities which can be moved about, measured out in discrete quantities, or adequately described in terms of energy flows.

They do, however, *feel* as if they could be, and the real ambiguity in Freud's system arises only when we recognize a second and more formidable trouble with such a vocabulary: not that it fails to explain mental experience, but that it fits all too well and provides a metaphor we find only too natural. The physics is really a phenomenology: it is our everyday

29. Recoeur, *Freud and Philosophy*, p. 6.

mythology raised to a science.[30] The myth is latent not only in Freudian neologisms like *cathexis*, *libido*, and *fixation*, but even in the most basic metaphors of his system, the ones that take the mind to be a space, ideas to be things, and emotions to be substances which can be dammed up or can overflow.[31] *Repression* and *sublimation*, after all, are the fates of liquids and gases. Or take the term *incorporation*, the mental act in which someone models himself after another person, feeling as if he had taken the other inside himself in some primitive oral, visual, or anal devouring. Roy Schafer has objected that incorporation is the fantasy accompanying such influence and not an explanation of it.[32] Analysts ought to be able to find some other way to describe what is going on besides saying "the patient ate his father," in Latinate vocabulary.

Schafer is not alone. The most energetic revisionists among the analysts today often focus on Freud's terminology as the source of the problem. Jacques Lacan, with his emphasis on language, preceded Schafer's more American emphasis on action, but both are making the same effort to rid psychoanalytic language of its reifications and metapsychological dinosaurs. Lacan and Schafer represent two poles of psychoanalysis and are as far apart in their view of man as structuralist and existentialist can be. But they share a concern for concentrating on the patient's words and implications and for avoiding hidden forces and substances lying behind them.

30. On myth and anthropomorphism in Freud's theory, see W. Grossman and B. Simon, "Anthropomorphism—Motive, Meaning and Causality in Psychoanalytic Theory," in *Psychoanalytic Study of the Child*, vol. 24 (New York: International Universities Press, 1969), pp. 78–111. On phenomenology, see Roy Schafer, *A New Language for Psychoanalysis* (New Haven: Yale University Press, 1976).

31. See, e.g., Schafer, *A New Language*.

32. Roy Schafer, *Aspects of Internalization* (New York: International Universities Press, 1969), which distinguishes introjection, identification, incorporation, internalization, and learning (see, e.g., definitions, pp. 13ff., to begin with). A similar objection has also been made by Jacques Derrida in "Fors" (an unpublished lecture on Wolfman).

Both see the analyst's translation of the patient's words into metapsychological terms as collusion with his illness.

However, the question is not merely one of inadequate vocabulary, but a much larger one about the status of psychoanalytic explanation: Is it explanation, or is it merely a parallel version of the experience it claims to explain—or, even more disturbing, a derivative version? Analysts have long been aware that Freud's vivid metaphors may merely restate mental experience, including the neurotic's fantasies. Edward Glover warned that one danger of an inexact interpretation using such terms is that the patient can adopt it as a satisfactory substitute for his original fantasy.[33] Tell a man that his passive sexual desires are really wishes to be fed by a masculine woman, and even if this is not the real explanation, it will perhaps "cure" the original fantasy by replacing it. Otherwise, how did all those people "get well" when their analysts offered them now-outmoded interpretations about birth traumas?

Some analysts have suggested that it is only a step from seeing inexact interpretation this way to seeing all psychoanalytic interpretation this way. Jean Laplanche and J. B. Pontalis, for example, have claimed that Freud's theories about infantile development (and the interpretations based on them) are really only restatements of infantile fantasies.[34] These fantasies, several analysts have claimed, not only fulfill wishes but actually themselves, in fact, resemble theories already.[35] A patient's symptoms can seem as alien to him as if they had been

33. Edward Glover, "The Therapeutic Effect of Inexact Interpretation: A Contribution to the Theory of Suggestion," *International Journal of Psychoanalysis* 12 (1931): 397–411. Critics of "Kleinian" analysis object that its explanations are fantasies themselves and work in just this way.

34. Jean Laplanche and J. B. Pontalis, "Fantasy and the Origins of Sexuality," *International Journal of Psychoanalysis* 49 (1968): 1–18.

35. See Heinz Kohut, *The Analysis of the Self: A Systematic Approach to the Psycho-analytic Treatment of Narcissistic Personality Disorders* (New York: International Universities Press, 1971); Laplanche and Pontalis, "Fantasy and the Origins of Sexuality"; Roy Schafer, "Mechanisms of Defense," *International Journal of Psychoanalysis* 49 (1968): 49–68.

commanded by a posthypnotic suggestion instead of by his own unconscious thought; his fantasies try to make sense of the symptoms. Like the victim of posthypnotic suggestion, the patient makes up an ad hoc explanation for what he is feeling: Little Hans at first no more understood his street phobia (he was afraid of horses) than his parents did, but he tried to explain it by linking it to fantasies about staying home to "coax" with his mother. Similarly, the oedipal child, upset by his own violent feelings, makes up a story blaming everything on somebody else ("I didn't know it was wrong!" or "My mother seduced *me!*"). Freud mistook these rationalizations, says Pontalis, for scientific explanations. It almost sounds as though Lévi-Strauss was correct in calling psychoanalysis a form of shamanism in which a medicine man simply substitutes a privileged myth for the sickman's private and eccentric confusion,[36] though there are, as we shall see, other ways of identifying the problem.

The collapse of metapsychological terms into merely descriptive or even derivative language—the fact that psychoanalytic explanantions do not explain in the way Freud meant them to—has been attributed to psychological factors by Schafer: analysts, like all people, tend to think in these terms, and they have trouble escaping the conditions of their own thought processes unless they work at it; Lacan attributes these difficulties in terminology to more fundamental linguistic necessities: language has rules, conditions, and implications of its own which are not in the control of the individual who uses it. And Derrida points to an even more basic logical—or grammatological—impossibility: the idea that one set of terms like those in Freud's metapsychology can explain another set which is supposedly derivative.

Whatever the explanation, the important fact is that the status of psychoanalytic statements is ambiguous, even within

36. Claude Lévi-Strauss, "The Effectiveness of Symbols," in *Structural Anthropology*, trans. Claire Jacobson and Brooke Schoept (New York: Doubleday/Anchor, 1967), pp. 181–202. See Wilden's comment on Lévi-Strauss's statement, in *The Language of the Self*, p. 231.

psychoanalysis itself. The tension between description and explanation will become particularly important in the model of the case history, where we will first raise the important question of the difference between psychoanalysis *of* literature and psychoanalysis in literature. This is not only a matter of confusing a representation of character with a diagnosis of character, but more fundamentally of confusing symbolic and discursive modes of consciousness and representation. Failure to recognize the tension can lead to reductive views of people, of texts, and of the relation between psychoanalyst and critic. If we take the tension into account, instead of trying to do away with it, however, it can become the "seminal ambiguity" which Herbert Fingarette saw giving life to psychoanalysis.[37]

The third and equally fertile ambiguity I want to mention here arises because psychoanalysis is changing to accommodate a growing body of data not only about "normal" neurotic adults but also about less familiar people like children, psychotics, and members of primitive societies. Psychoanalysis is moving outward from Freud's original concern with instinctual conflict (the definition of neurosis) to a much more general psychology of human development and experience. The more general concerns were always present in Freud's work, but he consistently maintained that "repression is the cornerstone of my theory,"[38] and he continued to look for the final explanation of human behavior in a battle between wish and repression. His implicit model for all experience was the one he had first taken from pathology: the model of neurotic hysteria, in which the symptom is caused by a repressed wish returning in distorted form, and instinctual conflict is the main determinant of behavior.

The movement toward a general psychology, by contrast,

---

37. Herbert Fingarette, "The Seminal Ambiguity of Psychoanalysis, " in *The Self in Transformation: Psychoanalysis, Philosophy and the Life of the Spirit* (New York: Basic Books, 1963).

38. Freud, "On the History of the Psychoanalytic Movement" (1914), *SE* 14:16; "Freud's Psychoanalytic Procedures" (1904 [1903]), *SE* 7:251.

has included two related shifts in emphasis—toward the earliest stages of development and toward the totality of experience rather than the instincts alone. The English school of psychoanalysis, in particular, has insisted on separating the fact that we suffer conflict from the fact that we have gone through various primitive stages of development, some of whose effects are naturally at odds with our current experience. As the child matures, he develops new ways of seeing himself and the word, building on the old ones and working against them in an interplay much more complicated than the battle between wish and defense which Freud had described. If we no longer indulge our oral wishes in original form, this is not necessarily because we have repressed them but at least partly because we have transformed them and replaced them with alternatives. When Freud called attention to the irrationality of everyday life, he explained it by referring to a collection of isolated, repressed, unconscious ideas; more recently analysts have begun to explain it by referring to other modes of consciousness at work.

Now when analysts look to the past, they look not only to past instinctual battles but to a whole global experience or mode of consciousness in which instinct and control were not fully separated from perception, cognition, and the child's relation to people around him. The battle between wish and defense—the cornerstone of Freud's psychoanalysis—is now seen to be only part of a larger experience. As W. R. D. Fairbairn has said, "The wish is not a kick in the pants administered out of the blue to a surprised ego, but somebody's impulse to do something to something or somebody."[39] The "oral stage" is not only a world of eating but a time of "oral greed" or "oral merging" in whole scenes where what the mouth does is merely a focus or symbol for the whole experience.[40] When Freud kept finding self-serving fantasies in his

---

39. W. R. D. Fairbairn, "Object Relations and Dynamic Structure," *International Journal of Psychoanalysis* 27 (1946): 36.

40. Michael Balint, "Changing Therapeutical Aims and Techniques in Psycho-analysis," *International Journal of Psychoanalysis* 31 (1950): 121.

patients' "memories" of childhood, he concluded that children lived by their wishes at the price of destroying reality. But in fact Freud was examining memories from a time when wish and reality made no sense as categories, because they were not yet differentiated from one another; nor were fiction and fact, self and other. Freud's emphasis on wish has shifted to an emphasis on whole fantasies about—or ways of seeing—experience. Psychoanalysis began as a study of the instincts, then widened to include defensive battles about instinct, and has gone on to encompass the whole person and his relation to the natural and social world. Analysts are now interested in tracing the emergence of the whole "self" and sense of reality, from its earliest infantile archetypes[41] to its current phenomenology.

The first disagreement we noted, concerning the logical status of psychoanalytic statements, is more a philosophical than a literary one; but this second disagreement, about the role of instinctual conflict, has immediate implications for practical literary criticism. Freud had attributed all content, all the strange modes of representation in dream work and primitive thinking, and all rhetorical strategy, to the agents of repression. As Ernest Jones flatly put in the case of symbolic expression, only what is repressed can be symbolized[42]—and therefore the only true symbols are symbols of repressed material. But according to the new views of the mind, this formula no longer holds. Freud discovered strange distortions of thought by studying their misuse in neurosis; but these now turn out to be necessary indirections by which we achieve a mature sense of ourselves and our world—some of these dis-

41. As in the increasing number of studies of the nature and development of narcissism, and in the renewed interest in borderline and psychotic conditions, which are defined by how they affect all thought, feeling, and experience rather than by a specific conflict between wishful and repressive forces—as "neurosis" long was. See, e.g., Kohut, *The Analysis of the Self*, and Otto Kernberg, *Borderline Conditions and Pathological Narcissim* (New York: Jason Aronson, 1975).

42. Ernest Jones, "The Theory of Symbolism" (1916), in *Papers on Psychoanalysis*, 5th ed. (Boston: Beacon Press, 1961), p. 97.

tortions may be used in repression, but they certainly need not be.

The analysts and critics who base their work on the older theory of repression carry on Freud's work of seeing all tensions, ambiguities, and rhetorical strategies in literature as the result of repression. These commentators, oddly enough, include both conservatives and revisionists. They include Norman Holland, who sees all literature as defensive or repressive transformation of fantasies, and the radical Jacques Lacan, for whom all tropes are defenses. By contrast, the analysts and critics basing their work on the newer developmental theories, instead of looking for the repressed meaning of specific symbols, tend to see literary ambiguities in the context of the whole development of symbolic discourse in children.[43] They look for peaceful evolution instead of violent repressions and revolutionary eruptions.

No one yet *has* finally understood how motives and meanings are related. None of the attempts so far has fully explored the relation between our pervasive bent toward symbolism and indirection, on the one hand, and our defensive conflicts, on the other. Freud and the orthodox followers of his instinctual theory no doubt simplify matters by assuming that all poetic indirections are caused by repression, but they simplify only at the price of misrepresenting them. Yet to go to the other extreme and merely look for benign transformations of meaning can also be reductive; it can "repress the idea of repression," as the French fear, and try to explain away the perverse effects of repressive forces. Neither system alone is sufficient to account for the full range of mental experience and its literary representations. But once again, we

---

43. See, e.g., Heinz Werner and Bernard Kaplan, *Symbol Formation: An Organismic-Development Approach to Language and the Expression of Thought* (New York: John Wiley, 1963), and Peter H. Wolff, "Cognitive Considerations for a Psychoanalytic Theory of Language Acquisition," in *Motives and Thought: Psychoanalytic Essays in Honor of David Rapaport*, ed. Robert R. Holt, Psychological Issues, vol. 5, no. 2/3 (New York: International Universities Press, 1966), pp. 299–343.

will find that the interaction *between* these systems can reveal much about the ways in which we structure experience. This interaction will arise first and most directly in the chapter on fantasies, but each of the models I have described has naturally been affected by the movement toward a general psychology. All aspects of a patient's discourse—or a literary text—are viewed differently if we are no longer trying to see them as determined solely by their function in the psychic economy but are willing to look for other, less predictable relations among them.

In the following chapters we shall see how the "unpredictable relations" in elements of content, psychic functions, mode of representation, and rhetorical function are vital to different kinds of interpretation—and how their interaction is necessary in order for us to feel that we have discovered something about what the text means. Morse Peckham has called meaning a scandalous term;[44] I hope that the following pages will provide more details about the scandal, even if they do not finally succeed in making it fully respectable.

44. Morse Peckham, "Psychology and Literature," in *Literary Criticism and Psychology, Yearbook of Comparative Criticism*, vol. 7, ed. Joseph P. Strelka (University Park: Pennsylvania State University Press, 1976), pp. 48–68.

2

Literature as Case History: Content

> After this long digression into literature let us return to
> clinical experience but only to establish in a few words
> the complete agreement between them.
>> —Freud on Lady Macbeth
>
> More needs she the divine than the physician.
>> —Doctor in *Macbeth*

The most obvious way to apply psychoanalysis to literature is
to begin with the fact that "the human nature of Freudian
psychology is exactly the stuff upon which the poet has always
exercised his art"[1] and to use the analyst's insights about people to analyze fictional characters. The text becomes case history, though now to be translated into other terms, with the
critic coaxing secrets from it which the poets only half-knew
they knew. Character analysis, however, has a bad reputation.
Though it had seemed only natural to Freud to treat characters like people, the New Critics were beginning to distrust all
character analysis even while he was writing; it was not long
before almost all critical realism gave way to a general belief
that characters, whose traits were determined not by analyz-
able "personalities" but by the requirements of the text, were
only parts of a design. And if we cannot even ask, "How many
children had Lady Macbeth?" as L. C. Knights warned in his

---

1. Lionel Trilling, "Freud and Literature" (1940), reprinted in *The Liberal
Imagination: Essays on Society and Literature* (New York: Anchor Books, 1953),
p. 32.

classic essay, then we certainly cannot ask how many complexes she had.[2] The analysts, then, who continue to explain
that Bartleby "prefers not to" because he is a psychotic de-
pressive, or who see unconscious motives for Hamlet's delay,
have no basis for their activities; they are perhaps enriching
psychoanalysis, but only at the price of misreading literature.

The question of character analysis has come up again, however, now that the new critical fastidiousness has abated. And
it is not only the traditional Freudians who keep it alive looking to literature for case histories to demonstrate their theories. It is also, more surprisingly, the most revisionary psychoanalytic critics who turn to character analysis. Geoffrey
Hartman, for example, has challenged the idea of wish
fulfillment, which underlies Freud's metapsychology, but
when he turns to an illustration for his own theory, he turns
to character analysis again.[3] Hartman brings a new version of
psychoanalysis to Coleridge's "Ancient Mariner" and watches
for moments of separation and individuation rather than for
phallic fantasies, but he is examining the Mariner's psychology nonetheless and momentarily puts aside the poem as
poem. Even Jacques Lacan's famous excursion into American
literature, admittedly not literary criticism per se, turns immediately to character analysis in the process of making a
more structural literary point.[4] His essay concerns the meaning of the purloined letter in Poe's story of that title, but in
proving that the letter is a floating signifier with no meaning
apart from the one given it by the situation, Lacan takes a de-
tour through character analysis and argues that the Minister

2. See Norman Holland, "Realism and the Psychological Critic; or, How
Many Complexes Had Lady Macbeth?" *Literature and Psychology* 10 (1960):
5–8; and see his expanded treatment of the problem in chapters 10 and 11 of
Psychoanalysis and Shakespeare (New York: McGraw-Hill, 1964).

3. Geoffrey Hartman, "I. A. Richards and the Dream of Communication,"
in *The Fate of Reading and Other Essays* (Chicago: University of Chicago Press,
1975), pp. 20–40.

4. Jacques Lacan, "Seminar on 'The Purloined Letter,'" trans. Jeffrey
Mehlman, in *French Freud: Structural Studies in Psychoanalysis*, Yale French
Studies 48 (1972): pp. 39–72.

D—— and Dupin, who are part of the situation, are also signifiers. He applies his theory of unconscious motivation to these characters as people.

Today, the problem of character analysis has taken new forms which challenge assumptions not only about analyzing characters but about the nature of character and of fiction. It is still as true for us as it was for Freud that the psychoanalytic truths in literature must be referred to truths of character; psychoanalysis still concerns people, and so does poetry. But now there is always a question about how the reference works. Interest in the unconscious existence of literary characters has led to questions about just where character, or the "self," is located, especially as new approaches to character are suggested not only in psychoanalysis itself but in philosophy, sociology, and anthropology. The character's distinction from his role and his world is no longer as clear as it once was. The old, sensible distinction between analyzing character, author, and reader has begun to give way, and heretofore uninteresting or "inappropriate" parts of the text have come to be seen as aspects of character portrayal. Frederick Crews's fairly traditional study of Hawthorne depends on an analysis of plots and landscapes as signs not only of Hawthorne's conflicts but also of the characters' conflicts: it is not clear just whom Crews is trying to psychoanalyze.[5] John Irwin's much more radical study of Faulkner, based on French models, sets out to examine the repetitions within and between texts that include Faulkner's novels and Freud's essays. But it merges this revisionary aim with a persistent attempt to psychoanalyze Quentin Compson as though he were a real person—using evidence which an analyst would refer back instead to Faulkner's own mind.[6]

5. Frederick Crews, *The Sins of the Fathers: Hawthorne's Psychological Themes* (New York: Oxford University Press, 1966).

6. John Irwin, *Doubling and Incest / Repetition and Revenge: A Speculative Reading of Faulkner* (Baltimore: Johns Hopkins University Press, 1975). For discussion of Irwin's repetition of traditional approaches, see the review of his book in *Diacritics* 7 (1977): 78–86.

The focus on character has even moved to nonfiction and is closely implicated in the recent interest in autobiography —an interest, that is, in works whose whole structure and significance are intimately connected with the character portrayed at their center.[7] It is also one aspect of Harold Bloom's ideas of influence, which transfer interest from the poem to the poet, who implicitly portrays himself as a speaking character within the poem.[8] The most recent manifestation of this concern with the location of character and the hidden aspects of the self goes still farther from narrative and from conventional characters by turning to philosophical prose, where there is no "character" except in the writer's implicit and often unwitting revelation of his own character and its conflicts.[9]

It is a matter no longer of trying to see a literary text as a case history but of treating it all too much like the raw material of an actual analysis—like the succession of stories, occasional lyric, autobiography, and discursive monologue which make up free associations. The critics imitate the analyst when they ignore the literal story or manifest argument in a text and try instead to see into it or through it and to relate its structure and conflicts to a drama within some human mind—a mind located ambiguously between the people mentioned in the text and the speaker himself. This is no longer old-fashioned character analysis, but its resemblance to that practice is not only a telling reminder of the continuity be-

---

7. See, e.g., Jeffrey Mehlman, *A Structural Study of Autobiography: Proust, Lewis, Sartre, Lévi-Strauss* (Ithaca, N.Y.: Cornell University Press, 1974), and Richard Onorato, *The Character of the Poet: Wordsworth in* The Prelude (Princeton, N.J.: Princeton University Press, 1971).

8. See, e.g., Harold Bloom, *The Anxiety of Influence: A Theory of Poetry* (New York: Oxford University Press, 1973), and *A Map of Misreading* (New York: Oxford University Press, 1975).

9. This is a "character" or "self" only in a sense very different from the traditional one, but even though it may consist only of the verbal unity bounded by the text, it is a self whose divisions Jacques Derrida and Paul de Man analyze in their rereadings of writers.

tween the new and the continuing critical concerns but a warning that distinctions which seem simple are not simple after all.

Character analysis, then, has more than historical importance; in fact it provides a vital meeting place for psychoanalysis and literature, where problems in interpretation arise with particular force and clarity. These problems have to do with the nature of both psychoanalytic statements and literary interpretation, and Freud's easy assumption that the poets discovered the unconscious before he did—like Trilling's claim that Freud and the poets practiced on the same human nature—merely bypasses the problems without solving them. Neither Freud nor the poets presented us with "human nature"; we as critics are left to compare human nature as Freud represented it to human nature as the poets represented it, and we face problems of translation whenever we try to confront their views of man.

In fact, not just one but two questions always come up in efforts to compare two such different attempts to capture the elusive totality of "human nature." First, which of many things is being said about "human nature" or about "the unconscious"? Then, even more important, what *form* does this insight take? Can we compare a scientific to a poetic one? What does it mean in each case to "exercise your art" upon the same material? The difference is not one of vocabulary alone.

These difficulties will arise again in the use of the other models. The examination of character, though, can serve as an introduction to the others, and in the following section I shall use the critical debate about Shakespeare's characters as the focus for discussion, since they have attracted more psychoanalytic attention than almost any others and have generated a controversy about the whole process of character analysis. The discussion will also lead, I hope, to a clarification of the problems inherent in applying psychoanalysis in other cases and in other ways.

METAPSYCHOLOGY AND THE CASE OF EVERYMAN

The primary connection between Freud and the poets is a shared mythology, a general insight into human nature and a confrontation with experience neither the poets nor Freud were afraid to see, though most of the rest of us were. In this sense the poets discovered the unconscious before Freud, and they did it in strikingly similar ways. Nonetheless, I shall argue, this fact gives us no basis for proceeding to talk about the unconscious mind of a specific character and representing it in the way Freud did when he analyzed people or literary characters. The discovery of the unconscious is not the same as the discovery of psychoanalysis.

By disagreeing with talk about the character's unconscious mind I certainly do not mean to suggest that Shakespeare's characters are either rational or simple. His plays explore the depths of human motivation. Shakespeare exposed the nerve; he never let us forget that there is a murderer in kindly Macbeth or gracious Othello, a madman in every lover, and both murderer and madman in those whose conscience is caught by what we see on stage. In more quiet revelations, too, Shakespearean characters betray their complexities and complex blindnesses. They respond to their situations in ways more complicated and devious than they know, ways which have nothing to do with logic and morality but with something more like passion and even sheer physical instinct. Their simple virtues become questionable: we begin to wonder about the heroism of a Coriolanus, the righteousness of an Angelo, and the self-sacrificing love of an Antonio willing, for no perceptible reason, to give a pound of flesh for his friend.

But in all of this, what Shakespeare shows us is not the unconscious but simply the irrational, which is the unconscious the poets have always known—that aspect of human nature which, from Plato's dark horse to Schwartz's "heavy bear that goes with me," has been seen as our other self. They have seen it as a biological force, as divine possession, and as both at once. From Dionysus sweeping up the Maenads, to D. H.

Lawrence's sexual currents, to the more purely negative depths of appetite in Conrad's *Heart of Darkness*, characters in literature have discovered "truths more intense than knowledge,"[10] as George Steiner described the force which drives Greek heroes to their fates. Other versions of the experience take it even farther from rational life, to something even more fundamental—Wordsworth's blind beggars and border creatures who are barely distinguishable from the landscape, the nothingness in E. M. Forster's Indian caves of Malabar, the cool impersonality of Mrs. Ramsay's retreat in the wedge of the lighthouse. The unconscious the poets discovered is not only irrational but often something which destroys ordinary selfhood; it is more an un*self*consciousness than an unconscious, whether it comes from above or from below, or touches both.

If Shakespeare is Freud's predecessor in all of this, it is as a creator of metapsychological theories rather than as a creator of clinical case histories. If he resembles Freud, it is Freud the philosopher and poet, who stood back from the messy and improbable details of experience to make his abstractions about human nature, who provided a metapsychological explanation for Everyman's behavior and a psychomachia to portray it. And he does so in much the same terms. The concrete drama in the plays, of course, is very different from the implicit drama in Freud's theories; but the similarities are striking. Where Freud seems to have pictured a heroic ego barely holding up the dam on the banks of the id, Shakespeare has his cities and encampments surrounded by Turks and oceans and witch-infested heaths. Again and again we see the boundaries of ordinary rational life breaking down, and with them the boundaries of the ordinary rational self, whatever the particular terms defining them in a particular play. The fragile intellectual order in *Love's Labour's Lost* falls with the first assault of love and death; even Lear's

---

10. George Steiner, *The Death of Tragedy* (New York: Alfred A Knopf, 1961), p. 7.

magnificently accommodating world gives way to the monstrous passions lurking not only on the heath and in the villains but in Lear himself. In the comedies and romances, Shakespeare dramatizes Freud's optimistic dictum, "Where id was, there shall ego become,"[11] as characters confront the extremes of both internal and external tempests to return more whole and calm. The forsworn scholars "lose [their] oaths to find [them]selves" (4.3.358), and the shipwrecked party in *The Tempest* lose everything but find themselves "when no man was his own" (5.1.213) before. Even in the tragedies, where return is not guaranteed, what matters is the passage; Lear is never so much a king as when he loses his kingdom and can say, "They told me I was every thing; 'tis a lie" (4.6.104–05).[12]

And if Freud sometimes anthropomorphizes the parts of the mind, so does Shakespeare. Ariel and Caliban may be seen as walking portraits of "the conscious" and "the unconscious" (and so might the earlier pair, Armado and Costard), down to the details that consciousness is associated with language and is willing to undergo some pain to gain its pleasure in the end. Freud added a three-part division to this original dichotomy; so does Shakespeare. In addition to the obvious psychomachia in the triple world of *Henry IV*, Part 2, where Hal has to choose between the id (Falstaff) and the superego (the Lord Chief Justice), many of Shakespeare's hierarchically organized multiple plots lend themselves to Freudian allegory, with the clownish id at the bottom in the subplot and the regal superego in the "overplot." Certainly a play like *Measure for Measure* suggests a kind of analytic self-scrutiny, as the Duke, like the analysand's "observing ego," withdraws from the action to oversee the battle between upright Angelo and the low life in the stews.

Shakespeare knew about wish fulfillment, too, and about

11. Sigmund Freud, Lecture 31, *New Introductory Lectures On Psycho-Analysis* (1933), *SE* 22:80.

12. All quotations from Shakespeare are taken from *The Riverside Shakespeare* (Boston: Houghton Mifflin, 1974).

the way it could assume hostile and perverse forms. The world at the center of his plays may not be pleasurable, but it is always the product of the characters' desires, spoken or unspoken. In the comedies, nearly all audiences recognize immediately the wish fulfillment which C. L. Barber has identified with festivals of release and which takes place in what Northrop Frye has called the green worlds of "desire."[13] Shakespeare explored the paradoxes of "will"—both "rational intention" and "lust"—and showed us worlds where people have things "as they like it" or get "what they will" without realizing what that means. He even came close to dramatizing Freud's hydraulic theory about the flow of libidinal cathexis which blindly drives the unconscious will from object to object, when he showed the lovers blindly "transferring" their loves from object to object in the forest, though he saw, instead of a flow of cathexis, a flow of juice from the flower "love-in-idleness."

Freud internalized Shakespeare's dramas; his nineteenth-century science made the poet's cosmology into a psychology. There are obvious differences, of course, between a drama and a theory. Both Freud and Shakespeare, nonetheless, were making mythologies, creations not very different from the fantasies and just-so stories we all invent to make sense of extraordinary experiences. These are the phenomenological versions of conflict, loss, and passion—the folklore rationalizations we need in order to cope with things that otherwise do not fit into our rational lives. To the degree that Freud's metapsychology is myth raised to a science, as was suggested in chapter 1, to the degree that his theorizing has its roots in commonsense psychology and folk anthropomorphism, his theories resemble Shakespeare's plays. It is no wonder that some of Freud's concretizing metaphors are like Shake-

13. C. L. Barber describes the relation throughout his *Shakespeare's Festive Comedy: A Study of Dramatic Form and Its Relationship to Social Custom* (Princeton, N.J.: Princeton University Press, 1959). Northorp Frye's discussion appears, e.g., in his *Anatomy of Criticism: Four Essays* (New York: Atheneum, 1966) pp. 43–52, 163–86.

speare's—so much so that when Jacques Lacan attacks such
reifications he draws on Shakespeare for his caricature of the
analyst's picture of the unconscious as a Caliban-like creature
that rises from the depths.

But Shakespeare's plays and Freud's metapsychological
theories, along with the common human fantasies underlying
both, differ greatly from the actuality of living with unconscious forces. To "discover the unconscious" and tell what we
all feel at times—that there is always something more than we
know in ourselves—is very different from uncovering the
quiet ways in which it is unconsciously working. The unconscious experiences which psychoanalysis traces are less coherently organized and less comprehensible than even the most
horrible and irrational passions in any poetic schema. They
are not located in some cellar of the mind or a forest outside
Athens; they infiltrate the ground and structure of Athens itself, in the most surprisingly unheroic and inconsequential
ways. Shakespeare's schema and Freud's theoretical map of
the mind resemble each other more than either of them resembles unconscious experience—or experience which is
brought to consciousness only in the special procedure which
is what Freud discovered, the psychoanalytic process. And it is
only in the psychoanalytic process that characters, and people, can be psychoanalyzed.

Case History or Fantasy: Literal or Figurative?

I have been suggesting that despite Shakespeare's discovery
about the nature of human motivation in general, we have no
basis for psychoanalyzing the characters who are part of its
expression. His plays are like Freud's metapsychology and
not like case histories; the "reality" of his characters, even
though it depends on their being irrational as well as rational
beings, does not include the kind of unconscious experience
on which an analysis is based. The analyst and the poet are,
after all, dealing with different aspects of human nature and
different manifestations of the unconscious. The analyst always deals with more of the mind than does either the poet or

the theoretician who makes maps of the mind. Like the poet, the analyst asks about a character's unacknowledged motives; but unlike the poet, he traces these back to other thoughts, other experiences, other contexts, which gave rise to motives and give them their only meaning. What is unique about psychoanalysis is that it not simply identifies strange behavior but also locates a source for behavior in something besides current experience—and these two goals are inseparable. By definition, the experiences the analyst deals with are independent of and often alien to current experience. They derive from fixations to periods sometimes so distant that we not only do not remember them but could not recognize a memory of them. These experiences are not responsive to the ongoing realities of life, even though they may find hiding places and even breeding places there.

In fact, the more realistic a character is, in the sense of responding fully and believably to his world, the more problematic it may be to assign an unconscious complex of motives to him—just as it is hard to know how to deal with insights into the unconscious minds of real people whose integrity is otherwise not in question. Even in life, evoking unconscious motives seems unrealistic, because it means invoking explanations which contradict felt experience and which require us to completely readjust our image of ourselves—and of human nature. It means invoking those alien trains of thought and preoccupations whose connections to reality are often illogical; the determining role of these motives in behavior is redundant, at least in "normal" people. What do you do when you find out that your friend's altruism derives from childhood rivalries, or that your surgeon's flawless operations satisfy his otherwise inactive sadistic fantasies from childhood? Any revision of our view of ourselves or other people implied by this new, discontinuous insight usually occurs in a psychoanalyst's office—and for the most part we do not go there unless we find that the self we thought we knew is inconsistent. We wait until the altruism goes sour or the surgeon botches a simple procedure. Even in the analyst's office, there is little room for diagnoses like the ones often offered as psychoanalysis of character—a psychoanalytic tag offered as explanation, as though the name made the behavior any more explicable—like J. I. M. Stewart's diagnosis of Leontes as homosexual.[14] There is no place for such wild analyses[15] or diagnostic cataloging, but only for the slow unraveling of all the disowned ideas and experiences leading from the forgotten past to present behavior. Yoking a hidden, otherwise invisible, motive from something called the unconscious to the surface is not enough. If purely unconscious motives *are* there, they are hard to locate: Is Brutus unconsciously killing his father when he kills Caesar? There is no room for these motives in the fully explained world of the play; or rather, there is room for too many of them. In actuality, almost nothing is absolutely "unconscious" in this way; the unconscious motive is always present in some form, however bizarre or disowned, and always provides the analyst with cues to its presence.

In Shakespeare's plays, however, there are no such cues, nothing which demands to be understood in terms other than the ones introduced by the world of play and the action it contains. His plays make sense of irrational behavior by externalizing it, as we have seen, in an explanatory myth. Even the characters who seem like psychiatrists' textbook cases when taken out of their plays have objective correlatives for their behavior. The play's world explains, even if it does not always justify, what the characters do. The behavior *is* irrational, and the characters *do* participate in the creation of comic or tragic chaos—but the causes of their behavior work on divine, natural, and social levels, as well as on the level of the individual divided will. The explanation lies in the context, not in some additional unseen shaper of the will, and certainly not in offstage, never-mentioned past events.

14. J. I. M. Stewart, *Character and Motive in Shakespeare: Some Recent Appraisals Examined* (London: Longmans, Green, 1949), pp. 30–37.
15. See Freud, "Wild Psycho-analysis" (1910), *SE* 11:221–27.

To invoke unconscious motives in such a fictional world is similar to invoking tragic flaws to explain tragedy—blaming a comfortably flawed agent who does not fit in with his environment instead of realizing that the agent is an essential part of it. To blame Hamlet's tragic flaw for his fate is to leave our sense of his world undisturbed; it allows us to overlook the painful contradictions in a flawed world, which is the only world we have, and to locate them in one easily identified part of one character's mind. In an even more reductive way, it hides the paradox that Hamlet's greatness is inseparable from his flaw. The homosexual label moves the flaw to the less visible unconscious level, but it nonetheless lodges the problem in a specific deviation. It comforts the audience by isolating Leontes from them, just as it isolates his flaw from his own heterosexual self; but it ignores the fact that Leontes' "homosexual" jealousy is inevitable in any world which is to know the value of passion at all. The cause of his jealousy is not found in an eccentric accident outside the current situation in Leontes' unique history, but forms an essential paradox within it. A crude diagnostic label which turns tragic experience into mere pathology is obviously inappropriate for Leontes, as it is for real people. But for characters enmeshed in their fictional worlds, even the most sensitive and carefully descriptive psychoanalysis is out of place, though it would not be in life. My expectations about a man next door who acted like Leontes would be very different from my expectations about Leontes in *The Winter's Tale*. For the man next door I would be more inclined to accept Stewart's diagnosis of homosexuality, at least as a starting point for investigation. My conventions for analyzing behavior in life include the assumptions that behavior has psychological determinants, often unconscious, and that certain clusters of visible traits in one person may well spring from the same source as in another. In *The Winter's Tale*, however, the clusters of traits can only mean what they mean in the play itself, just as Othello's blackness means only what it means in his play, not what it would mean in the world at large. One cannot follow Philip

Roth's autobiographical hero, who reflected upon his own
migraines "in the same supramedical way that I might consider the illness of a Milly Theale or a Hans Castorp,"[16] because those illnesses belong not to the characters alone but to
whole worlds.

Hamlet may seem an exception to this rule, which is perhaps
one reason why it continues to invite diagnosis and analysis.
We are especially tempted to talk about Hamlet's childhood
fixations, because he not only seems driven—with his compulsive humor, his obsessive use of sexual imagery, his sudden veerings from intensity to abstraction—but is thoroughly
entangled with his parents. However, while a real man with
an Oedipus complex is entangled with childish memories of
his parents, Hamlet must cope with two live human beings
who are actually provoking his strange behavior by their own.
Hamlet's whole world justifies his supposedly oedipal behavior, and everything he feels—excess and all—makes perfect
sense in a rotten world like Denmark. We can blame him only
for his idealism and his adolescent visions of what Denmark—
and a father—might be like; but even there Shakespeare gives
him some support by evoking for our mind's eye the old
Hamlet and Denmark as it used to be.

Hamlet is sensitive but not neurotic when he recoils from
his father's death, his mother's marriage to a boorish substitute, his betrayal by two old school friends, his desertion by
Ophelia and, worst of all, his failure to live up to his own expectations and become a perfect courtier or a revenge-play
hero. The objective correlative for his behavior is a world
fallen in his idealistic eyes; and Shakespeare makes it clear
that neither the ideals nor the fall are particular to Hamlet.
He is coming of age in a tragic world, feeling the thousand
natural shocks that flesh is heir to; it is no wonder he is sick of
action, sick of sexuality, sick of everything that means becoming an adult in such a world. There may be a suggestion that

16. Philip Roth, *My Life as a Man* (New York: Holt, Rinehart and Winston,
1970), p. 55.

his idealism is not pure, just as Brutus's rationalizations for sacrificing Caesar are not pure; but there are impurities enough in what we see of the world and of Hamlet's current motives without our having to invoke unconscious motives from a past world. Idealism always comes at the cost of more pragmatic and social virtues; one sometimes adopts idealism precisely because it precludes the less attractive necessities of life, as well as because one believes in it. But no matter how costly, idealism is not necessarily neurotic.

Shakespeare's plays explain and make sense of behavior by creating a context for it in just this way, even when the explanations are not so direct or explicit as in Hamlet's case. Nothing literally causes Leontes' jealousy or justifies Othello's in the way that Denmark causes Hamlet's melancholy, but Shakespeare gives us enough information to make sense of their jealousy nonetheless. Othello may be wrong about Desdemona, but he is right about Bianca; he lives in a world where women do sell themselves. In Leontes' case, the mere suddenness and irrationality of his jealousy is explanation enough. We know everything when we hear that he has seen the "spider in the cup"; his motiveless malignancy is a fact about his world, a human mystery as inexplicable as the suddenness of bear attacks or storms at sea. We must look to the human condition for an explanation of his behavior, not to an eccentricity in Leontes.

All Shakespeare's characters live in such worlds, even those who suffer more conflict, are more neurotic or are just plain mad. The current logic of Lady Macbeth's sleepwalking madness, for example, is absolutely clear and actually rather healthy. We might better investigate Macbeth's continued (neurotic?) sanity. Lady Macbeth's fixation is almost literally true to events; she really did have bloody hands earlier in the play, although of course she thought then that a little water would clear them. Compare a real case history which superficially seems so similar that Freud himself called it "a case of Lady Macbeth." This was a woman with a dirt phobia who kept washing her hands and would not touch doorknobs ex-

cept with her elbows. She had committed adultery, Freud discovered, and "the washing was symbolic, designed to replace
by physical purity the moral purity which she regretted having lost."[17] But despite Freud's diagnosis, this was not a case
of Lady Macbeth. It is true that both women imagined connections between their strange behavior and external events;
the vital difference, however, is that for Lady Macbeth, the
connections really existed. Of course, not all fictional characters have such a completely literal basis for their
symptoms. When the clerk Wemmick in *Great Expectations*
washes his hands, he too is scrubbing away purely moral dirt.
Still, the connection between symptom and events is always as
straightforward and essential in literary neurotics as it is in
their healthy fellows. Lady Macbeth's delusion, though presented as madness, is not very different from Othello's sane
enough words just before he kills himself: in Aleppo once,

> Where a malignant and a turban'd Turk
> Beat a Venetian and traduc'd the state,
> I took by th' throat the circumcised dog,
> And smote him—thus.

[5.2.352–56]

Her hands repeat their earlier deed, and so do his; the only
difference is that she takes the figure of speech literally. By
contrast, the real "madman," though some of his symptoms
express essential connections this way, suffers from the accidental and the devious—like Freud's patient's gratuitous use
of elbows to turn doorknobs.

Freud himself emphasized the difference in a later discussion of somnambulism. He maintained that people do not
express their guilt so openly in their sleep,[18] meaning that the
connection between symptom and the sleepwalker's world is

---

17. Freud, "Obsessions and Phobias" (1895), *SE* 3:79.
18. *Minutes of the Vienna Psychoanalytic Society*, ed. Herman Nunberg and
Ernst Federn, 3 vols. (New York: International Universities Press, 1962),
1:156–57.

not as evident as in Lady Macbeth's case. If we are to talk about her mental disturbance, Freud says, our discussion should have nothing to do with her obvious crime of murdering Duncan. Lady Macbeth must feel guilty about something else—about parricide or dashing her child's brains out or some other secret, outside, offstage burden which motivates her extreme reaction to the onstage act. Such guilt, whatever it is, always conceals itself cunningly in madness. Freud found parricidal guilt behind Rat Man's symptoms, but the symptoms themselves had nothing to do with fathers or death, at least not in an obvious symbolic way. The obsessive image which gave him his nickname was that of rats eating their way into the anus of some person he loved. The ultimate source of this symptom may have been his guilt, but its form condensed several experiences, wishes, and punishments into a pattern that had nothing to do with his current situation and had only an unrecognizable relation to his past. The image was further determined by his father's hateful gambling (*spielraten*) and his hateful marriage (*heiraten*). Rat Man may have found the idea of marriage "ratty," in another way as well, but the determining effect of the pun shows the tangential quality of real madness. Shakespeare's madmen stare directly into the centers of their worlds; real madmen are always looking somewhere else.

Lady Macbeth's symptoms, then, reveal not only a truth about her character but a truth about her world, or about character in general: blood does not wash off; nothing "clears us of this deed." This is not so much a psychological truth as a primitive moral truth, one that has often been put forth not only by religion but by folk wisdom and its secular guidelines for action. It is not so much a sign of personal motive as of a relationship which belongs neither strictly in cosmology nor in poetry, by means of which we talk about "poetic justice" and by which we anthropomorphize coincidences and see repetitions as revenges. And it is to this relationship that Freud finally appealed in his last treatment of the play, when he gave it back to critics and explained Lady Macbeth's state as the result of poetic justice, occurring in a pattern of events larger than any one character.[19]

Interpreting Lady Macbeth's symptoms in this manner removes her metamorphosis from the realm of the physician and into the realm not only of literary criticism but of the "divine," or rather into a realm which encompasses both. It places her with the characters whose metamorphoses Ovid and Dante described, in a realm where divine justice is the same as poetic justice, and the punishment is merely a repetition of the crime, in another key. Such spare, shapely logic is rarely apparent in real symptoms.

Freud said that he merely contributed the scientific language with which to discuss the poets' discoveries; and this is what he did in his theoretical statements. But in his psychoanalytic explorations of the mind, what he really contributed was a license to extend the poets' discoveries beyond the bounds of common sense. There are always reasons for behavior, but the reasons Shakespeare portrays always make sense and conform to our image of ourselves as fully human (though passionate, cruel, or lacking in self-knowledge). If Brutus has an unspoken motive, we can recognize it. But Rat Man's devious motives are harder to accept as models for our own, and what Freud did was tell us that they are models nonetheless. Actually, Shakespeare captures the spirit of the unconscious less in brutish Caliban than in Puck, who is best pleased by things that fall "preposterously," and in the riddling, elusive, second-rate sisters of ambivalence who unsettle Macbeth's world.

I do not wish to dismiss psychoanalytic commentary completely, however. It is easy enough to dispel the ghost of an Oedipus complex from Hamlet's mind, but not so easy to dismiss the sense that the drama which Freud describes is implicated in Shakespeare's. The two *are* connected, but not through character analysis: the evidence which argues against

19. Freud, "Some Character Types Met With in Psychoanalytic Work" (1916), *SE* 14:318–24.

Hamlet's having an Oedipus complex simultaneously suggests another role for the oedipal material in the play. Precisely because Hamlet's world justifies his responses, it also makes real the fantasies of a typical oedipal-stage child. An adolescent may have all of Hamlet's feelings, but he has no justification for them, except in his own fantasies. Such fantasies, of course, never include the subject's own inappropriate desires and certainly do not include oedipal complexes. They always create, instead, an external scene which makes sense of the adolescent hero's feelings, just as Freud's patients invented seduction scenes to rationalize their own desires: "My father made me do it." The fantasy, by its very nature, cannot be symptomatic unless the figure at its center is free from symptoms. The paranoiac never thinks that anything is wrong with him; and in his fantasies, nothing is. The young woman who dreams that her mother fell onto the railroad tracks is indignant when the analyst asks, "Why did you want to see your mother dead?" "It wasn't my fault!" the woman says. "I tried to save her but she wouldn't listen."[20]

In the play *Hamlet*—more than in any of the other major tragedies—the hero is not at fault. Whatever is wrong is wrong with Hamlet's entire world, a world which recreates every adolescent's fantasies about growing up. Not everyone is a prince in the midst of such parental decay, but everyone feels as if he were. All parents have been involved in mysterious, dirty crimes, which are to be hesitantly guessed at and reluctantly believed, though they compel the imagination and leave the child feeling foolish and left out. Every son's father, now degenerated into a bloated satire of himself, was a hero; and every mother shares Gertrude's blindness to his faults. Every son believes he has the best of reasons to tell his mother to stay out of his father's bed and the best, most externally imposed reasons for murdering his father. The difference is

20. Cited by Jacob Spanjaard in "The Manifest Dream Content and Its Significance in *The Interpretation of Dreams*," *International Journal of Psychoanalysis* 50 (1969): 227ff.

that, for Hamlet, this is all *true*. There is a fundamental difference between the fantasizer as he represents himself in his
fantasy and as he really is; *Hamlet* recreates the fantasy, not
the fantasizer.

THE ANALYST'S FIGURES AND THE POET'S

I have been arguing that Shakespeare's characters live out
their dramas in contexts which explain and even justify their
behavior, and that real, unconsciously shaped acts cannot be
explained this way. It might be objected, however, that my
distinction is not one of content but of form: of course, the
poets not only "simplified and abstracted," as Freud observed, but also expressed their discoveries symbolically,
rather than discursively. If the analyst can trace the oedipal
child's fantasies back to the child, why can't the critic trace
Hamlet's world back to Hamlet? Instead of writing an essay
on unconscious wishes, Sophocles dramatizes a man caught in
the power of an oracle. What is the difference?

Certainly Freud recognized very little difference. Like G.
K. Chesterton's analysis of one of Thackeray's women—"She
drank; Mr. Thackeray didn't know it, but she drank"—Freud
saw himself restating in scientific language what the poets
were able to express only in displaced and distorted form. He
saw only two poles of expression: that which was outright and
scientific, like his own diagnostic case histories; and that
which was repressed and distorted by subjective fantasy. All
poetic statement, according to Freud, could be measured by a
standard of objective truth like the scientific evidence about
the Oedipus complex. There were deviations from this standard because of repression, he admitted, but apart from that,
all oedipal works came out of the same "soil," and it was the
soil that mattered.

Yet Freud himself often had to sift through the soil in several ways before he could find what he was looking for. Not
only are his metapsychological essays different from his case
histories, but even within a case history itself, Freud nearly always presented three accounts of the material, each account

starting afresh: a realistic short story filling in the background chronologically; a record of the material in the order in which it came up during the analysis; and a final abstraction from the data, naming, categorizing, and diagnosing. The poets, too, have their individual ways of representing experience, their different conventions which cannot be explained simply by degrees of repression and cannot be reduced to one another. When the poets used what Freud called a different language, they were often saying something different as well, though he did not think so.

Take the oedipal stories themselves. Where Freud saw only differences in the degree of repression, we can see different aspects of human nature. For Freud, both Sophocles' *Oedipus Rex* and Shakespeare's *Hamlet* present the same Oedipus complex; they are different only in how openly they do so. Sophocles gives the more straightforward presentation, because Oedipus actually fulfills every child's wishes by murdering his father and marrying his mother. By Shakespeare's time, however, the "secular progress of repression among mankind"[21] had left us incapable of Sophocles' honesty. Hamlet can hardly bring himself to act at all, and when he does kill Claudius, he kills himself as well; Gertrude he never touches.

Yet when today we think of the oedipal child, caught in a triangle of intense, vaguely defined jealousies and attractions, a frustrated outsider mystified by adults, then *Hamlet* comes much closer to a straightforward presentation of his experience than does *Oedipus Rex*. If Sophocles presents anything we might recognize as an oedipal complex, it is not apparent in Oedipus's past crimes but in his triangular confrontation with Creon and Jocasta: first, when he arrived at Thebes after answering the Sphinx and found it ruled by Queen Jocasta and her brother; and second, on stage, when Creon and Jocasta question his present rashness and his authority. These scenes give us something of the feeling of what it is like to be an oedipal child, but they are transformed; here

21. Freud, *The Interpretation of Dreams* (1900), *SE* 4:264.

Oedipus is in charge, as the child never is. As for the two
deeds themselves, the very identification of two such well-
defined heroic acts distorts the child's experience of a diffuse
guilt and an unlocated evil—an experience which much more
closely resembles Hamlet's in Denmark. Such identification is
closer to metapsychology than to an open case history: Freud
transforms the immediacy and confusion of oedipal experience into abstract terms ("our first sexual impulse and our
first hatred"),[22] while Sophocles transforms them into concrete dramatic acts (murder at the crossroads and marriage at
the gates of Thebes), but both transformations distance the
acts. Sophocles' handling of the oedipal experience is not so
much an open wish fulfillment as a kind of repression. He
projects not only the impulse but the deeds themselves, so
that these deeds take place offstage and in the past; they are
facts to be discovered and discussed, not lived through. They
are acts rather than feelings and ideas. Psychology has been
transformed into history, phenomenology into cosmology.

Hamlet, by contrast, presents the phenomenological experience of an oedipal situation: the intense longings barely disguised as appropriate emotions, the jealousy though justi-
fied, the good intentions, and, perhaps most of all, the sense
of being only a child in someone else's world. When Oedipus
arrived at Thebes, Creon and Jocasta made way for him as
king; when Hamlet returns to Denmark for "th' election," he
is still only a prince in his uncle's world. While Oedipus's agony is shown as a conflict between present and disowned
past, Hamlet's is vividly portrayed as a present conflict
occurring completely within his own mind. Shakespeare gives
outward justification for the conflict, but unlike the conflict
in *Oedipus Rex*, it is an internal one.

A more modern, still more psychologically realistic version
of the Oedipus complex would detach it even further from its
context, as Henry James does in *The Princess Casamassima*.
James's small hero, Hyacinth, is an orphaned outsider in both

22. *Ibid.*, p. 262.

London worlds, social and socialist, from which his parents
came; but even this disadvantage does not explain his feelings. He suffers like Hamlet, but without the metaphysical
justification which Hamlet has. His problem is more pathological than philosophical, and the reader can feel superior to
him, as he cannot to Hamlet. Hyacinth is too bewildered, his
aspirations are too high, and his depressions are overdone.
He has a glimpse of the "royalty" governing each sphere, but
the figures he is in awe of are not kings and queens—only a
would-be prime minister from the slums and a somewhat dubious princess. He has what we might call a "duke complex,"
but it is comprised as much of childish envy as it is of revolutionary outrage. His finely felt bewilderment comes not only
from the mysteriousness of things and the paradoxes of civilization but also from a kind of neurotic blindness to the dark
truths about sexuality and violence in both the world and
himself. He half-creates this bewilderment. Hardly a brave
detective like Oedipus or even a wily madman like Hamlet,
Hyacinth is reduced to "surreptitious peepings" at the Princess's door. The original sin plaguing or poisoning the worlds
of Oedipus and Hamlet is present in Hyacinth's also; Oedipus's fated inheritance and Hamlet's serpentine uncle-mur-
derer are paralleled by the crimes of history which Hyacinth
discovers. But for Hyacinth there is no oracle or ghost to give
these substance, only his own self-imposed bewilderment.

The uniqueness of Sophocles' version is not in a psychological openness but in a prepsychological, primitive kind of
representation. Freud chooses to interpret the outright presentation of murder and incest as a fact about Oedipus the
character, but Sophocles has made it a fact about Oedipus's
world. The horrible deeds are not Oedipus's fault, but rather
a vast Freudian slip of the universe which exposes the unconscious truth, substituting father for stranger and mother for
wife in a story where they do not belong. The difference between the origin of the murders in Sophocles and in James is
telling. James's hero suddenly receives orders to kill a duke;
these come from the underground socialists, a force as inscru-

table as any Sophoclean oracle, and as unexpected. But unlike
Oedipus, Hyacinth himself has brought on the orders, by
associating with the revolutionaries in the first place.

There is no room for Oedipus's motives to exist separately
from his universe. Oedipus's world is one in which all potenti-
alities have already been translated into actions; thoughts and
wishes are accomplished facts. The confrontation between
Oedipus and Laius becomes a literal event: Oedipus meets
Laius in his coach and kills him. And this is all we are told;
feelings and judgments are left to implication. A comparison
with James's novel is again revealing. Here, there is never any
literal confrontation between father and son, only symbolic
displacements which Hyacinth himself creates, like the incident at the crossroads during one of Hyacinth's moods of ex-
clusion, when

> a young man in a white tie and a crush hat who dawdled
> by on his way to a dinner party in a hansom cab that
> nearly ran over one—these familiar phenomena became
> symbolic, insolent, defiant, took on themselves to make
> him smart with the sense that *he* was above all out of it.[23]

In Oedipus's world of action there are no subjunctives or
optatives, no ifs or buts, and no contradictions. To deny
something is to affirm it all the more strongly, as Oedipus
discovers when he wakes up in the arms of the fate he had
been running from. Nor are there analogies in his world, only
equivalences. This is true of primitive unconscious fantasies,
in which every man is "father," every woman is "mother," and
every sympathetic character is "me." The analyst's equation of
literary texts with such fantasies is what makes oedipal interpretations so boring in literature: in the play, Hamlet has one
father and kills another man, but according to the analyst the
two men are the same. What is different about *Oedipus* is that
here the two men really are the same. Despite Oedipus's ef-

23. Henry James, *The Princess Casamassima* (New York: Harper and Row,
1964), p. 125.

forts, the play presents a world without sublimation, and instincts without vicissitudes, a world (as Jocasta sees it) where dreams do not differ from the truth. It is a world as reductive as psychoanalytic interpretations can make literature seem. This is what comes out into the open: not a wish for something but, to the primitive mind, its eternal presence; not that little boys want to marry their mothers, or even that men still want to, but that on some level men always *do* marry them. Hamlet's world justifies his feelings; Hyacinth's is distorted by his; but Oedipus's world acts feelings out for him and makes it impossible to distinguish psychology from cosmology.

The question about Oedipus is really a question about how to read. For the most part Freud rejects a literal reading which would take at face value the work's division into our ordinary, expected categories of people, places, and events. Instead, he sees everything in the text as a displacement of psychological facts; its people, places, and events are to be seen as aspects of a character's mind or as the character's own subjective view of the external world. To a degree, this is nothing new. In a genre like allegory, for example, critics have often described the action of a literary work as an externalization of the hero's mind. They have seen book 1 of *The Faerie Queene* as Red Cross's dream, in which he "invents" the characters he meets. Freud and his followers differ first of all in the extent of their assumptions. "When nothing in [the character's] consciousness explains his behavior," Morton Kaplan and Robert Kloss generalize in their study *The Unspoken Motive*, then "it is in symbols" that we shall find evidence of unconscious motivation.[24]

Analysts also disagree about what the presence of symbolism implies. Having begun with the assumption that "this is a literal picture of the real world" or else "it is a symbolic picture of the hero's mind"—the analyst often views the text as a

---

24. *The Unspoken Motive: A Guide to Psychoanalytic Literary Criticism* (New York: Free Press, 1973), p. 83. See also pp. 35 and 85.

battleground for a war between two versions of reality. Depending on whether he favors the objective or the subjective version, he will see either of two forms of repression motivating the text's symbolism when it is present. Since Freud found reality only in an objective, "scientific" presentation of behavior, he saw anything else as an evasion, a distorted fantasy which not only was to be read back into the character's mind but was to be taken as evidence of repression on somebody's part. Frederick Crews goes even further and sees all landscapes specifically as repressed aspects of a character's mind. Crews not only reads symbolically; he interprets the presence of symbolism as a sign of repression. In Hawthorne's stories, for example, the characters may seem wooden, but "whatever is subtracted from overt psychology tends to reappear in imagery, even in the physical setting itself."[25] The key word here is *subtract*, implying that overt and covert expression are mutually incompatible, and that symbolic expression is necessarily a cowardly avoidance of the truth. So too, Crews finds that Conrad diverts us from "the hero's gloomy mind to his lush surroundings, which are stocked with misplaced energies; we expect confessions and get tropical storms."[26]

For a critic who values psychic reality over objective reality, the same conflict holds true, but in the opposite way. Leo Bersani, trying to explain a symbolic world somewhat like Hawthorne's, also sees the landscape as an aspect of the character's mind, but for him this is the "true" reality. The heath *is* Heathcliff; this is a courageously open expression of a primitive fantasy about self-as-world. To explain the correspondence between character and landscape as "only symbolic" would be to repress the fantasy of merging, in order to make the correspondence fit into our ordinary sense of real-

25. Crews, *The Sins of the Fathers*, p. 17.
26. Frederick Crews, "Conrad's Uneasiness—and Ours," in *Out of My System: Psychoanalysis, Ideology and Critical Method* (New York: Oxford University Press, 1975), p. 50.

ity. For Bersani, Crews's therapeutic "confession" is itself the repression.[27]

Whatever their differences, however, Freud, Crews, and Bersani all feel comfortable privileging one sort of reading and rejecting the literal. But in literature, as opposed to case history or fantasy, we are never sure which reading to choose. The literary text should be placed in the space between literal and symbolic reading. Even in so simple a case as landscapes, the fictional world depends on an easy transition from character to world. Shakespeare, for example, may on occasion show a dramatic change in landscape which is primarily a physical fact, like the sudden darkening of the woods when the murderers and mutilators begin their work in *Titus Andronicus*. He may also show changes which occur entirely in the beholder's eye, as in *The Tempest*, when good Gonzalo sees a pleasant island where the villainous Antonio sees only a rotten fen. But for the most part, the question about whether something is physical or psychological fact does not even arise. When Lear rages on the heath, there is no need to ask whether he has literally moved out of the palace to a heath; or whether he has created the heath by the force of his own state of mind. The correspondence simply makes sense. Shakespeare gives us psychic reality *as* reality; or rather, he creates worlds where the distinction does not exist. His distribution of landscape also illustrates the reverse of the relation we just saw, so that a character's private vision, like Lady Macbeth's hallucination, is also a part of the external world.

The play between character and world within the text is re-

27. Leo Bersani, *A Future for Astyanax: Character and Desire in Fiction* (Boston: Little, Brown, 1976), pp. 204–13, 221–23. Bersani is interested in the "mysterious scattering of the self" in a recreation of the child's original confusion between self and the world. He claims that only falsely "sublimated"—or "repressed," as he terms them—desires take the bland forms we recognize in adult life, and locate themselves solely *within* the mind. Bersani sees Brontë's *Wuthering Heights* as a presentation of "desublimated desire," returned to its original form, in which "character is only a piece of a person," with the other pieces scattered in the landscape and elsewhere.

ally one aspect of the more general tension between characters as characters, and characters as part of a state of mind
which pervades the work. The experience the characters undergo differs from the experience in the audience's life to
which the work refers. There is always a tension between the
two—between Hamlet and any young man coming of age, between Macbeth and any man confronting his own ability to
transgress laws he thought immutable. The man at the center
of these plays is not the same man the play is about. But we
must consider both if we are to understand literature at all. It
is the sense of discrepancy which makes the literary text different from both the impersonal, objective case history and
the subjective, unselfconscious fantasy. It is the unpsy-
chological nature of literature, its very outlandishness, that
makes it such an appropriate medium for truth about the
homely, psychological characters who are reading it. *Oedipus*
is about us, about people who do have our oracles inside our
heads, but we cannot understand the play unless we see that
Oedipus's oracles are real. The gap between what we actually
read in the story and the experience its vision illuminates is
not always the same size. In allegory we are made very conscious of the distance; in a realistic novel we can slip easily into
not noticing it; but it is always there.

While Freud's analysis, or Crews's, or Bersani's, does not allow for this play between story and experience, and insists instead on reducing the story to some other experience, there *is*
an exact equivalent to such interaction in the psychoanalytic
process. In this process no "story" is taken only at face value,
as a literal representation of reality; but neither is its manifest
face ignored. The analyst is always concerned with the relation between the fictional story and the narrator to whom it
ultimately refers. The relation is not always a matter of substitution, in which the patient makes up a substitute self as an
alternative to the real one. The location of the self is not that
simple and may be present in the entire narrative. Freud saw
fantasies as alternate worlds in which we create a satisfactory
self and a world appropriate to it; he told us that sometimes

we live in these alternate worlds. We find through the psychoanalytic process, however, that sometimes we do not live in any world whatsoever. The self lies not in a locatable scene with characters, however wish-fulfillingly fictional, but in a nonspatial, temporal play between scenes, and even in a changing narrative stance. The exchanges in the psychoanalytic process which lead to the gradual discovery of the patient's self are the same ones the reader entertains as he comes to understand the experience being portrayed—but not mimetically imitated—by literature. Each of the following models will illustrate one aspect of the recurring problem of the relation between a mimetic representation of experience and some other representation.

3

Literature as Fantasy:
Psychic Function

And there is no better reason for preferring this
elderberry bush than that it stirs an early memory,
that it is no novelty in my life, speaking to me
merely through my present sensibilities to form
and color, but the long companion of my existence
that wove itself into my joys when joys were vivid.
——George Eliot, *The Mill on the Floss*

Everyone knows that he has affective ties to his
parents or to his memories of them; the Freudian
contribution lies in the recognition that the ties are
mainly unconscious, and that they unconsciously
influence current personal relations, often in
quite mysterious ways.
——Stanley Leavy, "Psychoanalytic Interpretation"

Critics who have come to psychoanalysis for its insight into
fiction rather than into fictional characters have usually
drawn on the commonest psychoanalytic activity: its search
for unconscious wishes, which has gradually become a search
for the unconscious fantasies incorporating those wishes. The
difficulty with this kind of criticism lies in determining exactly what a fantasy is, and just what role it has in a text. I will
outline two stages of psychoanalytic thinking about the problem and suggest that they have fostered two different attitudes toward the literary text; the first—and probably best
known—has a limited usefulness, but the second is much
more promising.

The first stage was founded on Freud's thinking about fantasy, at a time when he was concerned primarily with fantasy as a wish-fulfilling device and generally assumed that apart from its psychic function it very much resembled the daydreams we know from adult life. The second state has been derived from psychoanalytic interest in the psychic function of fantasy, not only as a need satisfier but as a means of expression and perception—one whose infantile origins have made its cognitive, affective, and structural properties very different from an adult's stories.

With a better understanding of fantasies comes a more sensitive understanding of the many ways in which a fantasy can be related to the text it helps to shape. Freud virtually equated fantasy with text. He certainly equated fantasy with the crude daydream text, and he implied that the fantasy had a similarly intimate connection with the more artful manifest story in a literary text; at most, he suggested, the fantasy was distanced by an easily understood symbolism. But recently analysts have begun to distinguish between the primitive unconscious fantasy—"primal fantasy"[1]—and all its varied derivatives. The primal fantasy is a set of ingredients or a structure of conflict rather than a finished product. Its derivatives, however, can range from the most primitive obsessive images in dreams all the way up to the most rationalized misinterpretations of reality in everyday life—all of which the analyst loosely and confusingly refers to as *fantasies*.[2]

1. See discussion of the ambiguity in Jean Laplanche and J. B. Pontalis, "Fantasy and the Origins of Sexuality," *International Journal of Psychoanalysis* 49 (1968): 1–18; also see Joseph Sandler and Humberto Nagera, "Aspects of the Metapsychology of Fantasy," *Psychoanalytic Study of the Child* 18 (1963): 159–94.

2. Some analysts, however, have continued to call attention to the problem. See, e.g., Susan Isaacs, "The Nature and Function of Fantasy," *International Journal of Psychoanalysis* 29 (1948): 73–97, especially p. 80, and George S. Klein, "Peremptory Ideation: Structure and Force in Motivated Ideas," in *Perception, Motives and Personality* (New York: Alfred A. Knopf, 1970), pp. 399–400. See also C. S. Lewis's complaint about the confusion, in "Psycho-Analysis and Literary Criticism," in *They Asked for a Paper: Papers and Addresses* (London: Geoffrey Bles, 1962), pp. 120–39.

Once we have distinguished the manifest surface and the underlying fantasy structure of a text, it becomes clear that what matters, as we shall see again and again in each model, is not so much the presence of a certain kind of psychoanalytic raw material as the play between fantasy and surface, between two different ways of organizing the surface. This play does not necessarily correspond to Freud's original description of a simple battle between a latent wish and a manifest defensive disguise. The difference between *manifest* and *latent* is a difference not simply between defenses and hidden wish but between sophisticated and primitive ways of seeing things. Examining the play of fantasy—rather than its mere presence—can help the critic see how texts work. In this chapter I will look first at the daydream model, then at the fantasy model, and finally at application of these models to two novels.

DAYDREAMS: WISHES AND ANALOGIES

Though limited, the daydream makes a useful model for certain purposes, and it is historically important as the source of later fantasy models. The daydream was the model Freud chose automatically in his one essay on the psychoanalytic theory of literature, "Creative Writers and Day Dreaming [*das Phantasieren*]" (1908); it has remained surprisingly unchanged for seventy years. The terms Freud uses are familiar: something in the present reminds the writer of a childhood experience, which in turn awakens an old wish, and the writer makes up a story to fulfill the wish, using both present and past material. As in character analysis, this method emphasizes motives and looks to the past, but because these are the motives and the history of an entire text, the daydream model promises insight into literary structure. To a degree, it fulfills its promise, especially since it has benefited from increased psychoanalytic sophistication and is no longer the crudely reductive tool it once was. The first of the daydream's defining characteristics, its emphasis on motives or wishes as we know them from adult life, had made the earliest psychoanalytic studies of literature little more than exercises in biological or biographical determinism. The pioneers, like Otto Rank, who looked for incest motifs, and Marie Bonaparte, who looked for scraps of Poe's life in his work, were interested only in the hidden instinctual drive or the hidden memory behind a daydream, and when they turned to literature, they looked for the same things.[3] But analysts now see more than compulsive wish fulfillment or compulsive remembering in the repeated configuration which characterizes both daydreams and any given author's body of work.

The change began when analysts recognized that defenses are as important as wishes in shaping a work, and it has led to increasingly sensitive criticism as analysts have come to appreciate more and more of the activities involved when we not only defend ourselves against fantasies but respond to them "adaptively."[4] Within the safely marked off boundaries of the text, as in the daydream, we can resolve not only inner conflicts but also the conflict between our wishes and the world. A reader can then find an underlying pattern, as each daydreamer—or each author—repeats, varies, and generally develops increasingly effective solutions to the same old conflicts. We can trace "the myth of Jane Austen," the "Galton overlap" pattern in Mallarmé and Baudelaire, or the "identity theme" in H. D.'s poems.[5] And these patterns are

3. Otto Rank, *Das Inzest Motiv in Dichtung und Sage* (Leipzig: F. Deuticke, 1912); Marie Bonaparte, *Edgar Poe, étude psychoanalytique* (1933); English trans. John Rodker, *The Life and Works of Edgar Allan Poe* (London: Imago Publishing, 1949).

4. Ernst Kris, Simon Lesser, Norman Holland and, more recently, Albert Hutter, Jim Swan, and Murray Schwartz, all explore this aspect of literary texts in various essays.

5. Geoffrey Gorer, in "The Myth of Jane Austen," *American Imago* 2 (1941), traces a recurrent plot and iconography. Charles Mauron finds overlapping networks of images which vary and elaborate a continuing pattern, in *Introduction á la psychanalyse de Mallarmé* (Neuchâtel, Switzerland: Editions de la Baconniere, 1950). Norman Holland's description of "identity themes" includes not only repeated themes but stylistic traits analogous to

no longer seen as automatic reproductions of some wish fulfillment or some traumatic memory, but as shaped and subjective views of the world, determined neither by biology nor by biography, though drawing on both.[6] The gratification of a biological wish, which may ultimately motivate the author's effort, is postponed and distanced[7] while the author focuses on everything in the human context around it which gives it meaning. Or the supposed debt to biography is reversed, as an author shapes and "telescopes events to arouse effects even more profound and heightened than do the less dramatic and more gradual experiences they draw upon."[8] Edmund Wilson long ago provided an example of this kind of criticism at its best, when he linked the recurring scenes of childhood suffering in Dickens's novels to Dickens's own early experiences. The fictional scenes, he suggested, are "an attempt to digest these early shocks and hardships, to explain them, to justify himself in relation to them, to give an intelligible picture of a world in which such things could occur."[9] This is not mere wish fulfillment but the reworking of an entire experience; the daydream model suggest that *all* literature can be seen in part as just such an attempt "to give an intelligible picture" not only of the present but of the past as well.

In all of these developments, however, analysts still start

---

them (e.g., "passivity followed by sudden action"); for his analysis of H. D., see *Poems in Persons: An Introduction to the Psychoanalysis of Literature* (New York: W. W. Norton, 1973).

6. Thus Roland Barthes's version of psychoanalytic criticism is not so different from others as he suggests it is when he stresses his indifference to biographical facts, e.g., in *On Racine*, trans. Richard Howard (New York: Hill and Wang, 1964). (See especially the chapter "History or Literature?").

7. Ernst Kris, "Daydream and Fiction," in *Psychoanalytic Explorations in Art* (New York: Schocken Books, 1964), pp. 31–39.

8. Simon Lesser, *Fiction and the Unconscious* (New York: Random House, 1957), p. 233.

9. Edmund Wilson, "Dickens: The Two Scrooges," in *The Wound and the Bow: Seven Studies in Literature* (New York and London: Oxford University Press, 1941), p. 8.

with a theory about fiction based on one particular view of human existence—Freud's view that man must cope with wishes (and fears) in a world that denies them relief. Human beings "cannot subsist on the scanty satisfaction which they can extort from reality," Freud said.[10] Every fiction we make, then, is a more nourishing substitute for reality, an alternate world in which we work out our quarrel with the "reality principle" as it takes the form not only of *ananke* but also of *mimesis*. For daydreams, unlike more primitive fantasies and fairy tales, link us to reality, if only by offering an alternate version of it to keep us from escaping altogether. Ernest Kris tells about the men stranded on a desert island in the Pacific during the war who spent every spare moment of radio time listening to an adventure—about men stranded on a Pacific island.[11] No matter how farfetched Walter Mitty's secret life, or how exotic James Bond's histrionics, they take place in possible worlds. Even Quixote's imaginings are rationalized by the magicians, who collectively serve—like Bond's incredible gadgets—as deus ex machina (or in machina) to salvage an otherwise possible world by explaining a sudden shift that is not so possible.

The daydream model's limitations derive from this functional definition of literature as need satisfier. The precise function of literature has been, as we have seen, somewhat redefined; it is seen no longer as a simple instinctual catharsis but rather, as Norman Holland somewhere said, as a "vaccination" against larger indulgences outside the safe bounds of the text. Despite this change, however, the analyst is still as much interested in the "uses of enchantment"[12] as in its nature, and the use he finds most often is therapy: literature is therapy, and good literature is better therapy. The result is something closer to moral than to aesthetic criticism, though

10. Sigmund Freud, "Introductory Lectures on Psychoanalysis" (1916–17), *SE* 16:372.

11. Kris, "Approaches to Art," in *Psychoanalytic Explorations*, p. 45.

12. As is Bruno Bettelheim in *The Uses of Enchantment: The Meaning and Importance of Fairy Tales* (New York: Alfred A. Knopf, 1976).

not the kind of morality Freud was accused of flouting when
early reviewers found his interest in sex revolting, but moral
in the sense that Freud had, as Philip Rieff has put it, "the
mind of a moralist,"[13] and his whole intellectual development
can be seen as a series of increasingly complex answers to the
single and essentially moral question of how we can cope with
our uncivilized instincts.[14]

It is the moralist we hear in Freud's mild but barely disguised contempt for literature; he objected to texts which
merely allow us to escape into fantasy. If literature could not
provide a responsible "criticism of life," as Matthew Arnold
described it, then at least it could help prepare us for life by
exposing our fantasies and teaching us how to handle them.[15]
This morality is what early on allied liberal critics like Lionel
Trilling to Freud's cause. Even though Trilling saw that
Freud was concerned—perhaps at the heart of all his
work—with the vicissitudes of symbolic as well as instinctual
behavior, still in his own use of psychoanalysis, Trilling always
drew on Freud the moralist rather than Freud the
semiotician. He found in Freud someone who shared his own
concern with the necessities of sex and aggression, which
could be neither cured nor ignored: someone with a sense of
what he called the "biological nature of moral fact."[16]

With this sort of background, the analyst tends to see all literature as an allegory of civilization and its discontents, the
last step in the refinement of that battle between compulsion
and reality in which we handle our wishes and fears with

13. Philip Rieff, *Freud: The Mind of the Moralist* (New York: Viking Press,
1959).

14. Paul Ricoeur presents Freud's development this way in *Freud and Philosophy*, trans. Denis Savage (New Haven: Yale University Press, 1970).

15. Though Freud usually saw no use in literature except as a safety valve
for uncivilized emotions, he suggested at the end of his 1908 essay "Creative
Writers and Daydreaming" (*SE* 9:141–54) that a reader may learn through
the writer's fantasies how to accept and deal with his own.

16. Lionel Trilling, "The Bostonians," in *The Opposing Self: Nine Essays in
Criticism* (New York: Viking Press, 1959), p. 116.

increasing success, intelligence, and maturity. But in doing so, he has not progressed far from Freud's original suggestion about what makes literature different from daydreams: the suggestion that literature "softens the egoistic character" of the writer's fantasy. Even Ernst Kris, who recognized the formal as well as the factual and moral stringencies in a text, described the passage "from daydream to literature" as a passage from egotistical childishness to a balanced emotional maturity and distance from the battle; once again, the "aesthetic barrier" between primitive material and art is presented as a moral barrier.[17]

All this brings us close to something which critics have always been interested in; but that is the problem. The analyst has told us nothing new when he tells us that in literature we fight out our trial battles between our divided selves. The conflict between self and society, wish and repression, is, after all—in forms so varied and individual that psychoanalysis can hardly hope to catch their nuances in its single net—what stories have always been about. That poetry makes possible what Fulke Greville called a "balancing of passion," the Renaissance poets knew already.[18] Today René Girard describes the novel as "an obsession transcended,"[19] and Iris Murdoch defines the good novel as "therapy which resists the all-too-easy life of consolation and fantasy"; bad novels, she suggests, merely work out an author's "personal conflicts in a tightly conceived . . . myth," with no respect for things as they are rather than as the author might wish them to be.[20] Norman Holland, then, adds little when he argues that litera-

17. Kris, *Psychoanalytic Explorations*, pp. 35–39. Freud, "Creative Writers," *SE* 9:153.

18. Fulke Greville, *Poems and Dramas of Fulke Greville*, ed. Geoffrey Bullough, 2 vols. (New York, 1945), 1:182.

19. René Girard, *Deceit, Desire and the Novel: Self and Other in Literary Structure* (Baltimore: Johns Hopkins University Press, 1965), p. 300.

20. Quoted phrases taken, respectively, from "The Sublime and the Beautiful Revisited," *Yale Review* 49 (1959): 258, and "Against Dryness," *Encounter* 9 (1961): 20.

ture, like "all we know of living," is a "compromise of the mighty opposites of drive and defense."[21]

Even the more specific attempts to isolate fundamental narrative structures must inevitably build on the same essential conflict between wishing agent and resisting reality.[22] The universal myths which Northrop Frye anatomizes may have seasonal titles, but these myths can be better viewed as a series of positions determined not by the progress of the seasons but by the shape of a sphere graphed onto the axes of wish and reality, crossing the axes at romance (all positive wish, no reality), comedy (all positive reality), irony (negative wish), and tragedy (negative reality).[23]

Understandably, the psychoanalytic critics using this model have tended to pick works which deal explicitly with conflicts between opposing selves. The one literary text which Ernst Kris analyzes at length, for example, is Shakespeare's *Henry IV*,[24] which is a Renaissance psychomachia about the young prince who must choose between Falstaff's appetitive vices and the virtuous superego presiding as chief justice over his world. Others, such as Frederick Crews[25] and David Gordon,[26] come back repeatedly to writers like Hawthorne

21. Norman Holland, *The Dynamics of Literary Response* (New York: Oxford University Press, 1968), p. 53.

22. Thus, e.g., Vladimir Propp's analysis of folktales divides them into groups defined by the success or failure of the agent's struggle with reality (*Morphology of the Folk Tale* [Bloomington: Indiana Research Center in Anthropology, 1958], p. 92).

23. I do not claim that Northrop Frye would describe his wheel exactly this way, but he does see the romance mode as portraying all that man desires and the ironic mode as portraying all that man fears. See "Archetypal Criticism," in Frye's *Anatomy of Criticism: Four Essays* (New York: Atheneum, 1966), pp. 131–239.

24. Ernst Kris, "Prince Hal's Conflict," *Psychoanalytic Explorations*, pp. 273–85.

25. Frederick Crews has written on Hawthorne and Conrad in *The Sins of the Fathers: Hawthorne's Psychological Themes* (Oxford, London, and New York: Oxford University Press, 1966) and *Out of My System: Psychoanalysis, Ideology and Critical Method* (New York: Oxford University Press, 1975).

26. David J. Gordon examines a series of works about heroic and libidi-

and Lawrence, who were themselves explicitly concerned with very similar conflicts. The result is that the psychoanalytic critic often repeats what the literary critic has already said, though changing the vocabulary.

Of course psychoanalysis does promise to add something new to the critic's more traditional concern with the confrontation between desire and reality. Freud's second defining assumption about daydreams is that not only do they begin in wishes, but the wishes and fulfillments come partly from the past. The current battle is only the latest form of the confrontation, an adult and rationalized version of childhood fantasy battles about oral, anal, phallic, or childishly oedipal wishes; and the phantoms of the older battle haunt this one.[27] Reference to the past does add something new; we come closer to understanding the complexity of current literary experience by seeing that it draws on early expectations and experiences. The daydream model, however, does not show *how* it draws on them. It still leaves us with the problem of what to do with the childhood versions of experience—a puzzle which makes it all too tempting to see the primitive past as the "real" meaning behind the others: the birthmark which Hawthorne's mad scientist wants to remove from his wife is "really" the woman's sexual wound, as seen by the childish mind.[28]

Such reductions ignore the reality on the surface, and in doing so they paradoxically destroy the only context in which

nous rebellions in *Literary Art and the Unconscious* (Baton Rouge: Louisiana State University Press, 1976).

27. Ernst Kris and then Simon Lesser were the first to present and, in Lesser's case especially, fully to elaborate the role of infantile analogies in fiction. Their view of a psychoanalytic interpretation of literature coincides with what many have taken to be a description of psychoanalytic interpretation in general: they see psychoanalytic interpretation as putting literature in the context of infantile experience. (See, e.g., Roy Schafer, *Language and Insight* [New Haven: Yale University Press, 1978], and Marshall Edelson, *Language and Interpretation in Psychoanalysis* [New Haven: Yale University Press, 1975].)

28. See Lesser's analysis of Hawthorne's "The Birthmark," in *Fiction and the Unconscious*, pp. 87–91.

the depth can be effective; for the latent meanings exist only in a play with and against the manifest meanings. This is true even of simple anatomical symbols like birthmarks, which are much easier to deal with than whole texts and the network of fantasies evoked by them. There are, it is true, some trivially simple cases of double entendre in which the surface is merely a disguise for a symbol's "real" meaning, as in this *National Lampoon* "report from Washington":

> "I'm going to fill the loophole in your proposed legislation," he breathed, slipping his solid majority into my caucus. . . .[29]

But most cases are not this simple. No reader mistakes the pilgrimage the lover is making in Jean de Meun's *Romance of the Rose*, as he moves

> like a pilgrim most devout,
> Precipitate, but fervent and sincere,
> After that sweet permission, made my way
> Like loyal lover toward the loophole fair,
> The end of all my pilgrimage to achieve.
>   With greatest effort I conveyed with me
> My scrip and pilgrim staff so stiff and stout
> That it no ferrule needed to assure
> That it would hold the path and never slip.[30]

But none would be satisfied with a simple substitution which ignored the interaction between physical and spiritual progress. It is important that we know what role the latent meaning of the passage has, and that role may vary widely. Laurence Sterne reverses Ernest Jones's rules about the priority of sexual symbols,[31] for example, when he makes a "certain little family concernment" the symbol for winding the

29. *National Lampoon* (1973).
30. Guillaume de Lorris and Jean de Meun, *The Romance of the Rose*, trans. Harry W. Robbins (New York: E. P. Dutton, 1962), p. 454, 11. 21,347–55.
31. Ernest Jones, "The Theory of Symbolism" (1916), in *Papers on Psychoanalysis*, 5th ed. (Boston: Beacon Press, 1961).

clock in *Tristram Shandy*, because Mr. Shandy took care of both responsibilities on the first Sunday of every month. The two meanings may "blend imperceptibly" for Mrs. Shandy, when by association she suddenly is reminded to ask, "Pray you, my dear, have you not forgot to wind the clock?" But their relation is hardly so simple for her husband or for us—or for Sterne, who is manifestly playing with the fact that such mechanical symbolism is possible.

Although Sterne's symbolism fits too readily into the manifest story for Jonesian analysis, elsewhere Jones's method leaves us with a symbolic meaning that does not fit anywhere at all. Henry James introduces just such a problem with another timepiece, in *Watch and Ward*, the history of a delicate bachelor named Roger who has adopted a little girl and has secretly begun to hope that she will marry him. One night, when his manly friend Hubert is visiting, the girl surprises Roger by coming down in her nightgown:

> Her errand was to demand Roger's watch-key, her own having mysteriously vanished. . . . Roger's key proved a complete misfit, so that she had recourse to Hubert's. It hung in the watch-chain which depended from his waistcoat, and some rather intimate fumbling was needed to adjust it to Nora's diminutive timepiece. It worked admirably, and she stood looking at him with a little smile of caution as it creaked on the pivot.[32]

Every word solicits a Freudian reading, but there is no way to fit this interpretation directly into the story, as Nora's or Roger's secret wish, without distorting it. Nor can we readily attribute the unmistakable sexual electricity to James's purely irrelevant fantasies. Both these readings attempt to locate latent meaning while preserving the characters' psychological realism and both therefore fail to take account of the frankly ambiguous, hovering sexuality which really characterizes the

32. Henry James, *Watch and Ward* (1871), in *Watch and Ward, Longstaff's Marriage, Eugene Pickering, and Other Tales* (London: Macmillan, 1923), p. 83.

scene and which refuses to be located; but clearly the ambiguity here is more important than the sexuality. William Empson considers *all* Freudian interpretations as instances of his ultimate category of ambiguity, mutually exclusive meanings; his discussion of this category provides further instances of variously refined ironies in which no simple substitution will serve to explain, for example, Dryden's praise of God using scatological puns.

Simply identifying latent analogies is not sufficient, then, even to explain how isolated symbols work; it is still less satisfactory in explaining the role of fantasies evoked by an entire complex text. The psychoanalytic critic has never had much trouble identifying the "specular"[33] fantasy repetitions of the manifest story—a series of analogies going back to childhood, floating somewhere in the background of the story without touching it or forcing us to see it in new terms. He has had less success incorporating these phantoms into the body of the work and reconciling what he finds with what the ordinary reader takes to be the text. Of course, some psychoanalytic readers have not worried about the role of fantasies; for example, Erik Erikson describes a chain of analogies leading unbroken to earliest inchoate infantile memories.[34] He and others simply assume that, as Norman Holland says, "the psychoanalytic reading blends imperceptibly into the literary reading,"[35] just as the more primitive fantasy, presumably, blends imperceptibly into the later one. They see a swift and almost elegant movement up through the levels, a "progressively less fecaloid" series of displacements, as one analyst de-

33. The term "specular" is associated with Jacques Lacan's "imaginary" mode of thinking, one based on seeing resemblances and analogies between two things and tending to ignore the distinctions which keep the two things separate.

34. Erik Erikson, "The Dream Specimen of Psychoanalysis," *Journal of the American Psychoanalytic Association* 2 (1954): 5–56, where he talks about the process as it occurs in dreaming (see especially p. 15).

35. Norman Holland, *Psychoanalysis and Shakespeare* (New York: McGraw-Hill, 1964), p. 331.

scribed them, to mud, then to rocks, and finally to gems and gold for today's miser.[36]

Some psychoanalytic critics, however, have tried to define a more specific role for fantasy, and their suggestions are worth examining closely because most of the problems with psychoanalytic criticism have derived not from finding wild fantasies in the text but from claiming the wrong roles for them. Most notably, there have been two opposing theories about fantasy's role: either it is held to usurp the manifest text or else it is considered to be altogether irrelevant. In the first case, the fantasy is taken to be a part of the manifest story which has been repressed and must be brought back if we are to understand the text properly, just as Oedipus's past crimes must be brought back into the story. The tension between the manifest and the latent fantasy is then said to explain all the text's ambiguities, all the conflicts and tensions which the ordinary reader detects.

For readers who see repressed fantasies as benign and inherently interesting components in our lives, the psychoanalytic reading completes the ordinary one and leaves us with a whole and healthy text. Mark Kanzer, for example, finds in *Oedipus Rex* a fantasy common in children whose mothers are pregnant. He concludes that the fantasy can belong only to Oedipus, and since it must be stimulated by something going on in Oedipus's life, Jocasta must be pregnant.[37] Not many readers are willing to go this far in readjusting the literal facts in a story, but many, as we have seen, do readjust the facts about a character's mind in order to accommodate the evidence for a more general fantasy. On the other hand, for readers who find repressed meanings a more or less malignant growth on our otherwise integral lives, fitting the fantasy back into the literal story, though necessary, is truly a

---

36. Emile Rodrigué, "Notes on Symbolism," *International Journal of Psychoanalysis* 37 (1956): 157.

37. Mark Kanzer, "The Oedipus Trilogy," *Psychoanalytic Quarterly* 19 (1950): 561–72.

usurpation and can only result in distorting the text. This must lead, David Gordon says in his study *Literary Art and the Unconscious*, to "an interpretation which is not compatible with our interpretation of the artistic intention," as it does, for example, when Hardy's stoic logic in "Hap" is undermined by his unconsciously determined tone of despair in that poem.[38]

In the second case, fantasy is allowed *no* role at all in the manifest text, even as a disrupting force. "There is no unconscious irony," Wayne Booth says in his survey of that mode.[39] The fantasy is said to exist on some level separate from the manifest text, and there are various suggestions about what role it may play there. Norman Holland sees fantasy as the determining and ultimate meaning, with all the rest of the text functioning as a defense. If he were to apply his latest version of the theory, he would say that the fantasy and the defense belong not to the text but to the reader only; but the fantasy still determines the only "text" there is, namely, each reader's unique perception. Other critics admit the existence of fantasy in the text, but only as one of an almost infinite number of possible analogies, no one of which is more interesting or important than the others. The only plot which really matters is the one in the text; any childhood analogy is a separate and subsidiary matter.

The most fruitful suggestion about the role of fantasy lies at neither of these two extremes. It is the relatively modest claim that fantasies "resonate" with the manifest content of the work. *Resonate* is the word Gaston Bachelard chose in his early "psychoanalysis of fire,"[40] where he explored, though

38. Gordon, *Literary Art and the Unconscious*, p. 7.
39. Wayne Booth, *A Rhetoric of Irony* (Chicago: University of Chicago Press, 1974), p. 241. Contrast Jacques Lacan's casual claim that schizophrenics and neurotics always speak with irony, though an irony not always heard, in "Réponses à des étudiants en philosophie," *Cahiers pour l'Analyse* 3 (1966): 5–13.
40. Gaston Bachelard, *The Psychoanalysis of Fire*, trans. C.M. Ross (Boston: Beacon Press, 1964); see also *The Poetics of Space*, trans. Maria Jolas (New York: Orion Press, 1964); and *The Poetics of Reverie*, trans. Daniel Russell (Boston: Beacon Press, 1971).

not in an especially psychoanalytic way, the connotations of universally suggestive images. It is a word which other psychoanalytically inclined critics naturally turn to,[41] and it seems to capture the somehow subverbal effect of infantile analogies and the way in which earlier experience serves as what Charles Mauron calls the bass in a harmony of reference perhaps more musical than explicit.

Bachelard was talking about isolated images with set meanings apart from the text they were in; today analysts are more likely to talk about a structure of image patterns and entire scenes, but the idea of an infantile analogy to something in the text and now resonating behind it is the same. Marie Bonaparte saw the female anatomy resonating behind the double cheeks of the commissioner's fireplace in Poe's "Purloined Letter"; Lacan corrects her and points out a pattern of family relationships resonating behind the repeated configuration of relationships in the story.[42] But whether these commentators use element or whole structure as a base, each finds a resonance. Such resonating fantasies do not replace the surface; how could they? No one claims that Poe's "Descent into the Maelström" is really about a descent into the mother, or that Wordworth's feelings for nature were nothing more than a disguise for his feelings about his mother, or that when Matthew Arnold wrote "Dover Beach" he was actually remembering times when his mother withdrew to clash with her husband.

The fantasy does not replace adult experience but instead brings the intensities of childhood experience to bear on current adult life. It adds depth by evoking the unconscious

41. See, e.g., José Barchilon, "A Study of Camus' Mythopoetic Tale *The Fall*, with Some Comments about the Origin of Esthetic Feelings," *Jouranl of the American Psychoanalytic Association* 17 (1969): 193–240.

42. In fact, Bonaparte's piecemeal interpretations are not quite as far from Lacan's as he implies, especially when she looks for analogies to human beings and human relationships rather than for analogies to anatomy only. See Lacan's "Seminar on 'The Purloined Letter,'" translated by Jeffrey Mehlman in *French Freud: Structural Studies in Psychoanalysis*, Yale French Studies 48 (1972): 39–72, and Bonaparte's *The Life and Works of Edgar Allan Poe*.

remnants of infantile experience, without substituting that experience for an adult one. It evokes the feeling, not the mundane literal situation which created the feeling; Wordsworth described the process: "The soul, / Remembering how she felt, but what she felt / Remembering not, retains an obscure sense / Of possible sublimity." The analogy brings us back to "how" we felt, though not so self-consciously as Wordsworth. The resonance is more emotional than cognitive, and theorists have presented it as such. "The conventional critic tells us how [literature] *means*," Holland says, and "the psychological critic tells how it *moves* us."[43] Such insight is intended as a corrective to what Frederick Crews has called "anesthetic" or falsely objective criticism. The "meaning" revealed by psychoanalytic interpretation, in this theory, is, then, not only an unspoken motive but a special kind of unspoken metaphor, bringing what I. A. Richards has called the "transaction of contexts" which metaphor brings, though these contexts are emotional and not literal.

Take as an example a story which yields itself invitingly to psychoanalytic interpretation, yet finally resists any simplifying reduction: Conrad's story about Marlow journeying up the Congo to rescue the trader Kurtz, through increasingly dense and savage territory into the "heart of darkness." There he finds, instead of a brilliant young idealist, a corrupted Kurtz who has presided at "moonlit dances ending in unspeakable rites." Marlow is horrified, no less by his own fascination than by the rites themselves and by the metamorphosis of his idol into sinner.

Frederick Crews finds infantile fantasies beneath the surface of this story—analogies which tell the full truth but were repressed from Conrad's tale as written.[44] The story makes no sense, he says, unless we see its extensive ambiguity as a disguise and evasion of a repressed truth. The story's mysteri-

---

43. Holland, *Psychoanalysis and Shakespeare*, p. 320.
44. Frederick Crews, "Conrad's Uneasiness—and Ours," in *Out of My System*, pp. 42–62.

ousness about Kurtz (What exactly is he doing? What exactly is it that Marlow finds horrible?) is really Marlow's ambiguity about his own oedipal savagery, which he cannot come to terms with. Conrad, who cannot face it either, is colluding with him, evading the heroism he seems most to praise. As a result, "he is simultaneously terrified at existence and a connoisseur of its heightened moments, at once a nihilist and a raconteur."[45] The tension, Crews says, all derives from Conrad's struggle against his repressed fantasies; in particular, against a fantasied journey into the maternal body—a voyeuristic journey to observe the father, Kurtz, but at the same time an incestuous one, asserting the child's rights. Neither Marlow nor Conrad, who has manipulated this tale, is able to accept Kurtz's—the father's—act or Marlow's desire to repeat it. So the story first "represses" the details of the act and then disguises both characters' desires by insisting that Kurtz has sinned only with savage women ("not with my mother!") and that Marlow has come to rescue Kurtz, not to replace him. "It is startling to see how all the peculiarities of the Conradian world fall into place in this perspective,"[46] Crews says.

The problem with this perspective, as one of Crews's reviewers complained,[47] is that it is by no means the only unifying one for the text. Even Freud realized that there is "symbolism from above" as well as "from below,"[48] but Crews speaks as if all symbols, simply by virtue of being inexplicit, are symptoms of repressed infantile sexual material. Crews's reviewer objects to this reduction of all conflict in Marlow and his world to Conrad's personal neurotic conflicts. She

45. *Ibid.*, p. 48.
46. *Ibid.*, p. 47.
47. Rosemary Dinnage, *Times Literary Supplement*, 19 March 1976, pp. 319–20.
48. Sigmund Freud, *The Interpretation of Dreams* (1900), *SE* 5:524; "Remarks on the Theory and Practice of Dream Interpretation" (1923b), *SE* 19:111. In *An Outline of Psychoanalysis* (1940), Freud talks about dreams from the ego and from the id (*SE* 23:166).

sees the psychoanalytically observed fantasy as one analogy out of many, and not an especially privileged one which can replace or invade the literal story. She goes to the opposite extreme and refuses to grant special status to such fantasies at all. In fact, Crews himself later joins her (though not in remarks specifically about this story), when he retracts his earlier claims for analysis and warns that "a critic who may have been drawn toward Freud by the promise of a heightened sensitivity to conflict may, without ever knowing what has happened to him, become the purveyor of a peculiarly silly kind of allegory."[49] As the reviewer points out, the story is about "a confrontation with the self," and in it oedipal explorations of the maternal body, if not "silly," are no more relevant than references to a religious pilgrimage across a symbolic continent.

Surely neither approach is correct. The purposefully ambiguous outlines of a confrontation with the self cannot be reduced to one specific anatomical exploration; yet infantile experience is not just one more arbitrary analogy. The virtue of seeing only resonances is that it goes to neither of these extremes. The resonance theory about fantasies, however, can provide only a partial explanation for the way the early analogy works. Evoking an echo chamber of early fantasies behind the story can degenerate too easily into sentimentality, into unlimited proliferation of emotional associations, into memories of things that have once before moved us the way these events tend to move us now. The resonance theory, by showing how literature moves us, explains some facts about response, but it does not really come to terms with the text on its own terms. It does not show us how the text's meaning *depends on* how it moves us. And this theory cannot do so as long as it advocates search for "allegories of a particularly silly kind," in the sense that historical allegories are silly. So long as critics look for past experiences which are like the present

49. Frederick Crews, "Reductionism and Its Discontents," reprinted in *Out of My System*, pp. 166–85.

ones in every way except for exchangeable details, the value of the resonance theory is limited. It can only postulate that the man explores a river instead of his mother, or guzzles beer instead of nuzzling the breast, as if the simple displacement of an external object were all that mattered. We must turn away from the two expectations generated by the daydream model: that the manifest text will be shaped largely by a battle over wish fulfillment and that past experiences are almost exactly like present ones. We must look instead for fantasies deriving from the earliest stages of life, when wish fulfillment could not be separated from a whole way of seeing the world; and that way differs radically from any adult view.

THE BRANCHING TREE OF FANTASY

Since Freud wrote his essay on daydreams, analysts have been learning more about the rest of our fantasy life. Freud presented the wish-fulfilling, embattled daydream as the building block of the imagination, the foundation we should look for as the basis of more complex literature; but it is not that. The daydream is a polished and rationalized final product, not only because it already takes account of adult reality and includes defenses as well as wishes,[50] but also because it is organized enough to distinguish between wish and defense, in the first place, and between self and resisting reality. Instead of the kaleidoscope of images and scenes which characterize primitive fantasy—clusters which do not distinguish person, place, or time—the daydream presents a recognizable image of the world (though a more pleasing one), containing discrete events and separate individuals. It is already formulated into adult terms and public vocabulary. The daydream is, as Hanns Sachs said, only a Hollywood version of true fantasy.[51] Rather than recreating fantasies, the daydream saves

---

50. Kris, *Psychoanalytic Explorations*, p. 35, n. 43.

51. Hanns Sachs, *The Creative Unconscious* (Cambridge, Mass.: Sci-Art Publishers, 1964), p. 42. Similarly, well-identified daydreaming per se is only the final version of a much more general fantasizing activity which is "the

us from the terror they produce. Such fantasies take us back to an alien state of diffusion in its way more painful to the adult than any instinctual frustration. The daydream may satisfy wishes in a world where we no longer need be limited by—or even bored by—things as they are, and it may please us by letting us have our own way for a change. But we should realize that not the least of its gratifications, as Roy Schafer points out, is the way it represents us as stable and coherent enough to *have* a way of our own.[52]

The true building blocks of the imagination are not day-dreams but primitive fantasies. These are shaped not by wishes alone but by all aspects of early experience—not only instinctual, but cognitive, perceptual, and social (which analysts somewhat awkwardly call "object relations"). Primitive fantasies derive in fact from a period when these functions were not yet separated; and unlike wishes, they are not so much an alternative to rational thinking as a primitive form of thinking—or a primitive form of organizing all internal and external experience. Such fantasies are holistic experiences out of which all sense of self as opposed to the world, and all distinction between fiction and reality, will only later be precipitated.[53] But meanwhile the pattern matters more than the pieces, and the plot matters more than the "characters"—insofar as the pattern and the plot include real

baseline of [mental] activity," as Eric Klinger has called it in *Structure and Function of Fantasy* (New York: Wiley-Interscience, 1971), p. 348.

52. See Roy Schafer's discussion of fantasies in *Aspects of Internalization* (New York: International Universities Press, 1968), pp. 37–39, 85–89, 109–111.

53. Theories of global development emphasize the simultaneous emergence of symbolic and objective thinking out of a single undifferentiated matrix. See chapter 1, note 43, and also Margaret Mahler, *On Human Symbiosis and the Vicissitudes of Individuation* (New York: International Universities Press, 1968); René Spitz, *No and Yes: On the Genesis of Human Communication* (New York: International Universities Press, 1957) and *The First Year of Life* (New York: International Universities Press, 1965); D. W. Winnicott, *Collected Papers* (New York: Basic Books, 1958) and *The Maturational Process and the Facilitating Environment* (New York: International Universities Press, 1965).

people at all. In fantasies we "identify" with the whole scene, rather than locating ourselves within a single character or within a person. Emotions are registered as landscape; external intrusions seem as inescapable as do parts of the body; wishes and fears are magically realized as facts; and external objects or events do not exist, except in relation to the child.

The child himself is defined by relation rather than role—a phenomenon repeated in the analytic situation, where the patient alternates easily between playing himself as battered child and playing the omnipotent parent threatening to batter the analyst. So, too, the sadist can be content playing masochist, and the exhibitionist will walk round the door to the peephole if there is no one to look at him. These "projective identifications" are possible now, because the patterns of relationship were laid down before the child's sense of identity was, before he precipitated himself out of the whole experience. His sense of identity, indeed, is built on internalized relationships; today's inner battles are repetitions of childhood struggles with parents, and today's states of mind are learned from the ones he observed in childhood.

In the adult, these infantile confusions can be transformed into psychosis, if they take control, or into poetry, if they are self-consciously shaped and placed. But for the child they are the only way toward sanity and logic. This primitive form of fantasizing—this "fiction-making," as it seems from an objective point of view—is the child's first way of making contact with the outside world, as he gradually learns to separate internal and external from the original unified experience. At first he passes easily between the two. He moves outward by using images of (and fantasies about) his own body, which are almost the only reference points he has, to make sense of the outside world: Little Hans watches a box drop from the back of a truck and says it is "doing lumpf." Or the child takes a different approach and uses images from the outside world to understand his own feelings. Jacques Lacan has described the "mirror phase" which illustrates the child's alienation from himself—that moment when he sees "out there" an external image in the mirror and learns to take it as a picture of himself, a concrete recognition standing for the much more subtle and gradual process of exchanges in which the child's sense of himself is built up out of the play between his feelings and the world's responding reflection of them: his mother's impatience convinces him he is clumsy, or her delight tells him he is special.[54]

Each new stage of development, in fact, is characterized by its own particular degree of separation between self and world, internal and external experience, subjective symbolism and objective perceptions; and the child's fantasy life proliferates accordingly. Old concerns and images take on new and more mature forms as he grows. In addition, of course, each new stage of growth brings its own new fantasies, with new themes and new ways of seeing the world. The critic may put them in the same category, but oral, anal, phallic, and genital fantasies each arise at different times, in different contexts, and from different perspectives to generate their own branching derivatives. These terms do not simply refer to stages of instinctual development; they describe whole experiences, including the way the child feels, sees, and acts in the world—different "modes" of perception, feeling, and action, as Erik Erikson has called them.[55] The bodily activity is itself a

54. Jacques Lacan, "Le Stade du miroir" (1948); trans. Jean Roussel, "The Mirror-Phase as Formative of the Function of the I," *New Left Review* 51 (1968): 63–77; see also "Some Reflections on the Ego," *International Journal of Psychoanalysis* 34 (1953): 11–17. Lacan's description of the child's recognition of himself only through the revolutionary recognition of the "Other" in the mirror is closer than it might seem to the more gradual evolution of self and other that both the English and American analysts describe. See note 53 and, e.g., Hans Loewald, "Ego and Reality," *International Journal of Psychoanalysis* 32 (1951): 10–18.

55. Erik Erikson, *Childhood and Society* (New York: W. W. Norton, 1963), pp. 72–97. See also the more recent attempts to unify Freudian theories of instinctual development with Piaget's theories of cognitive development, especially in Heinz Werner and Bernard Kaplan, *Symbol Formation: An Organismic-Developmental Approach to Language and the Expression of Thought* (New York: John Wiley, 1963), and Peter Wolff, "Cognitive Considerations for a Psychoanalytic Theory of Language Acquisition," in *Motives and Thought: Psychoana-*

symbol of the whole mode, rather than its central defining quality; the issues in toilet training symbolize the more general issues an anal-stage child is concerned with—rule-consciousness, stubbornness and battle for control, a concern with simplistic dichotomies like "holding on" and "letting go," and a concern for precious objects, rather than for people. The adult's anality, as Edmund Wilson said, has nothing to do with sphincters; Ben Jonson's meticulously arranged plots and his pedantry can make an "anal" formal accompaniment to the miser's story in *The Alchemist*, without our ever having to refer to toilets to show why the configuration makes imaginative sense.[56]

The fact that not only are there many different fantasies but any one fantasy is really a series of fantasies from different stages of life is one subtlety that critics of psychoanalytic literary criticism sometimes overlook when they call it reductive. Any theory which finds the same fantasy in a *Playboy* joke and the *Wife of Bath's Tale*, one critic observed,[57] cannot be saying much about either. Naming the fantasy, however, is only the beginning. There are different stages of any fantasy—about love, about loss, about conflict—and the matter of Oedipus can be as varied a category as the matter of Troy. Finding a fantasy is not simply a matter of going back to progressively more fecaloid materials or of substituting the original breast for a beer. Later versions of a fantasy supposedly the "same" differ not only in one or two props but in

---

lytic Essays in Honor of David Rapaport, ed. Robert R. Hold, Psychological Issues, vol. 5, no. 2/3 (New York: International Universities Press, 1966). Howard Gardner has made such theories the basis for a general approach to the psychology of creativity in *The Arts and Human Development: A Psychological Study of the Artistic Process* (New York: John Wiley, 1973). For specific application of the theory of modes, see, e.g., Mark Shechner, *Joyce in Nighttown: A Psychoanalytic Inquiry into Ulysses* (Berkeley and Los Angeles: University of California Press, 1974).

56. Edmund Wilson, "Morose Ben Jonson," in *The Triple Thinkers: Twelve Essays on Literary Subjects*, (New York: Charles Scribner's, 1948), pp. 213–32.

57. Robert M. Adams, "Interfering with Literature," *New York Review of Books*, 10 April 1969, pp. 33–34.

their whole tone and design; they are increasingly realistic and elaborate. A primitive oral fantasy is a scene of oceanic longing or transcendental bliss, for which our adult thirsts and quenchings are only pallid approximations—and to which our adult notions of breasts are irrelevant.

As a result, the "same" fantasy is very different in an infant and an adolescent, in form as well as in content. Take for example the fantasy about losing a mother, so often invoked by psychoanalysts reading literature. Edgar Allan Poe's barren, icy landscapes capture the infant's sense of loss on a worldwide scale; his Berenices and Ligeias, returning from the dead to haunt the guilty narrator, are the products of an older child's imagination, while his theory that the death of a beautiful woman is the most poetic of all subjects is a still later and more rationalized response to loss. Poe's mother died when he was two; Wordsworth's mother died when he was seven, and his loss is reflected in a rather different way in *The Prelude*, as Richard Onorato has suggested.[58] Mother Nature is a gentler betrayer here than in Poe's stories, still as wide as the entire landscape but not as catastrophic or as threatening to the poet's very existence as it would be to a smaller child. The poem also includes a realistic picture of the child and mother; the experience is seen from an objective perspective, as it never is in Poe's total capitulations to fantasy. Loss takes still another form in Samuel Johnson's *Rasselas*, which he wrote to pay for expenses when his mother was dying. Whatever else we find in the fable, it is also a vision of the maternal happy valley, though highly distanced, rationalized, moralized, and stylized, and it shows the price one must pay when one leaves the valley.[59]

58. Richard Onorato, *The Character of the Poet: Wordsworth in* The Prelude (Princeton, N.J.: Princeton University Press, 1971).

59. See Bernard C. Meyer's speculations about *Rasselas* in "Some Reflections on the Contribution of Psychoanalysis to Biography," in *Psychoanalysis and Contemporary Science: An Annual of Integrative and Interdisciplinary Studies*, vol. 1 (New York: International Universities Press, 1972), pp. 382–85.

When he presented his model for literature, Freud evoked an image of a chain of fantasy running backward smoothly from the present. A more accurate image for the mind, however, is a branching tree, with its roots in the original fantasy and constantly branching derivatives all the way up, all still existing simultaneously. The trunk line may ascend in an unbroken chain of analogies. Often it does, in the case of core fantasies or "identity themes," so that the separate stages are no longer distinct, and the earlier ones are present—like the form of Aristotle's ship—only as structural echoes. But even in these cases, the main line is paralleled by partly detached and independent branches which can neither be severed from it nor forced back into it. Finding a derivative from the very top of the tree—for example, Paul mourning for his mother in *Sons and Lovers* or Stephen refusing to mourn for his in *Ulysses*—is very different from finding one sent out directly on a branch from lower down on the trunk, as in Poe's "Narrative of A. Gordon Pym," where the main character is tormented by thirst in the midst of a threatening sea. So different are the products of lower, early branches from those of the later ones that Freud used the difference to define two inverse forms of pathology.[60] The adult's attempt to live out a relatively early branch fantasy by taking it literally—recreating infantile unity by choosing a homosexual partner, for example—is "perversion"; the adult who lives out only a displaced and realistic version of the fantasy is "neurotic." The difference, for Freud, was functional and not a matter of definition alone, since, as he said, only the neurotic could be cured.

Freud's implicit value system is characteristic of literary

---

60. "Neuroses are the negative of perversions," Freud claims in "Three Essays on the Theory of Sexuality" (1905), *SE* 7:165, 231. Freud was distinguishing between the neurotic's use of repression, on one hand, and other forms of defense—rather than the failure of defense—in the pervisions, where the "open" fantasy could be tolerated because it was being "disavowed" or "split off." See note 67.

critics who use only the daydream model, with its single line of development that implicity becomes a measure of value: the daydream at the bottom of the line is transformed into increasingly civilized forms of literature. So Dickens's *Old Curiosity Shop* is mired in a masochistic daydream about Little Nell, while his later portrayal of a more realistic imprisonment of Little Dorrit in a complicated realistic world that provides a context for her experience makes *Little Dorrit* a much better novel. However, while such transformations are common, they are by no means the only paths from the raw material of our imagination to the finished literary work. In fact, daydreams and popular fiction, with their concern for a superficial realism, are not necessarily the bottom steps on a ladder leading upward toward literature. They are only one branch off the root of fantasy, a branch extended in the direction of the least resistance, as we try to accommodate ourselves to the external world. It is not a matter of moving upward and outward from raw fantasy to James Bond's rationalized heroics, and then farther upward to *Beowulf*. Quite the opposite; we would all agree that Fleming's novels are in some sense later derivatives[61] of the hero fantasy, farther out along the branch than *Beowulf*. Quality is not measured by distance from the root.

---

61. "Later" in the sense of having accommodated to an adult's recognition of the reality principle. Complex works that take account of the resistant world often *are* better than the purely self-indulgent fantasies from which they begin, as Lionel Trilling argues in his discussion of Keats's swoons and hypnotic trances, which, Trilling says, manifest a complex adult geniality but nonethless come out of "the passivity and self-reference of the infantile condition." ("The Poet as Hero: Keats in His Letters," in Trilling's *The Opposing Self: Nine Essays in Criticism* New York: Viking Press, 1959, pp. 3–49. Such versions of oral fantasies are certainly better than the crude literalizations in, for example, Robert Heinlein's *Stranger in a Strange Land*, where earthlings learn to "grok" in mysterious union and then lovingly eat the "stranger" in a scenitific version of the Last Supper. But the superiority of Keats's version depends on more than its acceptance of the reality principle.

FANTASY'S ROLE: IN THE TEXT

I do not mean to imply that the opposite simplification is true either, and that the more primitive the fantasy in a text, the better. There is no simple way to make such evaluations. There is not even a simple way to describe the fantasy's role or to locate it in a text. A primitive fantasy is not a story but a "schema for" a story, as one analyst described it; it is "peremptory ideation" about a particular conflict, with its characteristic feeling tone (often ambivalent) and its associated scenes and images, but with no fixed and final version.[62] Its role in literature is as varied and unpredictable as it is in human beings. In life, such peremptory ideation *can* take over current perception and turn it into endless versions of the same paranoid or narcissistic fantasy; or it can completely take over the "day residue" and shape dreams and daydreams. In literature, it can similarly preempt the writer's manifest plot; and then it is easiest to recognize, especially if a relatively primitive stage of fantasy, which has a local habitation and a name, is the one usurped. Jack kills the giant, chops down his beanstalk, and steals his jewels; little Johnnie is really fantasizing about killing and castrating his father and stealing his father's wife.

But even in a case like this, when one version of the fantasy takes over the plot or makes itself felt as a very close analogy, though we may sense the presence of fantasy, its role is not so easily described as Freud often made it sound. In many Freudian descriptions—like the ones we have been looking at—there is a fairly simple and consistent adversary relationship between fantasy and manifest text. Thus it is suggested that the fantasy is wish fulfilling (or fearsome), and the story is a disguise or a defensive transformation—at best an adaptive transformation. The fantasy is behind; the story is up front. The fantasy is unconsciously perceived; the story is

62. George S. Klein, *Perception, Motives and Personality* (New York: Alfred A. Knopf, 1970), pp. 357–412.

perceived consciously. The fantasy becomes apparent only through a symbolic or indirect reading, while the manifest story is available to a literal or "straight" reading.

Texts, however, are not this simple. Even in Conrad's *Heart of Darkness*, where we found a relatively simple analogy between the whole plot and the fantasy, the relation between the two cannot be described as a purely emotional resonance between two stories that have no cognitive connection except as open and hidden, or literal and figurative, versions of the same narrative. The difference between the reviewer's and the analyst's readings of *Heart of Darkness* is not the difference between a literal and a symbolic reading. The journey is a literal journey and not the "meaning" of the story, which even in the most scrupulously unpsychoanalytic approach requires a flexible reading not easily equated with or separated from the literal text. When the reviewer says that this is a story about the discovery of self, she is already making a symbolic equation between the physical journey and its analogous psychological movement. The psychoanalytic reading is in one sense more literal than the critic's. The analyst emphasizes the fact that in choosing this *particular* physical experience, Conrad is going back to the first form in which we experience anything resembling a confrontation with the self. The exploration of the "vast, fecund" continent, its fascination and abomination, *was* the exploration of the mother's body; and at an earlier stage, this voyeuristic or incestuous voyage was also an exploration of the self, then barely distinguished from the mother's body. The substitution of internal for external voyage is *now* a symbolic device, but *then* it was a literal equivalence. No outright sexual encounter with the mother could be so open a representation as this jungle river voyage, this internal voyage, because there was none in the infant's fantasy in the first place; the mother *was* the entire landscape, the lush jungle with its river entry. Conrad is not hiding a fantasy but going back to the most open, literal version of it. Presenting the experience this way is like emphasizing an etymologically important meaning for a word now used in a new sense and bringing a dead metaphor to life.

In *Heart of Darkness* the fantasy schema corresponds fairly closely in its details to the manifest story, but even there it does so only if we simplify, leaving out the plot twists and developments. Usually the fantasy does not predominate even to that degree or fit that neatly into the outline of the plot any more often than fantasy takes over the whole of a man's life and completely preempts perception. Rather than creating (and reinforcing) the manifest pattern, the fantasy often merely pulls the surface into new patterns. The unifying fantasy behind a text exhibits a different kind of unity from the mature, aesthetic unity which Ernst Kris describes as the artist's achievement when he balances conflicting psychic forces and identifies with the whole pattern in a text rather than with only the wish-fulfilling part. The patterns which Kris describes begin with discrete characters and events and then organize these into a larger unity. The patterns which fantasy brings are not "post-character," like Kris's, but "pre-character," both in the sense of focusing on only parts of people (for example, Poe's obsession with physical fragments such as eyes and teeth or the fairy tale's focus on psychological fragments of the split mother [witch and fairy godmother] and in the sense that people are not fully discriminated from the overall design. Kris's pattern is a balancing of characters and events, but the fantasy's pattern more closely resembles a merging. Kris's pattern is the difficult reward of escaping beyond the confines of self, while the fantasy's pattern is a relapse into seeing things as we did before we ever separated self from world.

Ernst Gombrich has made a similar distinction in the visual arts.[63] His manifest text is a cloyingly sweet version of "The Three Graces," which repels us, Gombrich says, not only because the graces are too naked but because the picture is too easy to read. He covers it with a wobbly glass, breaking up the too-obvious painting into alien chunks of shape and color in-

63. Ernst Gombrich, "Psychoanalysis and the History of Art," in *Meditations on a Hobby Horse and Other Essays on the Theory of Art* (London: Phaidon, 1963), pp. 40–41.

stead of a story, imposing on it a new and more interesting "latent" organization. Gombrich uses his glass as a parable for modern art, which takes us back to such patterns and, incidentally, back to the truly primitive libidinal gratifications which we find, for example, in the bright colors and phallic forms of Picasso's paintings and which appeal to us on some deeper level than do the smiling graces. For the analyst, Gombrich's demonstration is a parable for finding fantasies. The analyst suspends his interest in the realistic surface of a text, or of a cloying daydream, and ignores its rationalizations and the logical connections between elements. Like Gombrich, and like the structuralist, he avoids an itemizing or naive realism and looks for the less obvious fantasy structures which pull the surface elements into new patterns and reveal new emphases. He sees the manifest surface in new ways, rather than seeing through it to childhood analogies.

The commonest form of this readjustment of vision is the simple reassignment of values in the underlying fantasy, where the author is not located neatly within the hero of his story but is distributed over the whole design and can indeed be of the devil's party. Such contradictions of the manifest story are easy enough to find in clinical experience. Wolfman's intricate fantasy life reveals layers of fantasies which show just how slippery a simple tag like *castration* can be.[64] Wolfman, in his manifest symptomatology, was afraid he had a hole in his nose. It is not hard to believe that behind this fear lay a frightening fantasy about castration, and the far more general devastation to both mind and body which castration symbolizes. But in a still more primitive fantasy, the fear of castration turned out to be a disguise for Wolfman's *wish* to be castrated, so that he could be his father's lover. The manifest elements appear to be one thing from the perspective of the first fantasy and a very different thing from the perspective of the second.

---

64. As Freud says in his explanation of Wolfman's symptoms, "It was only a logical contradiction—which is not saying much." *From the History of an Infantile Neurosis*, SE 17:79.

The same thing can happen in a literary text. We have all found ourselves in the devil's party at one time or another, or have at least fleetingly seen the sacrificed hero as a tainted scapegoat best gotten out of the way. In addition to such reversals, however, the fantasy can suggest an even more radical readjustment of vision, in which it challenges not only the values assigned to characters and events but also their very identities. The critical approaches associated with the structuralists often call attention to counterstructures like this in texts, especially when such structures declare themselves on the manifest level and suggest doubts about the nature of personal identity in the stories. René Girard's study *Deceit, Desire and the Novel* explores the truism that people are affected by society and shows it to be a more radical paradox than suspected: individuals have not only their outward roles but their own desires—the defining qualities of their inner separateness—determined by others' desires. What seems to be a clearcut relationship between two independent people turns out to be a relationship determined by an absent third person; if Frédéric in Flaubert's *Sentimental Education* desires Mme Arnoux, this is because M. Arnoux already desires her. Frédéric's desire is really an identification with another's desire, determined by a prior relationship between two other people, with whom he forms a triangle. What I am suggesting here is that the priority of structures is nothing new to us; it is a priority which characterizes our earliest experiences and the fantasies which derive from them. Girard's triangular situation, as he notes briefly in a footnote to his book (which never mentions Freud),[65] has its origins in the complicated play between external and internal realities which characterizes the oedipal triangle.

The priority of structures is made even more explicit in the story whose interpretation Jacques Lacan has selected as the opening for his *Ecrits*: Poe's "The Purloined Letter."[66] Here,

65. Girard, *Deceit, Desire and the Novel*, p. 186.
66. His "Seminar on 'The Purloined Letter' " thus precedes the clinical seminars.

not only are characters defined by their role in a larger structure, but as they shift roles they also shift personalities: What
better demonstration could we find of our dependence on
relationship to know who we are? Poe's tale concerns the detective Dupin's recovery of a letter purloined from the
Queen. It is narrated by Dupin's friend, who heard it from
Dupin, and consists of two scenes, in each of which the letter
is stolen from a different person, but in the same way. In the
tale's first scene Minister D—— intrudes on the King and
Queen just after the Queen has received the embarrassing letter and kept it from the King's attention by casually pre-
tending it is irrelevant and *not* hiding it. The King is fooled,
but Minister D—— soon sees what is going on and takes the
letter, while the Queen of course can do nothing without
bringing the King's attention to the letter. In the second
scene, Minister D——, now put in the Queen's position, has
repeated the Queen's strategy of hiding the letter from the
eyes of the police, and has casually left it out among his own
letters. The police are fooled, but when Dupin enters, now
playing Minister D——'s old role in the original scene, he
sees what is going on and arranges to steal the letter. Lacan
suggests that each character's behavior—not only his acts but
his thoughts, feeling, and style—is shaped by the role he takes
in each scene. When he plays the thief, in the first scene,
Minister D—— exhibits a canny cleverness, but the moment
he possesses the letter and starts playing the Queen's role in
the second scene, he assumes her qualities. The same thing
happens to Dupin, as he moves from playing the thief in the
second scene to playing the Queen at the end of the story
when he has the letter and tells his friend—the narrator—
what happened. If Edgar Allan Poe, or the reader, identifies
with any character, Lacan says, it is not in the simple way
which Marie Bonaparte outlined when she analyzed the story
and suggested randomly scattered resemblances between Poe
and Dupin here or Poe and Minister D—— over there. We
identify with the whole structure of relationship rather than
with any particular personality.

In the examples we have just seen, a controlling fantasy either provides a complicated accompaniment to the manifest story, as in *Heart of Darkness*, or pulls the whole plot into new patterns, as in Poe's story. The role of fantasies, however, is still more varied than these cases suggest. Fantasy is brief and simple, and its effect is often felt locally, rather than in entire plots. What complicates—and enriches—its contribution is the fact that different versions of the fantasy affect different parts of the manifest story in entirely different ways. A single primal fantasy preempts first one and then another aspect of the text, repeating its own pattern beneath what otherwise appears to be a changing surface. The fantasy can even turn up in seemingly contradictory forms, forms which to the rational mind and the literal reader are distinct and perhaps mutually exclusive but which are all manifestations of its illogical cluster of ideas.

Interpretation becomes even more complicated because (especially in long and complex works) there is usually more than one fantasy, more than one determining psychic function and imaginative source (just as there is usually more than one external source) in a literary work. While one fantasy may parallel the main plot, others can work with and against it in a variety of ways. In *Jane Eyre*, for example, the manifest story about Jane's progress to adulthood is reinforced by a barely concealed female oedipal fantasy in which growing up means marrying daddy. But it is also contradicted by a more primitive oral-stage fantasy that repeats its own regressive wish fulfillment in the very events which supposedly show Jane's escape from such infantile indulgences. On the surface, the feminine bildungsroman shows Jane progressing from a stormy childhood in her foster family, to a somewhat less stormy adolescence in the larger "family" at Lowood School, where she moves from student to teacher, to an independent post as governess, and finally to her role as wife and mother in Rochester's house. This manifest plot is somewhat mechanically laden with a message: Jane leaves behind the crude moral dichotomies and the untamed passions of childhood and accommodates herself to an adult world of necessary pain, ethical decorum, and true Christianity. The oedipal fantasy is hardly moral, but it works in the same direction: Jane discards the childish role every little girl resents and is allowed to take her mother's place. Such is the world as every oedipal-stage girl sees it: every girl's mother is a raving lunatic in the attic, and every girl's heroic father loves her more than he loves the wife who is bound to him only by a legal fiction and who never deserved him in the first place.

The second fantasy cluster works in the opposite direction, however. Along with the oedipal story there is a story about an earlier and more primitive yearning for union with the mother, with all the intensity and exaggeration of an oral-stage infantile attachment: the landscape-wide desolation and revitalization, the magic telepathic empathy, and the promise of oceanic, transcendental union and bliss. In this earlier fantasy, rather than going through the difficult process of growing up, Jane is granted the pleasures of regression. The later, oedipal fantasy has to accommodate itself to the moral laws of Christianity (they live happily ever after, but only after a divine thunderbolt cripples Rochester and makes him pay for his sins); but in the earlier fantasy, Christianity represents a primitive religious union which is an infantile wish fulfillment. Instead of achieving a mature relationship with another, separate person, Jane regresses to a totally engulfing relationship of mutual identification and dependence. She and Rochester are not man and wife but mother and child, and as in all primitive fantasies, they take turns playing both roles. Rochester has represented a fierce and total maternal devotion all along: he actually appears disguised as a strange old gypsy woman in one scene, weirdly knowledgeable about Jane's whole life, who predicts Jane's future. By marrying him, Jane regains the totality every infant finds in his mother. It works the other way too, perhaps even more obviously, for Rochester's symbolic trimming and blinding at the end of the book makes him into a child in Jane's eyes, totally dependent on her. The ending has a function in both fantasies: Rochester's accident is the sad but liberating price mature lovers must pay, but it also returns them to a regressive world of mutual absorption in each other. Part of the novel's continuing attraction is its success in letting the reader have it both ways.

In addition to the play of multiple fantasies which we see in *Jane Eyre*, there is still another alternative to the simple hierarchy of closely analogous fantasies. This alternative can be seen in texts where different stages of the same fantasy appear side by side, primitive material taking its place next to later derivatives, so that the story demonstrates a "vertical split"[67] rather than a horizontal stratification. The splitting is obvious in the typical three-part movement in fairy tales, from home to forest and home again. The movement from the real world to the forest's magical world, where strange things start happening, is also a movement from a late, realistic version of fantasy to an earlier primitive version of the same fantasy. "Hansel and Gretel" begins with what resembles a child's typical, self-pitying daydream: "My mean mother is starving me to death and wants to leave me out in the cold." Here the subjective view of the world is carefully formulated in realistic terms and cleaned up, so that there is no sign of the child's anger or of destructive retaliations. Then the story moves to the forest, where the primitive feelings come out, and a more primitive version of the fantasy becomes literally true. There the children catch a glimpse of the perfect mother, who is all but literally an edible house, but then find her turned into the opposite, a witch who is going to eat *them* up instead. Not only the symbolism-turned-literal but

---

67. For discussion of such splitting and related defenses, see Sigmund Freud, "Fetishism" (1927), *SE* 21:149–57; "Constructions in Analysis" (1937), *SE* 23:255–69; "An Outline of Psychoanalysis" (1940 [1938]), *SE* 23:202–04; "Splitting of the Ego in the Process of Defense" (1940 [1938]), *SE* 23:275–78. See also Heinz Kohut, *The Analysis of the Self: A Systematic Approach to the Psycho-analytic Treatment of Narcissistic Personality Disorders* (New York: International Universities Press, 1971), pp. 176–78, 183–86.

also the extremes (either I eat you or you eat me) mark this as an early fantasy.

In a more sophisticated version of this fairy-tale movement, Dickens begins Pip's story in *Great Expectations* by portraying a real stepmother starving the poor boy physically and emotionally but then sends him off to Miss Havisham's fairy-tale "Satis House," with its deceptively nourishing feast spread for Pip and its final scene with Miss Havisham burned in her own hearth. The primitive fantasy of the second stage is only suggested, of course—by names and by some of the iconography of the original; but nonetheless we can feel a fantasy quality in these scenes that we do not notice in the stepmother's house at the beginning.

More often, the analogous fantasies exist side by side without being framed off as they are in "Hansel and Gretel," so that the interplay of several versions of an experience enriches the single presentation. In Gogol's story, "The Nose," Major Kavoliov awakens one morning to discover that his nose is gone and soon realizes that it has established a life and an identity to rival his own, indeed to take it over, for the nose is a much finer man than the Major ever was. The simple view of fantasy would lead us to name the fantasy supposedly underlying this story and make an easy substitution, as we might do in a simpler phallic anecdote like the Slawkenbergius tale in *Tristram Shandy*: there the whole joke lies in a simple substitution of the word *penis* every time Slawkenbergius's nose is mentioned. Tzvetan Todorov makes his case against psychoanalysis by equating *psychoanalytic* with just such an interpretation of stories. "The disappearance of the nose signifies, we are told, castration," he says—and quite rightly discards this reduction.[68] But the real explanation is that underlying fantasy material from different stages of development is affecting the text. In an early version of the fan-

---

68. Tzvetan Todorov, *The Fantastic: A Structural Approach to a Literary Genre*, trans. Richard Howard (Ithaca, N.Y.: Cornell University Press, 1975), p. 72.

tasy, castration is represented as loss of a body part, and the part is magically equated with a person. But in a later version of the fantasy, castration is represented more realistically as the Captain's loss of identity and his humiliation, particular concrete experiences symbolized in the child's world by a physical mutilation. The nose is something of a distraction: even the penis itself is only a phallic symbol, as Lacan would say. Yes, the story is about castration, but to say this much is only to ask a new question: What is castration? And the answer to this is a complicated one, made up of ideas and images from different stages of life.

Such interactions occur in more realistic texts as well. I have already mentioned Wilson's essay on the anality of *The Alchemist*, where he points out late adult derivatives of fantasy in both form and content—in the careful plotting and elaborate control on Jonson's part and in the similarly "anal" organizing concerns of his hero. But he also identifies what we now recognize as a somewhat more primitive symbolism, in the alchemist's fantasy of transforming worthless things into precious ones—a fantasy which also characterizes the child's ambivalence about his body. Finally, there is the literal reminder of anality, as the entire dramatic choreography leads to the privy in the climactic scene.

In answer to the first question I raised at the beginning of the chapter—What is a fantasy?—we have seen that fantasy is always fantas*ies*: one primal fantasy can potentially generate multiple permutations, endlessly fertile and careless of detail at any one state, and take on new forms at each new stage of development. "I eat you, you eat me, we both fall into a hole, the hole is an ocean, we are the ocean"; and later, "I feed you poison, you feed me poison"; or "I chew you out, you chew me out, I am remorseful." The fantasy serves other functions besides naturalistic mimetic truth-telling, but *wish fulfillment* is too limited a term to encompass the variety of psychic functions which remain after we eliminate "telling the truth." Daydreams may fulfill wishes because they have already sorted everything else out, but fantasy is partly defined by the way it reveals everything at once, indiscriminately: wishes, fears, defenses, subjective versions, from one point of view and then from another. A cluster of alternative fantasies can surround every element in a central situation, as Freud illustrated: a little girl's fantasy that "a child is being beaten" starts out as a wish-fulfilling triumph over a sibling ("My father is beating that child"), is transformed by guilt and passive desires into an exciting masochistic version ("My father is beating me"), and finally evolves into a socially and personally acceptable version ("The teacher is beating several little boys"), now shaped by still other jealousies and defenses against seeming vulnerable.[69]

The French psychoanalysts' emphasis on repetition rather than wish fulfillment as the primal motive in fantasizing is perhaps more accurate, since it does not prescribe relationships before the fact and does not identify a controlling fantasy at the cost of dismissing other versions as disguises and displacements. But we should remember that *repetition* too is a reductive term. It does not capture a sense of the kaleidoscopic recycling of partial, inverted, and contradictory forms of fantasy which serve a variety of functions and are ordered not simply in linear repetitions but in patterns determined by a primitive but precise logic.

The answer to the second question—What role does fantasy play?—must be similarly indeterminate. Fantasy's role cannot be predicted; it crops up wherever it can, taking over or slipping out like a taboo subject in polite conversation, and it affects not only the story or plot but the character configurations, the landscape, the props, the imagery, and the language. The presence of fantasy is anything but a mere substitution of a hidden story for an open one. Fantasy is present in the proliferation of scenes arising from different elements of the text, sometimes more, sometimes less directly and obviously; it is sometimes literally part of the text and sometimes only a distant echo.

69. Freud, "A Child is Being Beaten" (1919e), *SE* 17:175–204.

The best evidence for the presence of an oedipal fantasy in
Hamlet, for example, is not in the single analogy between the
play's plot and an oedipal fantasy but rather in the sheer mul-
titude of oedipally suggestive scenes, images, and configurations which emerge whole or in pieces from the ongoing action. The central oedipal images of unnatural murder
and unnatural sex proliferate and become inseparable, first
as a double aspect of Claudius's parental, secret crime and
then as aspects of Hamlet's own voyeuristic and retaliatory
desires. Finally, it becomes impossible to tell who is doing
what to whom, as the identities of criminal and victim merge
and switch in the primitive fantasies provoked by the play's
language and action. Claudius poisons both sword and cup;
he pours poison into the King's ear and drops poison into the
Queen's cup; murder and incest on the rational level become
the single crime of destructive sexuality in the fantasy. And
this crime spreads to "poison the ear of Denmark" and taint
all human communication, as people "take," "beg," or "assault" each others' ears throughout the dialogue. It is in this
context that Hamlet makes his own gestures toward sexuality
and murder, and we begin to see the several oedipal triangles
generated around the paternal apex as different men take the
role of Hamlet's "father." The fact that Polonius the father
spies on Hamlet's interview with his beloved Ophelia links this
scene to the later one when Polonius (now actually taken for
Hamlet's father) spies on Hamlet's interview with his beloved
mother. As in all primitive fantasies, it is hard to tell whether
the son is taking his father's place and repeating his crime, or
whether he is punishing his father and *un*doing his crime. Is
Hamlet taking Hamlet senior's place and repeating Claudius's
crime, or is he punishing Claudius and undoing Claudius's
crime? Is a brother (Claudius) pouring poison into his brother's (the older Hamlet's) ear, as in the play-within-a-play? Or
is a nephew (Hamlet) pouring poison into his uncle's
(Claudius's) ear, as in the dumb show? Or is the son pouring
poison in his father's ear, if we short-circuit the two actions?
It is also hard to determine whether Hamlet is attacking his

father murderously or attacking his mother sexually. He goes to Gertrude's room "speak[ing] daggers," and though he had vowed to use none, Gertrude finds soon enough that his words "like daggers enter in mine ears." Is Hamlet here imitating his father/uncle's incestuous attack on Gertrude? Or is he attacking that father by attacking his mother? "Father and mother are one flesh," as Hamlet explains when he calls Claudius "my loving mother," and Hamlet's attacks on his mother in the bedroom scene harm the images of Claudius, not Gertrude: first a picture of Claudius as a "mildew'd ear" and then a stand-in for Claudius, dead behind the arras where he was trying to "overhear." The confusion between murderous and sexual attacks is further complicated by a confusion between attack and suicide. In the last scene, Hamlet's revenge literally destroys him; elsewhere he is hoist with his own verbal petards, as when he admiringly calls up the image of a bloody young murderer: no sooner does he tell how Pyrrhus is about to murder Priam, than the citadel of Troy collapses and "takes prisoner Pyrrhus' ear."

The foregoing is just evidence of the *presence* of oedipal fantasy material in the play: I am not suggesting that these fantastic reversals and equivalences replace the more rational distinctions which "really" make up the action but that they enrich and complicate an already ambiguous world. Fantasy material is always present; it is, according to one investigator, the "baseline of [mental] activity,"[70] even on the higher preconscious level, and it dominates all unconscious thought. What makes literature special, however, is the way it draws on fantasies and yet escapes from the chaos of pure fantasy; the way it forms hierarchies so we can separate what is really going on from what might be going on and can distinguish the theme from the variation. What makes literature unique is neither the presence of nor the eradication of fantasy, but the play between kaleidoscopic patterns of fantasies on the one hand and, on the other, the impression we get of a stabler ac-

70. Klinger, *Structure and Functions of Fantasy*, p. 348.

tion which emerges from it. Sometimes the network of fantasy variations merely resonates with the stable manifest story, in the way I have described earlier. But most often there is a more concrete connection, and we can spot the crisis in the manifest story which has opened a path into the fantasy level. Things fall apart in Hamlet's world where love and murder ought to be separated, and we descend into a nightmare where they are inseparable, where echoes are the truth, ghosts are real, and the King is a liar. But the play, unlike a true nightmare, always maintains the distinction between fantasy and reality, however revealing—and accurate—the threat of their merger may be.

FANTASY'S ROLE: IN DIFFERENT TEXTS

The same fantasy can play entirely different roles in different texts. To suggest how the identification of fantasy's role can be useful to critics, I will now examine a victim fantasy whose derivatives have ranged from archaic myths to psychologically realistic novels. These derivatives typically elaborate a central trap scene in which an uncompromising villain closes in on an innocent and helpless victim—a scene important in both of the versions which I will examine more closely here: Richardson's *Clarissa* and Dickens's *Old Curiosity Shop*. The victim fantasy is superficially an unpleasant scene arousing pity, terror, or perhaps tears, but certainly nothing recognizably sexual. Neither *Clarissa* nor *Curiosity Shop*, as modern readers are amused to remind themselves, seemed suspiciously Freudian to their first readers. The same is true for some modern readers. Richardson's biographers dismiss Freudian approaches to the novel: "We see very little sex in it, surprisingly little," they explain, "considering the story."[71] *Clarissa* was taken to be a model of behavior for young ladies, and readers on both sides of the Atlantic found something

71. T. C. Duncan Eaves and Ben D. Kimpel, *Samuel Richardson: A Biography* (Oxford: Clarendon Press, 1971), p. 258.

"simply and severely grand," as Edgar Allan Poe said, in Little Nell's suffering.

But all versions of the victim fantasy have remained perversely attractive, and their darker side has subsequently made them the focus of psychoanalytic literary criticism. Mario Praz saw in *Clarissa* one of the commonest romantic agonies and suggested that sensuality lay beneath Richardson's moralizing veneer.[72] Leslie Fiedler saw Clarissa's story as the archetype for the sexually conflicted drama of love and death which preoccupies American novelists, and he found in Dickens's Nell a close cousin.[73] What I want to suggest is that much of the psychoanalysis applied to these two books up to this point has not been true analysis of fantasy but rather a much more constricted search for adult daydreams behind texts, a search for relatively realistic representations of adults with recognizable adult sexual desires and inhibitions. Applying psychoanalysis to these two novels, as in many similar psychoanalytic studies of other novels, has usually meant trying to find analogies to the story in the actions of real adults and then reducing the fiction to the terms of its real-life analogy. This method can be fascinating, but it can also be insensitive to the two novels' own terms and dynamics.

It has led critics in several cases, to attribute tensions in each of the novels to the characters' pathology. Clarissa, we are told, is really a masochist, dreaming about her own rape long before it happens, secretly enjoying Lovelace's tyranny, and finally unveiling her hidden sensual fantasies in her last, insane letters.[74] Lovelace is even more obviously a sadist,

72. Mario Praz, "The Shadow of the Divine Marquis," in *The Romantic Agony*, trans. Angus Davidson, 2nd ed. (London and New York: Oxford University Press, 1970), p. 97.

73. Leslie Fiedler, "Richardson and the Tragedy of Seduction," in *Love and Death in the American Novel* (New York: Criterion Books, 1960).

74. Dorothy Van Ghent, "On *Clarissa Harlowe*," in *The English Novel: Form and Function* (New York: Harper Perennial, 1967), pp. 78–83. Also Ian Watt, "Richardson as Novelist: *Clarissa*," in *The Rise of the Novel* (Berkeley and Los Angeles: University of California Press, 1965), pp. 222–38.

whose natural sexual desire has been perverted into the desire to dominate.[75] *Clarissa*, we are told, is a case history and has little to say about anything in the outside world (except what it may tell us indirectly about Richardson's own case and his Lovelacian tendencies).[76] The novel's only darkness lies in the characters' unconscious desires, then, and not in the nature of things or in the ambiguity of consciously approved values.

This attack on *Clarissa*, if reductive, is at least plausible. A similar attempt to psychoanalyze Dickens's characters turns the novel into a joke, because the characters are so patently unrealistic; Grandfather Trent and Little Nell no more need motives than do characters in a fairy tale. But ever since Mark Spilka discovered "the bones of an early Victorian *Lolita*"[77] under the corrupt flesh of *The Old Curiosity Shop*, even these flat characters have been suspect. It is suggested that Trent's devotion masks sadistic, incestuous desires, and that Nell's masochism is all that remains after she (like Clarissa) has tried to repress her natural sexuality.

There are, of course, some modern versions of the victim fantasy which *do* rationalize and internalize its ambiguities; but the result in such cases shows how inadequate psychological diagnosis is for the earlier novels. There is no mysterious truth about hurting the thing you love in John Fowles's *The Collector* for example; its increasingly repellent hero kidnaps

75. See, e.g., Morris Golden, *Richardson's Characters* (Ann Arbor: University of Michigan Press, 1963).

76. If anything, we might see Clarissa and Lovelace as embodiments of two different aspects of Richardson. It is interesting to note, for example, that the very first story Richardson remembered telling—one he remembered "particularly"—was a history "of a Servant-*Man* preferred by a fine young Lady (for his Goodness) to a Lord, who was a Libertine" (emphasis added) and that his account of his early years includes the undocumented story of a similar preference for Richardson himself on the part of a mysteriously unidentified "wealthy man." (Eaves and Kimpel, *Samuel Richardson*, pp. 10–13.)

77. Mark Spilka, "Little Nell Revisited," *Papers of the Michigan Academy of Science, Arts and Letters* 45 (1960): 427–37.

his victim and hides her away in a hole in the ground. His consuming excitement in capturing, keeping, and photographing his "specimen" is simply a perversion of the more physical consummation which he can neither achieve nor bear to think about. This demented hero is quite removed from the demonic Lovelace, in whom it is impossible to separate sickness from health, the mix-ups of perversion from the mysteries of sexuality.

The comparison of *Curiosity Shop* and *Lolita* is equally instructive. The psychoanalytic interpretation of Nell's character sounds like a parody, and that is exactly what *Lolita* is. Nabokov has taken the highly charged, ambivalent relationships in Dickens's novel (and, incidentally, in the equally infantile love life of Dickens's admirer, Poe) and translated them into one exactly describable, unambiguous physiological predilection. Humbert Humbert in *Lolita* is engaged in nothing more transcendent than indulging his taste for prepubescent bodies. The larger fascination is gone, once Nabokov transforms the relationship from something outside the bounds of rational adult experience into something all too familiar. Instead of the double sense of an interpretation which insists on itself and yet *cannot* be true ("The child is involved in a sexual relationship!"), we are left only with the sense that it is true after all, and none but the purely sexual fascination remains. ("But didn't you play this game when *you* were a child?" Lolita asks in bed, after Humbert's elaborate delicacies in trying to get her there without shocking her or letting her know what he is doing.)[78]

78. When Iris Murdoch retells the victim fantasy as a psychologically realistic novel in *The Black Prince*, she tries to recapture the fascination of the fantasy at the same time, but the realism kills it. Her hero Bradley is in love with a girl some forty years younger than he, and while we see the psychological reasons for this, we are also supposed to feel something more mysterious in their union—something like the eerie power of Trent's love for sickly Nell, or Poe's love for his dead child brides (or the love of any of the symbolic predecessors the novel evokes, like Aschenbach's love for Tadzio). But Murdoch has to insert the symbolism from above, and this does not quite work. The earlier novels convey a sense of the dark side of love to the degree that love is

Mario Praz and Leslie Fiedler, for the most part, avoid the simplicities of the earlier critics who tried to psychoanalyze characters and come closer to describing the quality of fantasy and its role in the two novels, because they focus on the whole pattern of relationships and situations. But both still talk in terms of a pattern of *adult* relationships. Praz explains that the satanic rebels he examines in his study cannot exist outside the context of a story about a moral order and its embodiment by a pure maiden; though we may relish only the details of violation, he says, our imaginations must paradoxically dwell on, and therefore even invent, images of perfection. This paradoxical mutuality of opposites is fantasy-like, but Praz's discussion implies that the paradox operates only in purely adult terms.[79] Fiedler explains our attraction to morally pure maidens (rather than to more sexually robust and interesting ones) as the result of a somewhat different conflict, one between passion and fear. Americans prefer a story where the sweet young thing dies before anything happens to one with a proper sexual triumph and union, he says, because their sexual fears make the death of a fragile, harmless heroine the only consummation they can begin to think about.[80] But again, the terms of the conflict are drawn from adult life; even in this displaced form, the battle is still between desire for and fear of full-blooded genital sexuality.

We must bypass these adult daydreams and go back to the whole branching tree of scenes and images which make up the victim fantasy, starting from the most infantile versions, to understand the different ways in which these components manifest themselves in the novels. The fantasy is not a product of the adult mind but derives from the earliest relations

---

not confined and explained away as neurosis in only one psyche: Trent's love for Nell and her submission to him, for example, are truly deathly. Murdoch, by contrast, must dress her heroine up in a Hamlet suit on the day of her seduction, and only by her costume does she become the black prince, the dark side of eros.

79. Praz, "The Shadow of the Divine Marquis," pp. 63–83.
80. Fiedler, "Richardson and the Tragedy of Seduction."

between a mother and child absorbed in one another and just
beginning to discover the child's separate existence. From the
beginning it is a fiercely ambivalent exchange. For the child,
the relationship promises a continually blissful union in
which, psychologically if not physically, the two really are one
being; but it also threatens to become a hellish suffocation if
the mother is too possessive and prevents the child's development as a separate being. The psychotic Dr. Schreber called
his adult version of the experience *soul murder*, and it is just
that: the total possessiveness which reduces people to things
and kills the spirit.[81] But for a child this suffocation first
takes physical form. The child is tied down, moved, filled,
and emptied by someone too strong to resist—an invasion of
the body which has its logical culmination in cannibalism and
vampirism, as Praz shows in his analysis of the victim fantasy's
gothic versions. The mother welcomes the child—and then
turns on him with open jaws. (Thus Fowles's *Collector*, despite
its superficial realism, returns obsessively to the infant's small
world of breathing, eating, and bathing; the hero ruins his
specimen's meals, denies her baths, and makes it impossible
for her to breathe.) The physicality in this novel includes a
diffuse sexuality, but this hardly differs from the child's other
urgencies of appetite and power. Adult sexuality appears
only in later versions of the fantasy, along with the distinction
between the sexes. Hansel and Gretel make up an androgy-
nous hero-heroine, and their mother's change is asexual. Little Red Riding-Hood acts out a later version of the fantasy;
she is definitely feminine (her red cap, like Sleeping Beauty's
drop of blood, is the sign of passage into womanhood), and
her feeble grandma turns into a masculine wolf. The mature
sexual relationship is even more explicit in "Beauty and the
Beast," where the husband himself has two opposite sides.
Still later and more sophisticated versions, of course, elabo-

81. See Freud's psychoanalysis of Schreber's *Memoirs*, in which Schreber
describes his soul murder: "Psychoanalytic Notes upon an Autobiographical
Account of a Case of Paranoia" (1911), *SE* 12:3–84.

rate the more familiar forms of adult sexual exchanges and adult perversions.

Meanwhile, though, because of the ambivalence of the mother-child relationship—the child is both drawn to and repelled by his mother—the child may seem masochistic. "What big teeth you have, grandma!" betrays Little Red Riding-Hood's perception of, and even excitement about, what is to come. But it is not so much that she wants to be hurt as that she wants someone strong enough to take care of her, even if that means someone strong enough to devour her. The child may also seem sadistic, because at this primitive stage, feelings have not been separated from facts or consistently located within the self. The child's inarticulate rage is as much an alien invasion of her peaceful state as a mother's punishment is. The toothy monster under grandma's lace cap is partly a projection of the child's own hostility and need to dominate, which she has not yet isolated and distinguished from the situation as a whole.

These illogical ambivalences and confusions, along with the exaggeration and emotional intensity of a scene, are what indicates the presence of fantasy material, whether it manifests itself in terms of a rational, adult experience or in the more bizarre terms of infantile experience. What we shall see in comparing the two novels, *Clarissa* and *The Old Curiosity Shop*, is that *Clarissa*'s manifest plot is a rationalized, fully elaborated adult version of the victim fantasy, while the plot in *Curiosity Shop*, with its impossibly good little heroine and its fairy-tale dwarf villain, more closely resembles earlier and cruder forms of the fantasy. Richardson's novel happens to be a success, while Dickens's is a notorious failure, but the difference has nothing to do with how much primitive wish fulfillment has been repressed or with how close to the surface the primitive fantasy comes; success or failure is a function of how well the fantasy material has been integrated into the rest of the novel. Both novels are shaped in part by recurring configurations from the primal fantasy situation, and both begin with successful though very different ways of integrating primal fantasy material: Richardson's method is realistic and Dickens's is more symbolic, perhaps mythic. But while Richardson continues to integrate the fantasy as it recurs, elaborating it in increasingly revealing ways, Dickens's repetitions become increasingly impoverished and less revealing. The wealth of fantasy material is reduced and frozen into one daydream script, and this finally takes over the novel. More seriously, it takes over the narrator's relation to his material, affecting the pace, the tone, and the style of the narrative.

Clarissa deals with complex adult experience, for which childhood fantasies are only analogies from long ago. But these fantasies do have two important effects: they contribute to the emotional "resonance" of the events and to the repetitiveness of the plot. It is true that the crude actions and emotions expressed in the early forms of the fantasy are not literally relevant to the mature version of the fantasy now being acted out in a complex world of realistic characters and varied issues. But the parallels between Clarissa's situation and the child's are extensive, detailed, and easily visible. Clarissa reenacts a version of the infantile fantasy with both her family and Lovelace, finding herself in each case stalemated in a conflict between attraction and destruction. Life in her family promises the prelapsarian bliss Clarissa experienced as a beloved child; but now it denies her everything and suffocates her with its demands. Life with Lovelace promises another kind of bliss, but it too comes only at the price of her freedom to be herself. In both cases, she is trapped, tricked, and treated less and less like a human being, denied even the decency of a response to her letters and pleas.

Worst of all is the hypocrisy of her enemies. Their orders are disguised as offers, and their selfish demands are presented as thoughtful considerations of her well-being. When she insists on the freedom she needs to survive, they take her plea as an insolent attack. They back her into corners and then punish her for reacting. Clarissa's family punishes her for supposedly loving Lovelace and then "forgives" her by pressing her to marry the rich and odious Solmes; but they refuse to see any reason for her reluctance except a forbidden attachment to Lovelace, for which they punish her. Lovelace steals her letters and then punishes her when she gets angry; he proposes when she cannot accept and then complains that she will not have him. For Clarissa this is "soul murder," a nightmare of being treated like an object, of being powerless in the hands of people who force her to play a game and then keep changing the rules. They even try to force her to accept their way of seeing things, not only denying her what she needs to exist as a human being but denying her the simple integrity of being allowed to name their actions and to have faith in her own perceptions.

Yet she cannot avoid contributing to the torture. Her goodness provokes both her family and Lovelace, and it makes her utterly inflexible. She refuses to see her family's weakness and therefore falls prey to their deceptions, passively, acceptingly, believing in their way of seeing things because they ask her to. She does this with Lovelace too, at first, allowing herself to write him letters to get closer to him, and finally to be enticed, against her better judgment, into a secret meeting, where he takes the opportunity to kidnap her. But later her contribution to the relationship works even more subtly, as the two are locked more and more closely into a pattern of mutual goads. Her impossibly high-minded idealism brings out the worst in Lovelace; it goads his need to destroy it and prevents her from meeting him halfway, giving him the encouragement he wants instead of her eternal "exasperating recriminations." They create each other. The worse he gets, the more courageously she tries to hold onto her solid belief in correct behavior; her goodness taunts him, as she escapes his possessive grasp, and tempts him even more into outrageous violations of it. They create one another symbolically, too: very early in the novel she has a dream in which Lovelace is the extreme literalization of himself; he stabs and buries her alive. And Lovelace dreams a dream at the end in which Clarissa is more angelic than we ever see her in the novel.

These paradoxes lie at the heart of Richardson's novel, and
any diagnosis of perversely interlocking sexual desires is of
course very much a reduction of the lovers' experience.
Clarissa explores the painful ironies which emerge when two
human beings as different as man and woman, and two aspects of human nature as different as idealistic love and erotic
love, meet in one relationship. The ironies of passion, the
necessary misunderstandings, the vulnerabilities and actual
dangerousness of goodness like Clarissa's, the fact that too
much altruism is as selfish and as threatening to human relations as too much selfishness, and in the same way—these
larger truths are the reason the situation interests us at all.
But so long as we do not reduce the novel's adult world to a
childish analogy, the psychoanalyst's reading is useful, because the fantasy analogies do have an important role in
adding to the sheer magnetism of the situation. Though painful for the adult, the sparring between Clarissa and Lovelace
nonetheless repeats the promise along with the pain of that
original relationship. It is easier to keep trying to establish
paradise, even at the cost of being punished again and again,
than it is to break away and set off alone in an ordinary world.
Clarissa's idealism has something of this stubbornly blind
quality, even if she herself does not. She does, of course,
finally question her human absolutes after she is raped, but
on the fantasy level she settles into another matrix in the end,
a religious one, and submits herself to that. She relinquishes
her selfhood to a larger cause than either family or Lovelace
and becomes the inanimate object they wanted when they
tried to subdue her will.

The fantasy makes itself felt not only in the quality of the
experience but even more strongly in its sheer repetitiveness.
One of *Clarissa*'s most impressive achievements is the way in
which it sustains its length. This achievement depends partly
on how the two main characters continue to develop and oc-
cupy the psychological space, but it also depends on a primitive rhythm of trap and escape which propels us through the
action from one magnetic scene in which Clarissa is faced with

disaster, to the next. Each time, her escape routes are cut off one by one—by Lovelace, with his tricks and traps, who lures her into the brothel; by her family, who allow her no way to communicate with them; by her own high standards of behavior, which make her reluctant to ask for help when help is available; and by Richardson himself, who eliminates whatever possibilities remain by ensuring that the friendly Hannah is sick. We think, "This time it is over, now she has no way out, now she must give in"; and then at the last minute something happens. Aunt Hervey intercedes, or Clarissa writes one more letter, or Lovelace thinks of another plan to placate her for awhile. And so we begin again.

The novel is a consummately achieved cliff-hanger—a psychological cliff-hanger, not a physical one—which the reader finds less like watching a thriller than like watching a couple caught up in a ritual of nagging, repetitive fights, a stalemate of repeated confrontations, each appearing ultimate but none exploding, and all sinking back into that cycle we have only recently learned to call a game. The characters see each scene as a disaster, an obstacle to be overcome on the way to happiness, but we come to view each scene as an end in itself, with its own stability and perverse appeal.

Such scenes belong properly at the climax of a story, but here they make up the story itself. One such scene occurs at the climax of *Othello*, and since Richardson cites Desdemona as one of Clarissa's inspirations, the difference is instructive. The murderous madness of Othello and the saintly passivity of Desdemona seem to anticipate the drama between Lovelace and Clarissa. Othello descends into a monstrous egotism, a failure of trust that staggers rational minds, and he exhibits a need for ocular proof which is just as insane as Lovelace's tests for Clarissa. He may not cart Desdemona away to a brothel, but he imagines her in one when he comes to accuse her, and for him imagination counts. Finally, after trying to stifle Desdemona's spirit, Othello literally smothers her. All of this, however, is the perversion of an originally pure love; it is a fall from grace, a distortion.

For Lovelace, things are very different. His monstrous behavior does not occur at the tragic climax of his love; it is, for him the very condition of his love. His behavior is not a distortion; it is the love itself. When Othello is overtaken by jealousy, his "occupation's gone"; he is a changed man. But tormenting suspicion is Lovelace's *only* occupation, and he realizes this. Shakespeare allows us to glimpse this state as the perversion of love, the extreme of love, love's dark potential for one who loves not wisely but too well. But Richardson shows us that love is always its opposite. Othello never meant to suffocate Desdemona; he loved her freely at first. But Lovelace's love suffocates from the very beginning, and that is why it is so attractive to him.

Nonetheless, Richardson's novel moves forward despite the repetition of these emotionally powerful infantile scenes. The characters change and begin to outgrow the stalemate in which they are caught. The novel's struggle to escape from this obsession is inseparable from the characters' attempts to deal with their own obsessions; gradually the stalemate takes on new forms as the lovers detach themselves from their original visions and eventually—despite the repetition of fantasy—transcend the terms of the deadlock.

The manifest story in *The Old Curiosity Shop* draws on more primitive versions of the victim fantasy, so that instead of being enacted between two complex people like Clarissa and Lovelace, it is spread out in a whole network of literal and symbolic relations among psychologically simpler characters. Nearly every human relationship in the novel recreates some aspect of the ambivalent infantile relation between mother and child, but the most prominent of these recreations is the one between Trent and Little Nell—the seemingly devoted grandfather and the even more devoted child who sacrifices herself to his dreams for her. While this mutual dedication may seem "most beautiful," as Poe said, it has (like much of the beauty Poe admired) another side. Trent's love is finally selfish; he justifies his obsession with gambling as a means to make Nell rich some day, but he is so consumed by it that means and ends become confused, and he hardly has the strength to care for her, or even to see her, as she really is. The main result of his parental concern in fact is to turn Nell into a parent caring for him. His uncontrollable vice, in addition, puts both of them into the power of the sadistic, sharp-toothed dwarf, Quilp, a moneylender who is the book's villain and who obviously symbolizes Trent's potential for evil.

The darker side of Trent symbolized by Quilp, however, is not simply an unwitting adult sexuality lurking behind his secretive, unbreakable midnight habit, as psychoanalytic critics first suggested.[82] It does have that tone—the dwarf bristles with phallic energy, smacking his lips over Nell, smoking his obscenely glowing cigar all night while his wife sits up, and writhing another night in Nell's bed. The moneylender is indeed part Rumpelstiltskin, that fairy-tale image for male sexuality embodied in the "penis-man," as Freud suggested;[83] he can do magic and spin straw into gold, and he comes to claim his price for doing so. But Quilp is primarily a more primitive demon—a possessive, manipulative, selfish, easily insulted, and outrageously revengeful will. He does not want to marry Nell so much as to possess her and even devour her. He is master of the gnawing ambivalence present in the fantasy—the selfishness posing as kindness, the teasing offer which is really a threat, the ironic husbandly sweetness apparent in his comment, "Have some more shrimp, my dear, do," when his wife knows he is furious at her for spending the money. Tyranny masquerades as love: Quilp purposely tortures his wife with politeness, but Trent's unwitting torture of Nell with his devotion is just as effective.

82. Spilka, "Little Nell Revisited."

83. Sigmund Freud, "The Occurrence in Dreams of Material from Fairy Tales" (1913), *SE* 12:281ff. Such figures lurk behind potential husbands elsewhere, too, for example in Thomas Mann's *Buddenbrooks*, where the red-faced, yellow-toothed Herr Kesselmeyer, the moneylender, turns out to have been the moving force behind Herr Grünlich's proposal to Tony Buddenbrooks.

Like Clarissa, however, Nell half-creates her situation, not by conscious or even unconscious intention (though she does have "secrets she didn't know herself") but because such things could not go on without her passive goodness to sustain them. In fact, it is she who—unwittingly, of course—betrays Trent to Quilp, when she allows Quilp to draw her grandfather's secret from her; she is the go-between for the two men, linking them together. But even more impressive than her actual role in events is the strength of what Henry James would call her imagination of disaster. She haunts churchyards, thinks people dead when they are not, and multiplies Quilp into "a legion of Quilps" hemming her in. She even imagines a peculiar version of the "persecuted maiden" scene, before it happens, when she worries that her grandfather will kill himself and that his blood will come creeping to her bedroom door. This is not, any more than Clarissa's dream, purely a sign of her internal ambivalence or sadomasochism. It is rather, as Gabriel Pearson has described it, "a state of mind [without] a person to suffer it."

> Dickens seems able to resuscitate childhood as a baf-
> fled, protean and fluid psychic economy in which peo-
> ple change, value, impulse and action are substitutes for
> each other, and absolutes clash and dissolve within the
> same personality. This state is closer to actually lived
> childhood than Pip's recollection of himself, whose very
> vividness and clarity are slightly illusory products of ret-
> rospect.[84]

It is not simply a matter of Nell's own guilt projected but of an ambivalent world—a world which, before long, plays back her own vision in a nightmarish scene where Nell wakes to find a figure creeping silently and stealthily to the end of her bed. It is her grandfather, come to steal her money; and this horrifies her even more:

84. Gabriel Pearson, "*The Old Curiosity Shop,*" in *Dickens and the Twentieth Century,* ed. John Gross and Gabriel Pearson (Toronto: University of Toronto Press, 1962), p. 82.

The terror she had lately felt was nothing compared with
that which now oppressed her. . . . She had no fear of her
dear old grandfather . . . but the man she had seen that
night . . . seemed like another creature in his shape, a
monstrous distortion of his image, a something to recoil
from, and be the more afraid of because it bore a likeness
to him.[85]

[Pp. 302–03]

Grandpa has turned into a wolf.

The human relationships in Dickens's *Old Curiosity Shop*,
then, are shaped by a fantasy in which there are only two possible roles. One is that of the loving parent, who may at any
moment turn Quilp and devour the child; the other is the innocent, loving child who has a gift for death. The fantasy goes
beyond shaping the characters' relationships, however, and
takes over the entire world of the novel, even the landscape.
Readers have always felt the starkness of Dickens's primitive
polarities in the book; youth and age, city and country, good
and evil, life and death; but the pairings have always been
seen to constitute a random, unstructured collection. On the
contrary, they are all versions of the human relationship we
have just seen, though as they continue to appear, they become increasingly stylized and less human.

There are three major versions of this polar relationship in
The Old Curiosity Shop, and they divide the novel into three distinct parts, serving to structure Nell's otherwise picaresque
adventures, as she moves from London to the Fairgrounds
and then to the country. The opposition in the first part of
the novel, in London, is defined primarily in human terms,
in the opposition between Quilp (or Trent/Quilp) and Nell:
one masters and devours, and the other submits and dies.
The opposition takes many forms and helps make this the
liveliest part of the novel, with its several plots and its variety
of characters.

85. Charles Dickens, *The Old Curiosity Shop*, ed. Angus Easson (Harmondsworth, Middlesex: Penguin Books, 1972).

When Nell and Trent escape from the city to the Fairgrounds, in the second part of the novel, they encounter a
second form of the opposition between two kinds of art,
embodied in the Punch show and the waxworks show, each of
which they join for a while. This form of opposition is at an
aesthetic remove from the conflicts in London, and it represents a conflict between images, not people. The action in
this section is correspondingly distanced, or at least dampened, though it has a kind of artificial "Jarley"-ness, like the
jolly Mrs. Jarley who runs the waxworks. Nonetheless, although the opposition here is more emblematic than dramatic (and so is the action), the opposing art works are still
closely associated with the original, human opposition between Quilp and Nell. Quilp is, after all, a living Punch (a
"grotesque puppet") who torments his wife, threatens ba-
bies, and drives dogs to frenzy. And Nell is actually called a
"wax works child" by Miss Monflathers. Although Miss
Monflathers is referring to Nell's job exhibiting wax figures,
Nell's waxy pallor has struck not only readers but the custom-
ers in the waxworks, who mistake her for one of the exhibitions. Everything we hear about the two competing shows
elaborates this opposition between Quilp's sadistic energy and
Nell's passive perfection. The Punch is a noisy, boisterous,
common show that is almost alive; the puppets have a comic
indestructibility (they first appear in the cemetery, like
"mirth in funeral," jauntily perched on gravestones) and a
way of dominating their supposed masters, who must mend,
repair, and carry them around, as Codlin the puppet master
complains. The waxworks, by contrast, as Mrs. Jarley (the
proprietor) explains, are "calm and classic" and utterly sub-
missive to their artist-master. It is but a moment's work for
Jarley to turn a disreputable wax clown into a schoolteacher
for a fastidious patron. It is interesting that only here in the
"unreality" of the Fairgrounds do Nell's worst fantasies—and
the novel's—emerge openly, as Trent creeps down to steal
her money (perhaps to kill her?) in the scene I cited earlier.

This suspended world of art does not last, however, and

Trent and Nell are forced on to the third section of the novel and the third version of opposition, this time in its least human and least dramatic form—a division of the world into two landscapes. Here the action almost stops, as Nell and Trent pass from the vibrant, destructive factory fires in the city into their opposite—the pastoral countryside crumbling in a passive, quiet decay. The fantasy has reduced everything to its own simplifying terms.

The fantasy plays still another role in the novel, besides shaping the characters' relationships and the structure of events. It also determines the relationship between the artist and his art, both within the novel and within the sketchy but important framing story about Master Humphrey, who is the purported author of the novel. *The Old Curiosity Shop* is in a way filled with nothing but artists, or shapers and manipulators. Nell is Trent's work of art, just as Midas's daughter was his, and it is not hard to see Quilp with all his scheming as a writer or at least a director—a parody of Dickens's untamed hunger for reality and his manipulation of characters like puppets. For all these artists, art is always a battle, a fight for control, as demonstrated vividly at the Fairgrounds, where the "artists" are more like keepers, trying to keep their giants, freaks, and performing dogs in order and hauling them around like curious objects.

Despite the threat, however, the artists for the most part keep control. So much so that what we see is not really art but something which borders on art: ritual magic. Its ultimate manifestation is Quilp dancing around in his larger-than-life voodoo doll, a masthead he calls Kit. This he torments in place of the boy, screwing in gimlets and pokers and, most telling of all, carving his own name into it, as a sign of total possession.[86] This is Pygmalion in reverse, no longer fiction

86. The masthead looks nothing like Kit, though Quilp frightens Samson Brass into agreeing, "Is it not like Kit?!" But the closer the idol is to an incarnation rather than a represenation, as Ernst Kris has suggested, the less it *needs* to look like the god whose name it bears. (Kris, *Psychoanalytic Explorations*, p. 49.).

but some strange lawless reality in which Kit has been turned into a statue.

Dickens's novel fails because the narrator falls into the same relation to his material as these manipulators have to theirs. His material threatens to get out of hand and sometimes does, but for the most part it is captured and pinned down, and it dies in the process. This has nothing to do with Dickens's private feelings about his novel, whatever they may have been. It is, rather, something *we* can feel in the style and shape of the novel. What is important here is that we can also see Dickens's desire to control acted out in the relation between the novel's fictional narrator, Master Humphrey, and his story.

Dickens began the novel as a short story, one of the "personal adventures" Master Humphrey included in his chatty journal, *Master Humphrey's Clock*.[87] It was to have been a mood piece rather than a story, in fact, with the center of interest being the narrator's own feelings and observations, and it was intended as only one of many pieces he was to share with his readers. In the several issues preceding the beginning of Nell's story, Humphrey tells readers a good deal about himself and his aims in the journal, and from his autobiographical revelations we can see his resemblance to the possessive artists in the novel; he, too, is a collector of objects and appearances, a manipulator of sorts, a man who wants control over things. *Master Humphrey's Clock* was intended as a miscellaneous collection of stories, letters, adventures, and reports. The journal, however modestly Humphrey defines it, was

---

87. *Master Humphrey's Clock*, the weekly periodical written entirely by Dickens himself, came out weekly from April 1840 until November 1841. The first installment of what was to grow into *The Old Curiosity Shop* appeared in the fourth issue of *Master Humphrey's Clock*, the second installment appeared in the seventh issue, and thereafter Little Nell's story was continued in every issue until its completion in February 1841. The two works were later published separately. For a discussion of the genesis of the novel, see Robert L. Patten, " 'The Story-Weaver at His Loom': Dickens and *The Old Curiosity Shop*," in *Dickens the Craftsman: Strategies of Presentation*, ed. Robert B. Partlow, Jr. (Carbondale: Southern Illinois University Press, 1970), pp. 44–64.

meant to assimilate the whole world, in bite-sized pieces of all periods of history and of all parts of the globe. Humphrey's intention is only a slight displacement of Dickens's own ambition to recreate in *Master Humphrey's Clock* a combination of *The Tatler, The Spectator, The Bee, Gulliver's Travels,* and *The Arabian Nights' Entertainments.* Humphrey is the nicest, most harmless embodiment of this urge to possess, but he unmistakably has it. He is "an old file in the queer house," as Dickens described him; a misshapen, withdrawn, contemplative old man who lives quietly alone, collecting odd tales and a very few friends and organizing a club which meets regularly as clockwork to share them. Even his prose is kept coolly under control as he tells us about himself; not a trace of Dickens can be detected.

In the first issue of his *Clock,* Humphrey warns that he will leave his neighbors' and readers' curiosity about him unsatisfied on many points (pp. 6, 7)[88] but he does tell us something about his background and especially about his "old cheerful companiable Clock"—a "quaint old thing . . . curiously and richly carved" (p. 9), which is the only possession left him from childhood except for the memory of his mother. It serves him as friend as well as timepiece and lends its name to the journal. It makes an interesting symbol and site for his imagination, too, because Humphrey's manuscripts are always kept "in the bottom of the old dark closet where the steady pendulum throbs and beats with healthy action" (p. 11). Dickens no doubt realized the implications of the throbbing pendulum ("Mr. Shandy's clock was nothing to mine," he wrote Walter Savage Landor in the heat of composition, "wind, wind, wind!"),[89] but in Humphrey's hands any earthy material put into this quaint closet comes out subli-

88. Charles Dickens, *Master Humphrey's Clock,* in *Master Humphrey's Clock and A Child's History of England,* ed., Derek Hudson (London: Oxford University Press, 1958). All quotations from *Master Humphrey's Clock* are taken from this edition.

89. See the letter for 26 July 1840, *Dickens' Letters,* ed. Madeline House and Graham Storey, Pilgrim edition, vol. 1 (Oxford: Clarendon Press, 1965).

mated; he "tempts coy Truth from her well in whatever airy forms she may take" and stresses the ability of his imagination to transform the "commonest matter" into something good.

Humphrey succeeds in keeping control of the first few issues of the *Clock*, presenting bits and pieces, including his "personal adventures," such as the account of his late-night walk, which was originally meant to be the whole of Nell's story. The story, however, having plucked him on the sleeve, in the form of Little Nell asking directions, soon leads him not only into strange parts of London but into much speculation. It makes him extremely curious, curious enough to take Nell home and see for himself where she lives, and curious enough to keep him awake at night. "It would be a curious speculation," he begins, or again, "It would be curious to find . . ." But he checks himself before he has been drawn too far into these imaginings, resisting the mystery of unknown and intractable material. Instead, he creates his own fixed image of Nell, which resembles a waxwork, and leaves it at that, "a sort of allegory": "I pictured to myself the child in her bed, alone, unwatched, uncared for. . . ." Humphrey means to leave her story at that, too, and actually does "detach himself" from the narrative at the end of the third chapter and allows it to take its own course—for it has indeed gotten out of hand, swelling out of its frame and nearly obliterating the frame altogether. *Master Humphrey's Clock* becomes nothing more than a medium for the serial publication of Nell's story. Humphrey seems to have lost control; the novel takes on a life of its own, branching out to incorporate Dick Swiveller and peripheral characters whom most modern readers have found the most interesting people in the novel.

In the end, however, Humphrey returns to tell us that he has never lost control after all. He had not really withdrawn but, unknown to us, had reentered the novel as an actor in the story. He was, it turns out, the mysterious Single Gentleman who appeared suddenly, midway into the plot, looking for Nell and chasing her across the countryside. In many ways, Humphrey and the Single Gentleman seem entirely opposite.

Humphrey is a solitary man; he ends his first and most important appearance by falling asleep; the Single Gentleman, on the other hand, begins his adventures by waking from an alarmingly long sleep ("We thought you was dead!") to set out after Nell. Humphrey withdraws from Nell and makes her into a little image, a story he can fit into his clock case; the Single Gentleman, for whom Nell seems ever out of reach, runs after her, just missing her, indulging his curiosity rather than checking it.

In *The Old Curiosity Shop*, the novel proper, the image of Humphrey as narrator is best illustrated by his quiet readings from manuscripts, at home on Thursday evening in his carefully arranged little club; the image we have of the Single Gentleman as narrator is derived from the only two glimpses we get of the narrator in his part of the novel: we see a man chasing after, flying over, being pulled and pushed by his material; a man always moving as the scene unrolls before him. His volume of the novel opens with an announcement:

> The historian takes the friendly reader by the hand and springing with him into the air, and cleaving the same at a greater rate than even Don Clephas Leandro Perez Zambullo and his familiar travelled . . . alights with him upon the pavement.
>
> [P. 319]

By the last chapter the narrator is back on the ground, but still moving:

> The magic reel, which, rolling on before, has led the chronicler thus far, now slackens in its pace, and stops. It lies before the goal; the pursuit is at an end.
>
> [P. 663]

No wonder that the careful Humphrey seems to emerge unscathed to tell another story from his clock, but the Single Gentleman has apparently been caught up in a repetition of Nell's story, like a somewhat jollier version of the ancient mariner who delighted to "travel in the footsteps of the old man and the child" and did so for a "long, long time" (p. 670). The difference between Humphrey and the Single Gentleman is the difference between journal and journey.

However, although the material in the last half of the plot gives the narrator a harder time, he controls it as well in his role as the Single Gentleman as in his role as Humphrey. While Humphrey indulged his sentimentality by imagining Nell asleep amid dangers, the Single Gentleman's efforts are rewarded by an almost exactly similar vision of Nell dead. His repetitions of her story are slightly more dynamic than Humphrey's original portrait, perhaps, but no less fixating and controlled. In both of his roles, Humphrey is engaged in a struggle with his material which resembles the manipulative struggle between the seducer and the pure maiden, or the parent and child—or between Quilp and Nell, along with all the other similar pairs in the plot. The fantasy shapes the narrator's story as well as that of his characters.

In light of what we know about this fantasy, it is interesting to note that ultimately Humphrey's success is a Pyrrhic victory. While *The Old Curiosity Shop*, though flawed, survives, *Master Humphrey's Clock*—which degenerated into a mere framework for serial publication—disappeared altogether after the *Barnaby Rudge* serial, which followed *Curiosity Shop*, ended. The two novels were eventually severed entirely from their foster parent, and Dickens had them published on their own without any of the framework from the original *Master Humphrey's Clock* issues. There is one final episode in Humphrey's story which foretells this fate and in a way explains it. Humphrey returns in the few issues following the end of Barnaby's story and reports on another meeting of the clock club, where he makes a careful distinction between stories derived from personal adventures and stories which are made up. Then he goes on to tell about one last adventure of his own, which shows just how dangerous it is to try to tame the chaos of experience into shapely "personal adventures," instead of staying safely home and drawing images out of one's own imagination.

Humphrey, we recall, started by putting away nicely shaped bits of experience in his clock case, always avoiding any chance that experience would swallow him up or that he would fall into "Truth's Well." But he narrates a story in which truth's well becomes first the "well of human misery" which Nell observes and then the nameless, bottomless well in the churchyard; and these are not so easy to deal with. Indeed, Humphrey is finally swallowed up. Instead of putting manuscripts into his clock, he himself decides to climb up *into* the giant clock on the top of St. Paul's. His harmless old friend is thereby replaced by something newly vital and destructive, with its

> complicated crowd of wheels and chains in iron and brass—great, sturdy, rattling engines—suggestive of breaking a finger put in here or there, and grinding a bone to powder—and these were the clock! (Its pulse measured every second) with one sledge-hammer beat, as if its business were to crush the seconds as they came trooping on, and remorselessly clear a path before the Day of Judgment.
>
> [P. 107]

Humphrey the devourer may at any moment be devoured if he is not careful.

This much we can actually see acted out in the plot of the novel. The novel's style and structure also bear witness to the hand of a controlling artist like Humphrey—or like Dickens. For Dickens, too, is a fixating narrator. Not surprisingly, the image of Nell was his own as well as Humphrey's ("I had always had it in mind to surround the lonely figure of the child with grotesque and wild, but not impossible companions"),[90] and it governs the whole book, even at moments when Master Humphrey disappears and we have only the prose before us.

---

90. Charles Dickens, preface to the first cheap edition of *The Old Curiosity Shop* (London: Chapman and Long, 1848); reprinted in Easson's edition, p. 42.

This visual fixation is offered as a mode of pity and devotion, but it is really a kind of destructive possessiveness. The narrator—Humphrey or Dickens—freezes Nell into a still-life picture from which she never emerges—a Sleeping Beauty preserved by her fairy godfather even from the intrusion of an awakening prince. He transforms her from a human child into a waxworks child and then into a stoneworks child, showing people around the monuments in the cemetery where she herself is slowly dying. He then fixes her into allegory, as Humphrey did.

Nell died before the novel began; her claim on Dickens's imagination was not only that she was "perfectly" good but also perfectly still and fixed in her goodness. *The Old Curiosity Shop* is a series of "violently static" images, to borrow a phrase Steven Marcus uses in reference to another Dickens novel,[91] and the violence is implied, however covertly, by the stasis which pervades. To call Dickens sadistic may be going too far; he never worried, as Hawthorne did, that allegorizing would "steal away the human warmth" of his creations.[92] But he did associate his allegories of perfection with waxworks and death, and he preferred a dead heroine. It was not Trent who killed Nell, but Dickens himself, when he fit her into her role. It is as if he threw corpses into the stream of his imagination, just as Gaffer Hexam might throw corpses into the Thames, because his work demanded that he pull them out again. If Dick Swiveller, in a moment of selfishness before his staggerers have refined him, can say smugly, "There's a young lady saving up for me," Dickens might well claim with equal satisfaction that there is a young lady dying for him.

Nell's death, though presented as a loss, brings some perverse satisfaction, too—the controller's satisfaction, which resembles Lovelace's satisfaction in capturing his charmer and

91. Steven Marcus, *Dickens from "Pickwick" to "Dombey"* (New York: Simon and Schuster, 1968), p. 73. Marcus is referring to *Oliver Twist*.
92. Nathaniel Hawthorne, Introduction to "Rappaccini's Daughter," in *Mosses from an Old Manse*, The Centenary Edition of the Works of Nathaniel Hawthorne, vol. 10 (Columbus: Ohio State University Press, 1974), 91–93.

subduing her to his will. Nell may die peacefully, but there is a sense that she has been trapped, just as Kit—at the very moment of Nell's death—is trapped by Quilp in London, branded falsely as a thief, and taken to jail. It is interesting that Dickens chose as an epigraph some sentimental lines about a grandfather who wanders lost after his grandchild has disappeared, but he gives no indication that the child "disappeared" by getting herself locked into a trunk on the day of her wedding and was not found for thirty years.[93] What better way to keep your child fixed at a perfect age?

It is not only Little Nell whom Dickens captures and stills, but the entire narrative. For his is a visualizing imagination rather than a narrative one, an attempt to capture and moralize about, rather than liberate, a story. Dickens took a great deal of trouble in dictating the production of the novel, especially the placement of the illustrations, asking that the woodcuts be "dropped in" the text at exactly the right place, rather than having other kinds of illustrations inserted as usual, on the facing page—as if the novel moved from static picture to static picture, rather than as a flowing narrative.[94] It is interesting to recall that the "idyll," which Steven Marcus so aptly identifies in the background of *The Old Curiosity Shop*, was still implied in the nineteenth century as not so much a pastoral as a "framed" picture. Dickens presents the idyllic as the merely still, and this affects all aspects of his style. He transforms curiosity into a collection of curiosities, and in the novel's movement we can feel a decline not only into death, but into the waxworks prose of the last chapters.

93. Dickens first acknowledged his debt to Samuel Rogers's "Ginevra" in his preface to *Barnaby Rudge*; a dedication to Rogers later appeared at the head of volume 1 of *Curiosity Shop*. See *Letters*, vol. 2, p. 125, 8? or 9? September 1840. It is interesting to note that exactly one month after dedicating the volume to Rogers, Dickens wrote a letter defending him against charges of being a dirty old man like the one the analysts see in Trent (*Letters*, vol. 2, pp. 139–42, 27 October 1840).

94. See Joan Stevens, " 'Woodcuts Dropped into the Text': The Illustrations in *The Old Curiosity Shop* and *Barnaby Rudge*," *Studies in Bibliography* 20 (1967): 113–33.

The Old Curiosity Shop is a failure not only because of its sentimental story but also because of its style and the deadly "allegory" which presides at the death of Little Nell and at the death of the reader's interest. The last parts of the story are simply too abstract. This is the narrator's "airy truth"; if Shakespeare gives it a local habitation and a name, Dickens seems to be going in the opposite direction here, erasing all names and details and presenting us with the barest abstractions and archetypes. We are given so few details that these are hardly "scenes" at all. Once Nell and Trent reach the country, they pass through one ruin after another and meet one nameless old man after another—the Clergyman, the Sexton, the second Sexton, the Bachelor. Even the portion of Kit's story, back in London, which alternates with this one runs out of energy at this point, and the verbs themselves lose their actuality, as Dickens employs the coy subjunctive for an entire chapter. The fantasy, in other words, has been acted out on the level of language as well as in the story and in the narrator's experience. On this level too, achieving control over the material entails a sacrifice of its life and energy. Fantasy has many roles; while it proved a resource for Richardson, it has preempted what might have been more complex, flexible and appropriate structures of organization in Dickens's novel.

4

Literature as Dream: Mode
of Representation

What it will be Questioned When the Sun rises do you
not see a round Disk of fire somewhat like a Guinea
O no no I see an Innumerable company of the Heavenly host crying Holy Holy Holy is the Lord God
Almighty.
> —William Blake, *A Vision of the Last Judgment*

[Secondary revision] behaves in the manner which the
poet maliciously ascribes to philosophers: it fills up the
gaps in the dream-structure with shreds and patches. As
a result . . . the dream loses its appearance of absurdity
. . . and approximates to the model of an intelligible experience.
> —Freud, *The Interpretation of Dreams*

Dreams and daydreams are often grouped together and said
to be two different instances of a single Freudian wish
fulfillment model based on the famous formula presented in
The Interpretation of Dreams: "Every dream is the (disguised)
fulfillment of a (repressed) wish."[1] But even though Freud
had introduced his suggestion about dreams by evoking the
folk wisdom connecting them to our more transparently
wishful daydreams, and even though he continued to link
them when he talked about wishes, the two are not the same.
Freud himself separated them elsewhere, when he warned

1. Sigmund Freud, *The Interpretation of Dreams* (1900), SE 4:160.

analysts to be careful about seemingly transparent dreams; a
daydream might be providing a misleadingly simple facade
for the complex dream structure underneath. Harriet Vane
knows this in Sayer's *Gaudy Night*, when she wakes up cha-
grined from a dream about embracing Lord Peter Wimsey
but is relieved to remember that "dreams never symbolize our
real wishes but always something Much Worse!" If she really
wanted to embrace Lord Peter, she says, she would have
dreamed about typewriters or spring cleaning.

Wish fulfillment in the daydream is obvious; the corresponding subjectivity in fantasies, as we saw in the last chapter, is equally obvious, though odd. Daydreams present a
recognizable reality, and fantasies present a recognizable psychic reality. Dreams, however, as Freud tried to impress on
his audience, present no recognizable reality at all, but only a
coded version of it. They less resemble paintings than they resemble writing. Though dreams, like daydreams, present
wishful material, what makes them different is the *way* they
present it—their special "dream-work" language or mode of
represenation. Freud added a footnote to the 1925 edition of
Dreams, correcting earlier readers who had begun to reduce
dreams to nothing but their wishful latent thoughts. "At bottom, dreams are nothing other than a particular *form* of
thinking," he said. "It is the *dream-work* which creates that
form, and it alone is the essence of dreaming."[2]

Already, in the original version of *Dreams*, Freud had emphasized the uniqueness of the dream language he had discovered. He distinguished it very carefully from the more
natural language of symbolism present in daydreams, and
from the allegories which previous interpreters had tried to
find in dreams. The traditional interpreter had read a dream
in its own terms, or in terms of some close analogy: Pharaoh's
seven lean cattle are seven lean years, and the fat cattle represent fat years. This is symbolic interpretation, Freud says, and

2. *Ibid.*, SE 5:506–07.

he dismisses it;[3] the dream will require a much less intuitively natural mode of reading.

It is odd how persistently Freud is associated with precisely the sort of symbol hunting he was trying to supersede, not only in the cliché visions of analysts rooting up phallic symbols but in more sophisticated applications of psychoanalysis as well. One critic, for example, has identified what he calls Dickens's "dreamer's stance," which he claims makes psychoanalytic interpretation necessary.[4] But what he identifies as the dreamer's stance is simply the fact that Dickens's plots must be read on two levels, the literal and the symbolic: not only is Magwitch a criminal but symbolically he is Pip's father and an aspect of Pip himself. True as this is, however, it has less to do with dreams than with daydreams and fantasies. What Freud meant was that we ought not read dreams literally *or* symbolically; they are not naturalistic efforts at mimesis. The dream takes place, in Freud's words, on that "other stage" (*auf dem anderen Schauplatz*) of psychic reality, not because it is fictional or surrealistic or visionary, but because it works according to different rules of representation.

In making these distinctions and thus calling attention to the dream's mode of representation, Freud was calling attention to an entirely new dimension of the dream material. He simultaneously provided the basis for a new view of psychic conflict which is much more useful than the old for thinking about literature. He shifted our attention away from a battle between wish and repression as a model for dreams and other

3. The terminology can be confusing. Freud's use of *symbolic* makes it closer to what we now generally mean by *allegorical* interpretation—the assignation of fixed meanings. That sort of interpretation is, in fact, often defined now by its difference from what most critics would call *symbolic* interpretation. See, e.g., C. S. Lewis's distinction between allegory and symbolism in *The Allegory of Love* (New York: Oxford University Press, 1958), p. 50. Jacques Lacan would call the same kind of interpretation "imaginary" and would counter it to still another sort of "symbolic" interpretation.

4. Taylor Stoehr, *Dickens: The Dreamer's Stance* (Ithaca, N.Y.: Cornell University Press, 1965).

fictions, to a much more general tension between two entirely different ways of seeing things and representing experience. It is true that Freud retained his primary conception of dreams as wish fulfillments even while he spoke of them as a new language; he tried to reduce his two discoveries—about motive and language—to a single one, by showing that the dream's strange language was a function of the struggle between wish and censor and that the dream could be entirely explained by the neatly arranged dichotomies in his formula: the dream is a "(disguised) fulfillment of a (repressed) wish." Thus the difference between ordinary thinking and dreamwork thinking was to be explained as the difference between wish and disguised manifestation.

Nonetheless, although Freud maintained his wish fulfillment formula for dreams, much of what he says—and certainly much of what he *does* in the course of actual dream interpretations—implies that it is the more general conflict which defines the dream's special nature and which must be dealt with in interpreting it. This larger conflict between two different ways of "thinking," or of seeing and representing experience, reveals itself most dramatically in Freud's self-contradictory descriptions of the quality which he said most distinguished dreams from waking experience and which he was the first to emphasize: their regressive quality which, according to Freud, explained both the dream's motive and its special language.

In the first of the following sections I will reexamine Freud's formlua and show that his original dicotomy between wish and disguise does not hold true, even within itself; and that the other tensions between ordinary and special language, and between maturity and regression, certainly cannot be reduced to functions of the original. As we shall see, the concepts of wish and disguise were quickly expanded in Freud's actual practice to imply a much more general conflict in dreams. The second section demonstrates this widened conflict by reexamining one of Freud's most important sample dream analyses. In the third section, I will suggest that the conflict in dreams can be a useful starting point for understanding the way certain literary texts work.

BEYOND "THE (DISGUISED) FULFILLMENT OF A (REPRESSED) WISH": MOTIVES, LANGUAGE, AND REGRESSION

Freud's formula depends on the existence of an obvious distinction between wish and disguise, but neither of these concepts is simple, as we saw in our discussion of fantasies in the last chapter. They become even more complex in Freud's discussion of dreams; part of the whole puzzle about dreams lies in deciding just what the wish is and what fulfillment would be, and in distinguishing fulfillment from its supposed disguise.

Let us examine the wish. For Freud, the wish is the thing itself, the original source and meaning behind the manifest dream's false facade. Without the censor's interference, every dream would be as simple as Freud's paradigm "dream of convenience," in which the thirsty sleeper dreams that he is drinking so he will not have to wake up and get himself a drink. It is "a dream I can produce as often as I like in myself—experimentally, as it were," Freud says, "if I eat anchovies or olives . . . in the evening [before bed]."[5] In practice, however, it is not as easy as Freud suggests to separate the primitive wish from the other elements in the dream. Nor is any wish, even a physiological one like thirst, so easily separable from its later associations outside the dream; indeed, the wish's own meaning and power for the adult, far from being literally obvious, may actually derive from its own supposed derivatives.

Even Freud's example of the "experimental" convenience dream demonstrates these complications.[6] After eating anchovies one night, Freud did dream about drinking—but that was not all he dreamed. His wife was giving him a drink from a valuable urn which he had in reality just given away as

---

5. Freud, *The Interpretation of Dreams*, SE 4:123.
6. *Ibid.*, p. 124.

a present. The difference between this and an unadorned glass of water, which would have done just as well to fulfill his physiological need, is no accident, and it is not easy to isolate the original wish from its supposedly accidental context. Freud wanted the water, but his physiological need was inseparable from his more complex aesthetic desires for the urn and from his wish to be served by his wife.[7] Who is to say which of these wishes is ultimate? The physical act of drinking is a common denominator for several different wishes and the occasion for several differnet *kinds* of "wishing" in the dream.

Perhaps with Freud's anchovies in mind, Serge Leclaire and Jean Laplanche have even reported a dream "which fulfills the need to drink but without *any* reference to drinking."[8] Here the original wish disappears altogether from the dream of convenience, not because of any simple censorship but rather because of the complexity of what *wish* means. The dreamer was a boy named Philippe, who woke up thirsty from a dream about walking through the woods with a girl friend. The fulfillment of "drinking" was involved only in Philippe's associations to the walk, which included memories of drinks and people who gave him drinks, and of the time he learned to cup his hands and scoop water up for himself. The wish to drink was here inseparable from its later derivatives

7. Not only are these wishes different; they are different *kinds* of wishes. This difference has led Jacques Lacan to distinguish between simple "need," which is a physiological condition with an object as its goal; "demand," which is a desired relationship with another who will provide the object; and desire per se, which he defines as a mutually determined relationship (unlike the monolithic demand) in which needs are satisfied. See, e.g., J. B. Pontalis, "Les formations de l'inconscient," reports of seminars, 1957–58, *Bulletin de Psychologie*, vol. 11, no. 4/5; vol. 12, nos. 2/3 and 4 (1958); and Anthony Wilden's editorial comments in his translation of Jacques Lacan, *The Language of the Self: The Function of Language in Psychoanalysis* (Baltimore: Johns Hopkins University Press, 1968), pp. 189–92.

8. Serge Leclaire and Jean Laplanche, "The Unconscious: A Psychoanalytic Study," trans. Patrick Coleman, in *French Freud: Structural Studies in Psychoanalysis*, Yale French Studies 48 (1972): 118–75.

(wishes to seduce people into serving him, to be independent and get drinks for himself, and so forth). The fulfillment in the manifest dream was not so much disguised as elaborated to correspond to the elaboration of the wish.

Not only is the wish sometimes inseparable from its derivatives, but it may even turn out to be a symbolic disguise for one of its derivatives. In a dream about a related convenience, for example, Freud reports waking with a "pressing need to micturate" and remembers that he was just dreaming about bringing his father a urinal. This time, however, he suggests that his painful thoughts about his father's weakness came first and then called up his own physiological need as a distraction—or disguise—for those thoughts.[9]

Clearly, the physiological model is not suitable to represent complex psychological motives. And in fact, though Freud ostensibly uses this model throughout *The Interpretation of Dreams*, he unobtrusively complicates it until it becomes almost a reverse of itself. The first wishes he points to are simple, recognizable adult wishes: to be famous, to pursue forbidden hobbies. But soon he has to talk about the wishes which lie behind frightening and unpleasant dreams—wishes, he explains, "from another part of the mind."[10] While perfectly plausible, this claim modifies *wish* to include the very censorship which was supposed to oppose wishes. In addition, Freud soon admits that even the first sort of wishes are important only because they draw on regressive infantile wishes,[11] which are hardly recognizable as wishes any more

9. Freud, *The Interpretation of Dreams*, SE 4:208ff, esp. 218.
10. *Ibid.*, pp. 145–57.
11. Although the dream formula presented in *The Interpretation of Dreams* thus refers to repressed infantile wishes, Freud's sample analyses seldom go further than uncovering the more recognizable adult wish associated with and covering for the infantile wish. Freud reveals the formula itself only in stages. First he says that dreams fulfill wishes (chapters 2 and 3), then that they do so only in a distorted way (chapter 4); and only at the end of chapter 4 does the full formula, indicating that the wishes are repressed wishes, emerge (p. 160). Not until well into chapter 5 does he suggest that these re-

and may even offend; their gratifying quality, in other words, is inseparable from the childhood way of seeing things. Then Freud goes on to talk about the *ego's* wish to sleep,[12] and he moves entirely out of the realm of specific wishes into a discussion about general conditions of experience and our ways of coping with wishes in general.

At this point it is quite clear that Freud's wish is very different from a basic physiological sensation which can be satisfied with a simple physical act. *Wish-fulfilling* no longer means "gratifying" but simply "psychologically meaningful and determined."[13] Freud has moved from the supposedly unique regressed wish to the larger network of "dream thoughts" which mutually determine the manifest dream. When he called the dream *wish-fulfilling*, he was finally contrasting it not to "painful" but to "accidental" experiences and representations of them. The wish pleasure principle no longer means "pleasure-seeking,"[14] and Freud's goal is not to find the regressive pleasures of the text but the reasons for them—reasons which, as we shall see, include *adult* play with infantile wishes.

Just as problems arise in trying to find the dream's source and meaning in a single regressive wish, there are problems in viewing its surface as the product of a single adult motive of disguise or censorship. Freud, however, generally tried to do this. "The kernel of my theory of dreams lies in my deriva-

---

pressed wishes may go back to childhood in every case (p. 219), and not until chapter 7 does he make the full claim.

12. Freud, *The Interpretation of Dreams*, SE 5:570.

13. Or as Roy Schafer has suggested, the wish is better described as an "affirmation." ("The Idea of Resistance," *International Journal of Psychoanalysis* 54 [1973]: 259–85). Freud's own more general assertion that "the ego is at the center of every dream" comes closer to describing the nature of motivation in dreams than does the concept of *wish*, and even his own word for the "wish" in a joke—*tendency*—seems more accurate than "wish" itself.

14. Joseph H. Smith, "The Psychoanalytic Understanding of Human Freedom: Freedom From and Freedom For" (paper delivered at the Mark Kanzer Seminar on Psychoanalysis and the Humanities, Yale University, New Haven, 1976).

tion of dream distortion from the censorship,"[15] he stated; the dream's strangeness comes from the use of regressive modes of thinking to distort, not to express a more primitive truth. We shall see, however, that just as the wish is inseparable from an entire context of thoughts, censorship is inseparable from a more general mode of seeing and communicating. Like wish fulfillment, censorship comes to mean something more general, like "psychological determination." We may be able to talk about psychic *conflict* in dreams, but it is impossible to identify a wish and a censoring force as the components of that conflict.[16]

Freud's political censor paradigm is just as simple—and just as inadequate—as his convenience dream paradigm for wishes: the censor is an exclusively destructive force, which mindlessly rearranges the real wish-fulfilling dream thoughts to produce a meaningless surface. It breaks the dream up and repacks the pieces randomly, "like pack ice," making use of accidental and trivial connections between the thoughts to condense and displace them. The censor's activity is no more related to meaningful communication than was Lewis Carroll's paranoid ritual of cutting up his manuscript pages into arbitrarily numbered strips, pasting them randomly together to form new pages, and sending them to his publisher while carefully keeping to himself the key to the sequence. Even if the manifest dream

> has an apparently sensible exterior, we know that this has only come about through dream-distortion and can have as little organic relation to the internal content of the dream as the façade of an Italian church has to its structure and plan. . . . In general one must avoid seeking to

15. Freud, *The Interpretation of Dreams*, SE 4:308 and implied throughout the book.

16. See Jacob Spanjaard's careful examination of Freud's contradictory statements about "wish" and "defense" in relation to latent and manifest dream content, in "The Manifest Dream Content and Its Significance for the Interpretation of Dreams," *International Journal of Psychoanalysis* 50 (1969): 221–35, esp. 224.

explain one part of the manifest dream by another, as though the dream had been coherently conceived and was a logicaly arranged narrative. On the contrary, it is as a rule like a piece of breccia, composed of various fragments of rock held together by a binding medium, so that the designs that appear on it do not belong to the original rocks imbedded in it.[17]

The resulting image is a *bricolage*, a patchwork made out of other images, or a Viennese *geshnas* trick picture, as Freud calls it. The image cannot be taken as a whole (if strangely regressive) thought but can only be decoded piece by piece. At best, the facade may be related to dream thoughts like a rebus, punningly revealing a message once the elements are turned into words: the young man who dreams that the radiator overflowed when he turned the spigot is really saying, "Every time I let off steam I get into hot water." But more often the elements lead outward in several different ways, and one of the difficulties in interpreting dreams, Freud notes, is knowing just how to read each one. The one rule, for Freud, is to distrust a literal or even a symbolic reading. A lion in a dream is probably not a lion; nor is it a symbol for Hercules or even for courage, as it might be in a poem. And once we ignore these obvious meanings, the lion may mean any number of things. It may be a rebus-like reference to the dreamer's desire to "lie on" certain couches; it may be an allusion to the dreamer's cousin Daniel, or to his recent trip to the zoo. Or its dark mane—in contrast to the almost white mane of the lion the dreamer had actually seen—may even signal that "everything in this dream is a reversal of the truth." But whatever it means, the censor is responsible for the distance between meaning and lion.

As in the case of wishes, however, the paradigm does not always work, and Freud begins to contradict himself. Just as he ultimately invoked many different wishes and wishing

17. Freud, *Introductory Lectures on Psychoanalysis* (1915–17), *SE* 15:181–82. See also *The Interpretation of Dreams*, *SE* 4:104, and *SE* 5:449–500.

agencies, he invokes several kinds of disguise and constraint in the dream and attributes them all to the censor. As a result, he paradoxically claims that all distortions are due to the censor. ("He did the deed who gained by it," Freud explains),[18] but he also suggests at times that the distortions may have another source and may even help express latent thoughts.[19]

In the dream I cited earlier about hot water and the radiator, for example, the manifest imagery is *not* just a disguise; it actually calls up infantile urination fantasies associated with the more adult thoughts about "letting off steam," conveying them in the only symbolic terms which can possibly represent the infantile, exaggerated intensity of such early fantasies. If two ideas have been—from an adult point of view— "condensed," this is because the infantile memory being expressed comes from a time when the two concepts were not separated: the stream of urine *is* a burning jet of steam. The image expresses the thought rather than destroying it. Or more accurately, it works in two different ways. What seems like a disguise, from one point of view, is a way of saying something, from another—just as what seems like a wish can serve as a disguise. Freud tried to describe the conflict in dreams by setting up a dichotomy between wish and disguise, but what we have found instead is a dichotomy between two ways of representing the experience of "letting off steam," both of them vying for control of the manifest dream, pulling it in different directions and making different use of it.

As I suggested earlier, this conflict between two entirely different ways of seeing things comes out most clearly when Freud talks about regression, the phenomenon which forms

18. Freud, *The Interpretation of Dreams*, SE 4:308.

19. See discussions of contradictions in Freud's writings about dreams and primary process thinking, in Merton Gill, "The Primary Process," in *Motives and Thought: Psychoanalytic Essays in Honor of David Rapaport*, ed. Robert R. Holt, Psychological Issues, vol. 5, no. 2/3 (New York: International Universities Press, 1967), pp. 260–98; and in Marshall Edelson, "Language and Dreams: The Interpretation of Dreams Revisited," *Psychoanalytic Study of the Child* 27 (1972): 269ff.

the basis of his argument that dreams are unique creations and not just nighttime varieties of daydreams.

What allows Freud to distinguish between dreams and day-dreams is his interpretation of the two vital qualifiers to his wish fulfillment formula, the parenthetical stipulations that wishes are repressed and fulfillment is disguised. Both of these he attributes to regression; the contrast between waking and dreaming, Freud says, is the contrast between our mature, civilized selves and our infantile selves. The dreamer, Freud explains, removes his civilized extensions one by one, like a man taking out his false teeth and removing his eye-glasses before he goes to bed, and regresses to his infantile wishes and his infantile forms of expression, visual hallucination and concrete thinking.[20]

This makes sense and has the immediate appeal of other simplifying dichotomies—not only the one between wish and disguise but also the ones that pervade Freud's dream theory, like the dichotomy between *conscious* and *unconscious*. But as we have seen, such dichotomies seldom withstand scrutiny, and just as we had to learn to ask, not "Is a given thought conscious or unconscious?" but "What *kind* of consciousness?" so we will finally ask, not "Is the dream mature or regressed?" but "What *kind* of regression?" For once Freud goes on to explain how the regression in dreams works, he makes two contradictory claims. In the case of regressing to an infantile wish, Freud reductively assumes that the *literal* wish (for the breast or for some infantile masturbation fantasy-object, for example) is the ultimate meaning of and source for the dream. But when Freud talks about the dreamer's regression to infantile forms of representation, he makes it clear that these are not to be assumed to be final in themselves. "Regression" to a visual scene does not mean that the ultimate meaning of a dream is an infantile visual experience. Visual or pictorial representation, according to Freud, is only an old

20. Freud, "A Metapsychological Supplement to the Theory of Dreams" (1917), *SE* 14:222.

tool used somewhat restrictedly, in the absence of a better and
more modern one, for new adult purposes. The dreamer, like
the political cartoonist, is forced to condense, distort, and simplify his ideas so that they fit into cartoon form.[21] This is very
different from a person who has regressed to a state where all
he *knows* is pictorial and sensual experience.

In the one case the regression is absolute and ultimate; in
the other it is only a vehicle for expressing something else. In
the case of the infantile wish, we get closer to the "truth"; in
the case of infantile modes of representation, we are dis-
tracted from the truth: it has been translated into an alien and
inappropriate language. Despite Freud's smooth generaliza-
tion about regression in the dream, there is, finally, no way to
segregate its two roles. In fact, as we shall see, the contradictory functions of regression permeate every aspect of the
dream, including motive and means of representation. Regression is important not just because it takes place but because it inevitably causes confusion as it forces the interpreter
to switch from one mode of reading to another. Freud
claimed that dreams differ from waking life by discarding
mature meaning and motives in their regression, but the
source of the dream's unique quality is rather the way it
makes us uncertain about meaning and motive, playing each
one against a more primitive, regressed counterpart.

And there always *is* confusion. Dreams always seem to
mean more than the wakened dreamer can discern. In part
this is because he never has the original dream directly before
him. Dreams, if told, are always *re*told; we know about them
only after we have lost them—and lost our original "reading"
of the hallucinatory experience, which we did not realize we
had to interpret at all. We look back on our dreams, puzzled.
What seemed so horrifying last night now seems only
puzzling: Why was I terrified by the way the sunlight fell
across my mother's hands? And what we took for granted last
night now seems absurd. Sometimes the gap between dream

21. Freud, *The Interpretation of Dreams, SE* 5:339–40.

experience and the attempt at retelling it seems unbridgeable, and we cannot put the dream into words. Oddly enough, it is not always clear whether the dream or the retelling comes first in this strange relationship where the play *between* two versions of the dream is more important than either version. In the "hot water" dream, the dreamer's nighttime experience initially seems to come first, but as soon as he translates it into the derivative narrative and overhears his own words—"let off steam" and "into hot water"—the verbal statement seems to assume the original meaning, and the original dream appears to be only a code for it. The play between these two possibilities is the dream's defining quality and a main source of its unsettling power.

The gap between dreaming and telling is only partly responsible for the confusion, however. Even if the wakened dreamer seems to describe his dream exactly, he always misreads it at first, if he takes it literally. There is always another gap as well—a gap between the commonsense interpretation of the dream and some other interpretation which hovers behind it. Freud cited regressive mechanisms as the determinants of this other meaning, but this explanation will not always work. It is true that the dreamer has access to a primitive, nonmimetic mode of representation; this is what makes even the most mundane dream surface so different from life. But the primitive dream surface functions in different ways. In some instances it indicates that the dreamer has actually gone back to a primitive way of seeing and representing the world, to a time when feelings were part of the landscape, parents were kings and queens, penises were telephone poles, and a stream of urine was an explosive jet of steam. This reversion is not a denial of reality but a return to a mode of thinking in which wish, fear, and other subjective, emotionally tinged views have not been distinguished from reality.

Freud's claim that dreams fulfill wishes rather than telling the truth describes only the most obvious of several possible distortions resulting from such regression. In dreams, not only does the wishful imperative merge with the factual statement ("You must finish the book, Freud!" becomes a dream in which the book is finished); the subjunctive also merges with the factual ("If Irma had been a better patient, my reputation would be better" becomes a dream in which Irma *is* a better patient). Subjective, metaphorical versions of reality come to be presented as if they were literally true. The dreamer not only cannot distinguish between "I wish" and "It is true"; he cannot even tell the difference between "I think" and "It is true." Since much of the dreamer's thinking is regressive, this last confusion for the most part means returning to the child's concrete, physical way of grasping ideas: the ego was first a body ego, as Freud said. So Freud dreamed that he was dissecting his own pelvis when he felt that he was "spilling out his guts" to the readers of his dream book; and in his dream of the "botanical monograph," the difficult intellectual achievement of finishing the book became the physical achievement of turning its pages.[22] The dreamer is not bothered by this conflation while he sleeps; the wakened dreamer, however, finds that his commonsense, literal-minded insistence on one meaning for his dream gets him into trouble. He resembles the dim-witted narrator in Chaucer's *Book of the Duchess*, who when exploring his own dream world, could not tell the difference between a literal and a figurative game of chess, when the man in black talked about losing his queen.[23]

Simple regression like this, however, is not always sufficient to explain the dream's concrete imagery. In some cases, the dream's pictures, instead of reproducing infantile impressions, are used for some other nonmimetic, coded presentation of experience. Rather than being used primitively, as direct portrayals of experience, the pictures are put

22. *Ibid.*, SE 5:454, and *SE* 4:172.
23. Geoffrey Chaucer, *The Works of Geoffrey Chaucer*, edited by F. N. Robinson (Boston: Houghton Mifflin, 1957), pp. 273–74, ll. 652–56 and ll. 740–41.

to secondary use as diagrams, emblems, or hieroglyphs. Instead of returning to primitive infantile visual experience, these images reflect intellectual schema that no infant could understand. In other words, the dream draws not only on infantile consciousness but also on intellectual and sophisticated ways of seeing and thinking about things—on all the modes of consciousness which sort things out; which make judgments, diagrams, hierarchies, and anatomies; and which see things from all perspectives, as they really are, rather than subjectively. These sophisticated modes conflict with a natural, subjective view because they depend on acquired skills and knowledge, on familiarity with all the inherited social, literary, and linguistic conventions which gradually organize a child's natural and immediate consciousness. In other words, allegories draw on both the "barbarian" and the "bookish" views of the world, as C. S. Lewis has pointed out.[24] These views may seem opposite, but what is important for our purposes is that they nonetheless are similar in their common indifference to reality as we ordinarily perceive it. Regressive modes of consciousness may ignore the conventions of realism the way a child does, out of ignorance; the more intellectual modes ignore the conventions of realism the way a pedant or a philosopher does, out of another order of preconception altogether. But both ignore them.

The interplay among these different modes of consciousness imposes more than a simple uncertainty about not knowing how to interpret a given dream symbol. It is a more basic disorientation, like every child's reorientation when he moves from picture books to books containing nothing but printed words and has to learn the artificial conventions which will turn black marks into meaningful communications. We all had to learn to use our senses—our primary connection with the world—for secondary purposes. Everyone has had the experience of constraining natural responses to fit the artifices

24. C. S. Lewis, *The Discarded Image: An Introduction to Medieval and Renaissance Literature* (Cambridge: Cambridge University Press, 1964), p. 5.

of language. We have all had to resee our more impulsive and natural ways of understanding experience, in terms of civilization's artificial conventions; we had to learn these artifices so thoroughly that they finally became second nature,[25] the schemata were taken for reality, and childhood confusions were forgotten. Only in moments of alienation, disorientation, and sleepiness do we regress into a state in which we are unsure of the rules again. Only at threshold moments can we regain the old modes of consciousness while retaining the new modes; at these times, we can see their interplay and feel the old confusion. The sleeping dreamer, who does not know that his dreams are symbolic, may be capable of only one reading, and he feels no ambivalence; but of course we have no contact with him.

For the wakened dreamer reviewing his dream, the situation is always more confusing. He straddles the worlds of remembered dream and waking consciousness, and for him there is always a struggle between the two ways of reading the dream. Freud continually argued that we must ignore the ordinary, waking, commonsense way of reading dreams, but both methods are necessary. What Freud's work established was not the existence of a simple battle between wish and censor but the fact that the dream is multiply determined and lends itself to multiple, contradictory readings. This conflict is less like the tug-of-war implied by the dream formula than like the perceptual conflict caused by ambiguous duck-rabbit drawings or the intellectual conflict in a debate or a sequence of textual interpretations. Freud came closest to describing this conflict not when he talked about wishes and censors but when he singled out an oddly separate "factor" shaping the dream after "the dream has been presented before consciousness as an object of perception."[26] He called this factor the

25. James Nohrnberg's phrase, describing how the reader's experience internalizing Spenser's conventions in *The Faerie Queene* repeats the child's original experience. *The Analogy of* The Faerie Queene (Princeton, N.J.: Princeton University Press, 1976), p. 655.

26. Freud, *New Introductory Lectures on Psychoanalysis* (1933), *SE* 22:21.

"secondary revision" or "secondary elaboration" (*Bearbeitung*): it comes on the scene after the struggle and tries to pull the pieces together and shape the *geshnas* into something that makes sense in adult terms. The conflict here is less like the conflict between two moose clashing head on than like the dilemma of the passerby who encounters the animals afterward and wonders what the two-headed beast is called. This secondary factor is the passerby who introduces the dream's first misreading, and it is the interplay between primary and secondary readings that makes the dream what it is.

EXAMPLE: THE DREAM OF THE BOTANICAL MONOGRAPH

Freud, as I have suggested, tended to dismiss the commonsense reading of dreams and considered the secondary revision a superficial, rationalizing sugarcoating. Rather than stressing the mixture of strange and familiar elements in dreams, his primary interest was to surprise us and show us something new about the strangeness of dreams. Of course everyone had always thought dreams strange, but Freud was pointing up a different kind of strangeness. Traditionally, dreams had been seen as prophetic, otherworldly, perhaps surrealistic; and this is the way they are portrayed in literature. But the literary dream is more often a symbol for some other extraordinary experience than it is a realistic representation of dreams; damsels with dulcimers and talking flowers rarely appear in most people's dreams. Some dreams, if not visionary, are strange in that they are physically or psychologically impossible. But in most cases the dream, rather than being flagrantly impossible, is just a little odd and does not *seem* to call for special interpretation at all. It may simply give irrelevant details with an irritating insistence (Why a botanical monograph?), or it may omit the important details ("I couldn't see his face to tell who it was"). It may distort pictorial and narrative conventions, even if it does not flout them ("Then, somehow, it was not Berlin but Rome"). The dream may go too fast or too slow, or it may fail to locate itself firmly in time and space. Or it may be too ridiculously *un*strange ("I dreamed about having the piano tuned, which is exactly what happened yesterday").

Freud tried to draw attention away from the surface of all these dreams, whether they were outright ridiculous or suspiciously innocuous. His stated aim was to get to the real meaning behind the dream, to decode its clever language and find its hidden message—the wish behind it. But he did not follow his own program. In fact, Freud's search for the infantile wish, the one hallucinatory image misrepresented and distorted in the dream, was replaced by his search for and demonstration of a different way of reading the surface. Freud's point was that whether the dream is extravagantly ridiculous or trivially ordinary, it is necessary to ignore its obvious meaning and read it in a special way in order to discover the dream thoughts encoded in it. But Freud nonetheless also makes use of the obvious reading of the dream and our own final interpretation of the dream will always depend on the interaction of the two methods of reading.

The sample dream itself is quite unassuming; indeed, an obvious reading does not go far:

> I had written a monograph on a certain plant. The book lay before me and I was at the moment turning over a . . . colored plate. Bound up in each copy there was a dried specimen of the plant, as though it had been taken from a herbarium.[27]

But why should Freud dream about just this bit of trivia? According to him the thoughts behind the dream ultimately deal with profound concerns about work and love, but the surface gives no clue to these if it is read in the ordinary way. Instead, he says, we must read it like a code and see how the elements

27. Freud, *The Interpretation of Dreams*, SE 4:169–76; 180, n. 3, 191, 281–84, 305; SE 5:467. Freud refers to the dream several times, each time making different points about it. My analysis is based both on his interpretations and on several biographers' suggestions, particularly those about using Freud's less discretely edited paper, "Screen Memories" (1899), as an association to the dream. I have indicated in the text where my interpretation (but not the facts on which it is based) differs from both these sources.

work together. The dream consists of separate pieces, like
"botanical," "monograph," and "turning pages," and these
have been cleverly glued together to form a scene, as in a
parlor game where the contestant is given three words and
must make them into a sentence. But the real meaning is elsewhere, and we will not find it unless we are willing to follow
strange associational paths very different from intuitive ones.
These associational paths first take Freud through a series of
"botanical" thoughts. He starts with a perfectly indifferent experience of the previous morning when he happened to notice a botanical monograph in a window; then there is the
woman whose husband "forgot" to bring her flowers on her
birthday; there is Freud's own failure to bring his wife
flowers, though she remembers to bring him his favorite
"flowers," artichokes, from the market; there is the conversation of the previous night in which the forgotten lady was
mentioned, as were those important topics in the dream
thoughts, work and love—although these had nothing whatsoever to do with flowers, except in a ridiculously tenuous
way, since they concerned Freud's monograph on cocaine, a
"flower" of sorts; and there is Professor Gärtner and his
"blooming" wife, who interrupted that conversation. The
other memories which come to mind are just as tenuously
connected, it would seem.

Freud tries to make the connections between the associations sound as superficial as possible, but it turns out that elements in the questionable category (which includes artichokes
to eat, bouquets to bring his wife, cocaine, and Professor
Gärtner's blooming wife) are connected in more important
and familiar ways as well. What Freud has done is to stress
superficial links and ignore more important ones. These, it is
true, may sometimes be the only associations to escape the patient's resistance in analysis; but the others are always there. It
is as if a reader were to pick out the liquid images in *Twelfth
Night* and present them as the play's only organizing device,
without explaining the relation which oceans, rain, urine, and
tears have to the rest of the action. For it turns out that the

tenuous string of botanical references plays a more essential role in organizing the dream thoughts than Freud assigned.

In fact, the associations reveal nothing less than a series of crises in Freud's life, all of which are concerned with having to choose between self-indulgence and discipline, between sensual pleasure (or a favorite hobby) and hard work. They begin with a very early crisis, a scene of infantile masturbation and its forbidden fantasies; this is represented by a more innocent memory, in which Freud and his sister are mischievously pulling apart a book with colored leaves or plates ("like an artichoke," Freud says)—but with their father's unexpected encouragement.[28] Later adult crises develop out of Freud's subsequent love of monographs and his failures in botany. In his youth, Freud spent his time doing things like removing bookworms from the school herbarium, and in fact he himself was a "bookworm," collecting expensive monographs with colored plates, much to his father's disapproval. He could not marry his cousin in the flowery countryside because he had to spend his time studying; she was the girl he remembered visiting and stealing flowers from—or "deflowering." Much later, when he did interrupt his study of cocaine, in order to visit his fiancée, he paid for it by missing out on an important discovery about the plant's anesthetic properties. Finally, there was Freud's latest "botanical monograph," the book on dreams, which was causing him trouble. Freud was discouraged about finishing it, and his friend Fliess had just written encouragingly that he could "see himself turning over its pages" already—even though Freud had as yet sent him only pieces of the manuscript.[29] The dream

28. The connection between masturbation and pulling apart a book or an artichoke is suggested by the phrase *sich einen herunterreissen*, or *ausreissen*, "to pull one out," and by its dream symbol of breaking off a branch. Freud discusses the symbolism both in his autobiographical paper on "screen memories"—to which he directs the reader in his analysis of the botanical monograph (*SE* 3:319)—and in *The Interpretation of Dreams* (*SE* 5:348, n. 2, and 388).

29. Freud, *The Interpretation of Dreams, SE* 4:172, n. 1. It is also interesting

book was the latest "flower of his invention," we might say without stretching the associations too far. Dreams are not flowers, but Freud called his sample dream at the beginning of his book a "specimen" dream, like the specimens in the herbarium.

The crises, when considered as a group, reveal an interesting and paradoxical relationship in which the dichotomy between self-indulgence and hard work is partly resolved, as Freud turns away from real flowers to an analysis of them in his work. The manifest dream then becomes not only a hermeneutical puzzle but a symbolic image of Freud's lifelong conflict—the image of Freud turning over the dead leaves of a botanical monograph. The flowers that are alive in the fields come into his dry-as-dust academic book as dead things, "dried specimens." Freud's study has taken him away from life, courtship, flowers, deflowering, and eating artichokes. At the same time, however, it has taken him paradoxically toward all these. Freud in the dream is unfolding a colored plate; his books have in a way become his flowers, and he takes sensual pleasure in looking at their colored leaves —and in possessing them. He may have pulled the flower apart, but in doing so he has created it again in the book. He may analyze dreams, but he recreates them in his book; he pulls them apart in order to treasure them.

It is now clear that although the dream destroys the original thoughts (it does not reproduce them literally), it also creates something new, despite what Freud says. As T. S. Eliot says of poetry, dreams

> communicate—if it is communication, for the word may beg the question—an experience which is not an experience in the ordinary sense, for it may only exist, formed out of many personal experiences ordered in some way

---

that in "The Psychopathology of Everyday Life" (1901), Freud mentions a man who "remembered" seeing a certain monograph in a bookshop window but could not relocate the book; Freud confidently explained that the monograph existed only in fantasy: the man *intended* to write it himself (*SE* 6:151).

which may be very different from the way of valuation of practical life, in the expression of it. . . . that which is to be communicated is the (poem) itself, and only incidentally the experience and the thought which have gone into it.[30]

Freud slighted the "dream itself," because he expected it to communicate what Eliot calls "the experience and thought which have gone into it" in a very direct and literal way. He looked for the reproduction of a single, explanatory wish and saw only censorship if he failed to find that wish. We can see, however, that the dream's indirections not only disguise wishes but sometimes express something otherwise inexpressible. The dream is not about a single wish (which it has failed to represent) but about a whole network of associations, thoughts, and images related to each other and represented in the dream in the strangest, most diverse ways. Freud believed that he had discovered the meaning of the dream in a single wish behind it, but what he really discovered was that the thoughts motivating a dream are connected in such a way as to create the illusion of a single source or wish when they were psychoanalyzed by Freud's methods, although they yield other meanings when approached from different modes of consciousness or read in different ways. Freud discovered that we all resort to these strange ways of seeing and representing things at night;[31] but we also hold onto the ordinary

30. T. S. Eliot, *The Use of Poetry and the Use of Criticism* (Cambridge, Mass.: Harvard University Press, 1933), p. 21.

31. Nor does this occur only at night. Daytime perception itself cannot be described simply in terms of what we are conscious or unconscious of but requires a specification of *how* we are conscious of things. The familiar ambiguous duck-rabbit design shows how much individual subjectivity enters into our perception of the drawing as one or the other animal; Ernst Gombrich, especially, has shown how cultural subjectivity and inherited schema affect an individual's supposedly objective perception. But psychoanalysts have demonstrated an even more fundamental ambiguity in perception. In the case of the duck-rabbit design, the alternatives become possible when viewers are forced into new modes of consciousness. Charles Fisher and I. H. Paul, for example, forced an audience into another mode of perception by flashing a

modes of perception and the strangest thing of all is that
these two approaches can coexist.

DREAMS AND LITERATURE

Despite Freud's claim that the dream-work was entirely different from mature, well-shaped, purposeful communication—not to mention the poet's art—others have claimed,
on the basis of the same data, that dream-work is no different
from poetic thinking. According to them, Freud gave us a
"science of tropes" (Kenneth Burke); his was the one psychology that "makes poetry indigenous to the human mind," according to Lionel Trilling. The two fundamental dream
mechanisms are equivalent to the two kinds of figural language: *condensation* and *displacement* are other names for metaphor and metonymy (Jacques Lacan). From a somewhat
different perspective, Harold Bloom maintains that Freud's
list of defensive distortions can be mapped onto our poetic
tropes.[32]

Surely the equation is not quite this simple, whether we
wish to equate poetry with primitive thought processes, as
Lacan does, or with the censor, as Bloom does. Dream thinking includes elements closer to schizophrenic language than

---

similarly ambiguous design across a screen so quickly that none of the audience consciously saw it ("The Effect of Subliminal Visual Stimulation on Images and Dreams: A Validation Study," *Journal of the American Psychoanalytic
Association* 7 [1959]: 35–83). Nonetheless, nearly all the viewers had been
somehow aware of the design, and they even reproduced it in their supposedly random doodles, dreams, and conversations afterward. What is interesting is that under these special conditions, the normal laws of perception were
suspended: instead of seeing the equivalent of either a duck or a rabbit, for
example—what people in ordinary modes of consciousness see—some subjects saw only the meaningless outline determining both.

32. Kenneth Burke, "Freud—and the Analysis of Poetry," in *The Philosophy
of Literary Form* (New York: Vintage Books, 1957); Lionel Trilling, "Freud
and Literature," in *The Liberal Imagination* (New York: Viking Press, 1950);
Jacques Lacan, "The Insistence of the Letter in the Unconscious," trans. Jan
Miehl, in *Structuralism*, Yale French Studies 36/37 (1966); Harold Bloom, *A
Map of Misreading* (New York: Oxford University Press, 1975).

to poetry, and dream rhetoric includes figures so devious that no handbook has a name for them.[33] Along with poetic floral fantasies, it encompasses, for example, the ashtray which one man said represented his fellow patients because it was six-sided or "sick-sided."[34] But there is a connection between dreams and certain kinds of literature that insist, like the dream, on a gap between what the text seems to mean and the deeper meaning it seems to imply. I am not referring to what might seem to be an obvious parallel in the works of the symbolists or surrealists, who claimed to write directly from "the unconscious." The surrealists' famous "chance encounter" of a sewing machine and an umbrella is far too disjointed; we stop expecting it to make sense and so we lose the special tension between the promise of sense and the muteness of events, which characterizes dreams. The literary parallels are not to be found in these artless modes, where all logic and ordinary representation break down, but rather in

33. It is interesting that both William Empson (*Seven Types of Ambiguity* [New York: Meridian Books, 1955], pp. 217–63), and Ernst Kris ("Aesthetic Ambiguity," in *Psychoanalytic Explorations in Art* [New York: Schocken Books, 1964], pp. 243–64), who describe rhetorical figures in terms of *semantic* ambiguity between two different meanings, both reserve a special category for the "Freudian" ambiguity characteristic of dream thinking. Other forms of ambiguity consist of two or more logically related alternative meanings; Freudian ambiguity, according to Empson and Kris, consists of an alogical pairing of contradictory meanings. Dream logic is assigned a special place in still another approach to describing rhetorical figures—Jonathan Culler's operational definition, which identifies figures by the way in which we have to read them in order to understand them. Culler describes the several legitimate moves involved, for example in the figure of metaphor: in metaphor we move from a specific member of a class to the class itself, and then to another member—from "oak" to "tall things" to "Abraham Lincoln," for example. Some moves, however, are illegitimate—moves from class to member to class, for example: "dog" to "brown dog" to "brown things." Dream thinking often locates itself in this separate, "illegitimate" category. See Jonathan Culler, *Structuralist Poetics: Structuralism, Linguistics, and The Study of Literature* (Ithaca, N.Y.: Cornell University Press, 1975), pp. 179–83.

34. Harold Searles cites this example in "The Differentiation between Concrete and Metaphysical Thinking in the Recovering Schizophrenic Patient," *Journal of the American Psychoanalytic Association* 11 (1963): 35–36.

the more highly wrought, emblematic and artificial modes like allegory. Sophisticated, consciously shaped and publicly available art may seem to be at the other end of the scale of human production from the unsophisticated, unconsciously shaped, private dream. But dreams too use artifice, and the artifice used in both cases turns out to be strikingly similar.

Before turning to purely literary examples, let us consider for a moment some that, though not quite literary, are even more obviously similar to dreams. These are the medieval and Renaissance memory systems that Frances Yates has been exploring recently—constructs in the service of memory, which produce images like those Freud attributed to the dream's censorship or its artful "forgetting." The memory systems were visual devices for remembering long lists and arguments by inserting them, piece by piece, into a perfectly memorized mental picture of some complicated scene or building. In other words, to remember a list of virtues and vices—if one's memory building were the campus library —one would insert Pride shoving his way into the entry, Lust in the catalog bank doing something appropriate, and Envy in the form of an old hag ogling the books that borrowers are checking out at the circulation desk (perhaps with eyes painted on her dress, to signal her Latin origins). The more details in each case—and the more striking they were—the better the system worked. My point is that the result looks very much like a scene out of a dream, despite the fact that the memory system was a hard-won, consciously organized achievement in the service of communication, while the dream, in Freud's description, was a regressive escape, distorted in the service of censorship. The dichotomies between remembering and censoring, maturity and regressions, do not remain intact; both the memory system and the dream derive from the attempt to translate ideas into pictures and to reconcile two different ways of seeing and representing things, neither of which is pure memory or pure censorship. In both cases the created image hovers uncertainly between picture and diagram, or between narrative and hieroglyphic;

and in both cases what matters is the interpreter's fluctuation between the two ways of seeing the image.

A similar ambivalence, though more subtle in form, provides the parallel between the dream and allegory. Allegory, like dreams, depends on "the gap between what it means and what we'd normally expect it to mean," as Rosamund Tuve has pointed out in her study of the genre.[35] Its strangeness, like the dream's, does not depend on inherently strange objects and events but on this curious double perspective. Scenes which, when read one way, reveal nothing more than visionary plainness—a wide field, a house, an old man, a book—demand another way of reading by their promise of something more than what we would normally expect them to mean. Interestingly enough, the history of theory about allegory parallels the history of psychoanalytic attitudes toward the double perspective in the dream. Literary theorists first tried to explain the contradictory quality of allegory as a simple interaction between open expression and censorship, with both battling for control of the picture. Allegory presented a transcendent revelatory truth, and the "veil" of allegory shrouded its "misteries . . . lest by prophane wits it should be abused," as Sir Philip Sidney explained[36]—just as the dream's censor was supposed to veil its taboo visions.

In addition to the similarity of moral tone, there has been, until recently, a curious consistency in allegory and dream interpretation, as interpreters in both realms try to bridge the gap between meanings by discarding the sensuous surface and getting down to (or up to?) the simple abstractions which supposedly generate it. True allegory is assumed to deal with the ultimate truths and values in our lives (whether seen from a medieval or a Kafkaesque point of view), and the particular events in any allegorical story are always said to point beyond

35. Rosamund Tuve, *Allegorical Imagery: Some Medieval Books and Their Posterity* (Princeton, N.J.: Princeton University Press, 1966), p. 397.

36. Philip Sidney, *The Defense of Poesy* (Boston and New York: Ginn, 1890), p. 57.

themselves to their divine source or metaphysical base. No
wonder Tuve finds that so many allegories "mean the same
thing." Actually Freud's claim that every dream fulfilled a repressed wish was also, as he knew, a claim that all dreams
mean the same thing: they draw on the same tedious reser-
voir of infantile concerns, the wishes and feelings that are ultimately the source and basis for the rest of our lives. Freud's
ultimate truths are psychological rather than metaphysical,
but of course he would make no distinction between the two.
Whatever the nature of ultimate truths, in any case, both
Freud and the allegorical theorists often saw such a great gap
between the ultimate meaning of a text and its surface that
the surface seemed little more than a form of writing or a
code. The purported picture was really a hieroglyph or a rebus recording a prior truth in convenient (if regressive) pictures, and its surface story could mislead all but those who
knew the special rules for reading it.

But the real "gap" in allegory, like the gap in dreams, is not
between the surface and some truer meaning but between
different ways of reading the surface. Earlier theorists each
chose one way of reading allegories and claimed that this way
led to the ultimate truth: naive readers chose a literal reading;
moralists chose to see the action as an illustrated lesson, which
showed the rewards for behaving virtuously and the punishment for failing to do so. A third group, composed of more
learned theorists, followed Dante and the biblical interpreters, examining the surface story for analogies not only to our
own lives but also to the New Testament and to divine truths.
Sometimes this meant translating the surface story into symbols; in *The Faerie Queene*, Guyon's resistance to Mammon's
temptations is like Christ's rejection of Satan in the wil-
derness. At other times this approach meant translating the
surface into a rebus-like sentence in which each allegorical
character represented a word, and the character's interaction
was determined more by grammar than by dramatic truth:
thus in *The Faerie Queene* Guyon (Temperance) overcomes

Pyrocles (Angry Passion) by resisting the old Lady Occasion.[37] But until recently theorists were more interested in the ultimate message contained in allegory than in the particular means of expression. Lately, however, critics have become more interested in the play between surface and meaning; and in the particular *way* in which meanings are expressed. They have pointed out a more supple and sophisticated play between language and picture and have explored the "secret wit" of allegory's varied puns.[38]

Most recently, critics have even suggested that it is the play between these various ways of reading allegory that makes it work the way it does.[39] Unless the allegory is as simple and uninteresting as Freud's ideal dream of convenience, no one method of reading is sufficient, because the allegory draws on more than one mode of representation. Not even the traditional search for four "levels" of interpretation is enough, because each of these levels is just another example of the same analogical or symbolic representation; and a sheerly symbolic interpretation is no more appropriate here than in Freud's dream. The "associations" to allegory cannot be lined up as a simple series of analogies any more than Freud's associations can be arranged in a series.

What we learn from a comparison of allegory with dreams is that, first of all, allegorical representation is not unnatural or artificial, though critics have always taken it to be so. It

37. Freud discusses the dream as sentence in *The Interpretation of Dreams*, *SE* 4:314–19 and 323. For a discussion of allegory as sentence, see Morton Bloomfield, "A Grammatical Approach to Personification Allegory," *Modern Philology* 40 (1963): 161–71.

38. Martha Craig's dissertation on the centrality of Spenser's puns, part of which was published as "The Secret Wit of Spenser's Language," in *Elizabethan Poetry: Modern Essays in Criticism*, ed. Paul J. Alpers (New York: Oxford University Press, 1967), has been evoked and elaborated by nearly every critic of Spenser's allegory.

39. See various essays on Spenser by Paul J. Alpers and Harry Berger and other critics concerned with "reader response."

simply draws on the resources of a kind of thinking that differs from the one in which we construct a naturalistic, mimetic picture of reality. Like dreams, allegories make use of
pictorial narratives for nonmimetic purposes.[40] And even
more important, like dreams, they use the pictures in contradictory ways. In both cases the reader is disoriented at first,
and even for some time afterward; but the disorientation in
allegory is no more attributable to its artificiality than is the
disorientation in a dream. This disorientation results from
conflicting rules for understanding and from confusion
about how to read. Allegories, like dreams, make both regressive and intellectual use of their images. On the one hand, the
allegory recreates the simplest, most concrete infantile form
of thinking. It creates a House of Fame or a House of Pride in
order to bring home the intellectual abstraction in familiar
physical terms. Allegory is often described as a story dominated by ideas, but in these instances it actually presents ideas
felt directly and tangibly, as a child feels them.[41]

40. Freud's examination of dream-work techniques is newly important, in
fact, to recent trends in the study of both visual and literary representation,
where critics are focusing on nonmimetic techniques and are reexamining
the relation between ordinary perception and pictorial or literary experience
in art.

41. All this suggests that allegory, contrary to many of the traditional theories, is not artificial or unnatural but as natural as dreaming. As A. D. Nuttall
suggests about emblematic imagery, we must reexamine our concepts of what
is natural and probable: "If we must find a probability test for the bizarre imagery of seventeenth-century poetry, let us ask, not 'What would it be like to
see this happening in actual fact?' but rather, 'What would it be like to *dream*
this?' " (*Two Concepts of Allegory: A Study of Shakespeare's "The Tempest" and the
Logic of Allegorical Expression* [New York: Barnes and Noble, 1967], p. 88.)
Charles Dickens has even suggested that the primitive images in certain
dreams are the source of all allegory (Letter to Dr. Stone, 2 February 1851,
reprinted in *Nonesuch Dickens*, vol. 2 [London, 1938], pp. 267–70). Certainly
the images Dickens identifies—in which, for example, a writer's difficulties
with his story turn into a dream "of trying to shut a door that *will* fly open, or
to screw something that *will* be loose"—resemble the images in allegory as
well as the "hypogogic images" that Otto Silberer identified as characterizing
the dreamy state between sleeping and waking. On Silberer, see Freud, *The
Interpretation of Dreams*, SE 5:503ff.

On the other hand, the allegory does use its pictorial surface in a more artificial way to encode ideas. It draws on intellectual modes that are not mimetic but go in the opposite direction, away from regressive concretizing imagination to a highly abstract form of conceptualization. In Spenser's *Faerie Queene*, for example, Lucifera's House of Pride is an abstraction made visible so that its qualities take tangible form in its glittering, overbearing architecture and its glittering, overbearing owner. But this simple "regressive" concretization becomes more like an intellectual diagram, as we are told about parts of the house whose meanings are not so immediately and sensually obvious—the various compartments or categories of pride, or the various stages of pridefulness whose identification is not a matter of feeling and perception but a matter of disciplined thought.

Like the dream, allegory presents experience from several points of view other than the objective mimetic one. It presents the feel of pride, its source, its effect, its relation to other qualities—all the aspects of an abstract idea correspond to the variety of ways we become aware of it and represent it to ourselves. Allegory involves many ways of moving from text to meaning, just as dreams require a range of ways of moving from surface to its underlying associations. And part of what we mean by *allegorical* is the temptation to move in the wrong way, just as the dream's special quality is partly defined by the temptation to read dreams in the wrong way.

What is the difference, then, between dreams and allegories? How do we distinguish between one man's private, tendentious dream about his own predicament and the poet's portrayal of more pervasive contradictions in the human predicament, except to say that the poet's version is somehow "better"? Freud's well-known answer, in "Creative Writers and Daydreaming" (1908),[42] was that the poet first softens the egoistic character of his wish fulfillment and makes it more publicly available and then gives us a bonus of aesthetic

---

42. Freud, "Creative Writers and Daydreaming," *SE* 9:143–53.

pleasure. This theory does not help us very much. It has the virtue of not reducing art to wish fulfillment, but it puts us back where we started by perceiving a poem as the simple sum of its aesthetic and wish-fulfilling aspects.

I would like to suggest that we can glean more than Freud did from the comparison of dreams and poetry; that in the case of dreams and allegories, at least, we can better define what is special about the literary text if we compare the different ways in which dream and allegory embody the switch of representational modes I have been describing. Let us now look at two allegorical scenes which present a conflict not unlike the one Freud dreamed about in the dream of the botanical monograph: a scene from Chaucer's prologue to *The Legend of Good Women* and a scene from Spenser's "Legend of Temperance," from book 2 of *The Faerie Queene*. By comparing these allegories to Freud's dream we can see some specific differences between the representational interaction in dreams and allegories, and a much more general and more important difference in the degree of self-consciousness about this interaction.

Chaucer's *Legend of Good Women* is a series of stories that are much less interesting than their prologue. There the stories' "origin in a dream" is explained as an act of penance to the god of Love for having rejected love, to write books about not-so-good women. The prologue contains both dream and associations. It begins with Chaucer describing himself as torn between his bookish pursuits and the attractions of nature in May. Chaucer's favorite flower is the daisy, not the cyclamen, compositae, or cruciferae that haunt Freud's dream, but its traditional associations are similarly natural and amorous, and he plays on them just as Freud does, though in a somewhat different way. One morning in May, Chaucer tells us, he abandoned his books in order to observe the daisy; and the conflict must have been revived because it manifests itself in his dream that night, when the god of Love, accompanied by the daisy in the form of a queenly virgin, comes forth to chide Chaucer. The woman comes to Chaucer's defense, and the

solution to his conflict, like the solution to Freud's, is a compromise: he will continue to write books, but these will be
dedicated to praising the good women from whom he had
turned.

A reader may paraphrase both Freud's dream and
Chaucer's poem in the form of logical statements. In Freud's
dream there are two statements: "If you had accepted any of
the floral or feminine temptations your life would be much
more pleasant," and, "Every time you turn away from your
books to these attractive hobbies, you have been punished."
For Chaucer's poem there is one: "because you have sinned
against the floral and feminine world to write your books,
you must atone." Neither Freud's nor Chaucer's dream is a
mimetic portrayal of the experiences described in these para-
phrases, but the first difference we notice between them is
that Chaucer's comes closer to portraying its experience in a
recognizable way. Chaucer's conflict takes a dramatically and
phenomenologically appropriate form in the verbal debate,
with logical arguments on each side. Freud's dream is more
like an emblem of conflict than a dramatization of it; the tension between flowers and books can be *understood* in it but not
felt, as it is in Chaucer's personified drama. Freud presents a
static solution while Chaucer presents the drama leading up
to the solution.

Not only is the play between surface and underlying meaning in Chaucer's poem less contradictory than in Freud's
dream (the literal reading is closer to the others required); it
is also more firmly tied to a rational, adult point of view: the
debate takes a verbal form, in which the claims on each side
are neatly separated and analyzed. The dominance of an
adult point of view is related to another difference between
these two passages—a difference that apparently holds for
other dreams and allegories as well: there are no person-
ifications in the dream that resemble those appearing in the
allegory. Dreams rarely portray either specific people who
actually represent themselves, or personified abstractions,
like love, which exist entirely apart from the dreamer's expe-

rience of them.[43] The dream always falls somewhere between Dante's realistic gossip and the degenerate allegories of socialism and poverty in political cartoons. The dream is dominated by the dreamer's relation to or subjective view of some experience, not by the experience itself. It is as if the dreamer, unlike the allegorist, does not abstract the *essence* from several different things or people, although he may abstract the essence of their special relation to himself. Instead, he combines his images in another way. Chaucer's allegorical daisy, for example, is also the loyal and loving Queen Alceste and simultaneously represents the Virgin Mary, both of whom share the traits that are important in his allegory. Compare these with the little girl with yellow flowers who appears in a screen memory behind Freud's dream. Freud remembers taking the flowers away from her, or "deflowering" her, in his childhood. The girl is his cousin, and the yellow flowers represent the yellow dress of another young woman Freud once loved madly, so that deflowering the little girl represents pulling the petal-dress from the older one. This is metonymy, not metaphor. Chaucer's associations are between things similar in nature; Freud's are between things alike in time and space and superficial sensory details, like the color yellow. Chaucer's subject is an objective category (beautiful, loving women); Freud's is a subjective category: "I have seen both women in the country, where I have also seen yellow flowers."[44]

43. In John Bunyan's *Pilgrim's Progress*, for example, Christian meets a figure called Idle Talk. Portraying a similar experience in one of his dreams, however, Freud discusses a dream about seeing a book written by a *specific* man he knows, a Dr. Lecher. The meaning of the dream emerges only when Freud realizes that he considers Lecher a "non-stop talker" and fears he will become one himself. Dreams nearly always choose a specific character like Dr. Lecher over an abstract figure like Idle Talk.

44. In marginal cases, of course, the distinction between "objective" and "subjective," or between metaphor and metonymy, is questionable ("objective" by *whose* standards?), but the general difference is clear. It has been offered by psychoanalytic theorist Pinchas Noy as the defining difference between "primary process" thinking and "secondary process" thinking.

The most interesting difference between Freud's dream and Chaucer's allegory, however, lies not in the obvious accessibility of Chaucer's poem or even in Chaucer's specific technique of personification, but in his self-consciousness about interaction of different kinds of representation in the allegory. Dream and allegory require similar shifts in reading, but in the allegory, the very fact of the shifting becomes part of the experience being portrayed.

We can see this clearly in the nature of Chaucer's debate with Love in the *Legend* prologue. The medieval *débat* was an established genre on which all allegories drew (and which has been seen as a protoallegorical mode out of which allegory developed).[45] But when we compare this debate to the debate between the lover and the god of Love in *The Romance of the Rose*, it becomes clear that Chaucer has not only cast his conflict in the form of a debate (the traditional way of portraying it) but has also given us a delightful sketch of just what kind of lover would think of his love in this way, rationalizing its tensions and turning them into a perfectly civilized, sublimated conversation. There is no equivalent self-consciousness about tactics in Freud's dream.

Even more intriguing, Chaucer purposefully prevented easy symbolic translation of his experience by making the dream in a way *more* realistic than the experience that prompted it. Whereas Freud's dream presents a flower as a relatively traditional symbol of the women in his life (however complicated the relation between specific remembered women and flowers may be), Chaucer reverses tradition and presents a woman as a symbol of the flower in his life. The reader becomes pleasantly giddy trying to sort out the priorities: the dream-daisy personified represents the "real" women that the woman in Chaucer's dream displays. The im-

---

(Pinchas Noy, "A Revision of the Psychoanalytic Theory of the Primary Process," *International Journal of Psychoanalysis* 50 [1969]: 155–78.)

45. Charles Muscatine, "The Emergence of Psychological Allegory in Old French Romance," *PMLA* 68 (1953): 1160–82.

possibility of an easy separation of the experience from its representation is part of what the poem is about: even the most modest of poets knows that his books about love do not merely imitate love falsely but somehow come closer to the heart of it than random experience can. While Freud's dream required us to alter the way we understood *flower*, the change was not itself part of the dream's content, as it is in Chaucer's poem.

There is a similar and even more pervasive self-consciousness about switching modes of perception in Spenser's "Legend of Temperance" in *The Faerie Queene*. This book, like Freud's dream, deals with a conflict between sensual dissipation and spiritual and intellectual discipline, as the hero of the legend, Sir Guyon, learns what true temperance is.[46] Spenser does not present Guyon's conflict directly in terms of flowers and books, but he weaves this imagery into the story nonetheless. Guyon's assigned task is to destroy Acrasia's Bower of Bliss and its floral attractions, and the image of temptation that recurs throughout the legend, though not embodied in a flower, is often a fruit—apples golden and black or gold and purple grapes. In one scene in particular, which we shall examine closely, these false temptations are countered by the true one in the form of a history book Guyon takes down from its shelf.

Both in itself and in the context of the two sections that surround it, this scene demonstrates Spenser's self-conscious control of the switches of perception necessary to understand it fully. The scene itself—we might call it the scene of the historical monographs—is the climax of Guyon's adventure. He has endured numerous trials and temptations, both alone and with the help of the more perfect Sir Arthur; now the two

---

46. Interestingly, Guyon's temptations, like Freud's, include not only the obvious ones of sloth and self-indulgence but their opposite: proud ambition. Freud had to resist not only sensual distractions but also the proud ambition to triumph in botany exams, in writing the cocaine monograph and the dream book. Guyon must resist not only the loose delights in Acrasia's false Eden but also the ambitious pride and possessiveness in Mammon's cave.

knights have finally arrived at the Castle of Alma, the state of achieved temperance. They are led through the house in what is obviously a tour of the temperate body: through the stomach-kitchen and parlor-heart to the turret-brain, itself neatly divided into chambers of fantasy, judgment, and memory. In the last of these, a book-lined chamber where old man Eumenestes tosses constantly in his chair while sifting through the volumes, Guyon and Arthur happen upon historical accounts of their respective nations and take them down to read.

The action in Alma's Castle has an obvious literal meaning: the dramatic action of looking at, discovering, and exchanging words with the people therein. It also has an obvious symbolic meaning as a representation of the state of being within a well-tempered body. The drama and the symbolism do not quite coincide, of course: the former is a narrative about discovery and the latter is a static diagram or chart of temperance that has nothing to do with *discovering* how to be temperate; and as Spenser's critics have noted,[47] there are interesting ways in which these two modes, literal drama and symbolic chart, interact. Nonetheless, this section of the legend has been generally taken to be primarily a simple (even simpleminded) symbolic representation of temperance. The symbolism is so natural that little effort is required to make the translation from house to body or to a temperate state of mind. All three states are naturally conceived in spatial terms; the "goodly frame of temperance" brings to mind not only our physical frame but also our frame of mind, and the highest and most important part of the house, the mind, is appropriately represented by the three chambers, a miniature body which corresponds to the physical image most people have of their minds.

47. Harry Berger, Jr., *The Allegorical Temper: Vision and Reality in Book II of Spenser's* Faerie Queene (Hamden, Conn.: Archon Books, 1967), pp. 34–35; Paul J. Alpers, *The Poetry of* The Faerie Queene (Princeton, N.J.: Princeton University Press, 1967), pp. 4–5, 279.

The criticism of the allegory here may hold true for Spenser's other symbolic houses as well, but the Castle of Alma seems to involve a more extreme use of simple symbolism. Unlike the House of Holiness or the House of Pride, for example, it represents not something more abstract than itself but something more concrete; something more familiar than itself, not less familiar; something more directly available to the senses, not less available. The body is so close to us (as Freud said, "the ego was first a body ego"), so much a part of our sense of things, that it provides the first standard by which we accustom ourselves to the world and also some of our lasting metaphors, by which we continue to know the arms of sleep, the head of state, the heart of the matter. It is odd that the source of metaphor should here be metaphorized; but that is precisely the point of Spenser's passage. The state of temperance is a state of perfect harmony in which the "tenor" and "vehicle" can switch places without loss: the perfect body could just as easily have been used to symbolize the House of Temperance in a spiritual sense (as, indeed, the body already does). Body and mind are in perfect harmony in the Castle of Alma, and so are the literal and figurative meanings of the experience. The very effortlessness with which the reader can switch from literal to symbolic readings of the text is part of what the passage is about.

The harmonious perception does not last very long, however, for immediately after this scene ends with the two knights opening their books, the next reveals the contents of each book. Suddenly we are swept away from an introspective exploration to the outward and impersonal flow of history; from the detailed and static images of a single symbolic place to the sweep of generations; from the ideal to the actuality of temperance.

But an even more unsettling switch of perspective is required after the two historical narratives are finished. The achievement of temperance seems complete, at last, and the episode at Alma's Castle seems over. In fact, Guyon actually leaves the house finally prepared to undertake his assigned quest. But it is just at this point that Alma's Castle is attacked by Maleger and an army of villains, and we begin a new scene with an entirely different—and more difficult—mode of representation, as Arthur fights off the attackers. The scene begins as if Spenser were employing the same kind of symbolism he used in the visit to Alma's house, where abstract and concrete, figurative and literal significances of the action merge into one another, so that intellectual and physical (or "practical") apprehension work together: As soon as Guyon (the "temperate soul") leaves, the ragged army assaults Alma's Castle, just as temptations to sin assault the body. Seven of Maleger's troops attack the main gate, suggesting the general threat of the seven deadly sins, and five others take on the outposts of sight, hearing, smell, taste, and touch. But we notice a discrepancy in this simple symbolism almost immediately: the temptations include not only deceptive attractions like wealth and flattery but outright repulsive ones, like toads assaulting the gate of lustful touch. This is a discrepancy between temptations as judged by the intellect and as felt by the senses, and it soon grows more obvious. The army, we hear, is not only a mighty force but also a flock of insubstantial shadows. Temptation feels like a battle with a mighty army, though we know the temptations would evaporate if only we could comprehend them properly. So too sin is powerful enough when felt as an impulse, though theologically it is "nothing," since it is defined as the mere absence of good, at least in the theology informing the poem.

The discrepancy becomes flagrant paradox when Maleger appears. We have just been told of the army of sins, and we expect its captain to be the captain of sin: if not Satan, then he ought at least to have some direct relation to the sins in his command. Just as Alma embodies the spirit of her castle, so should he embody the spirit of his army. But though Alma is manifestly temperate, Malegar displays no real sinfulness and embodies no obvious temptation. He may occasionally invite the identifying tags of Satan and Original Sin that have been hung on him, but on the whole he resists interpretation. Maleger is there and not there; he fights by running away and is strongest in his weakness; apart from his tiger, he calls to mind no comfortably familiar iconographic associations, and even the tiger is not readily interpreted.

What Maleger represents is not sin itself but a sick desire ("evil eagerness") for sin; or the sickness of desire; or someone sick of desire, who hates the things he most desires. The weakness that is strength is the weakness of the flesh that someone like the modest, quiet Guyon can resist, but that the outgoing and ambitious Arthur finds hard to fight, because it does not take the form of the physical enemies he knows how to handle. Maleger, then, neither personifies sinful temptation nor enacts it but represents a relation to temptation different from the one we have seen earlier in book 2. We must change our perspective to understand this scene; the dramatic story no longer works as harmoniously with its symbolic underpinnings as it has before. In fact, if the Castle of Alma is the archetype of simple allegorical representation, this scene is its antitype.[48] Alma's Castle represents one almost purely physical presence with another; Maleger, on the other hand, represents only an absence. Whether we see him as a failure of temperance (with Guyon's departure from the Castle) or as an absence of will, he does not exist physically; he is an intellectual category, a mental symbol only. He exists on a different metaphysical plane from the one on which the castle is built and is an example of a different kind of representation. We must switch our way of reading as we move from one canto to the next and switch from a natural symbolism to a rather uncomfortable and unnatural one.

The discrepancy between the two ways of understanding the text also points up a discrepancy in our conception of temperance. Temperance is a passive virtue; Guyon's heroic achievement in Mammon's Cave is that he does nothing; his

48. See James Nohrnberg's discussion of this episode as an allegory of allegorizing, *The Analogy of* The Faerie Queene, pp. 320–22.

trial would have been awkwardly represented by a battle.[49] But temperance is also an active virtue, and in Arthur's confrontation with Maleger, Spenser purposely chose a battle to represent what is objectively very inappropriate for such representation. Changing the use of symbolism is necessary to distinguish between two kinds of passivity, to separate proper activity from the wrong kind of activity, and to distinguish easy versions of temperance from the seemingly contradictory and difficult but truer versions.

In a much quoted comment, Northrop Frye has claimed that allegory interprets itself.[50] If it does, it interprets itself in the same way the wakened dreamer interprets his dream: by presenting it in different ways, employing different modes of representation and different points of view. In the case of the dream and the dreamer, the switch takes place when we move from the isolated dream-as-dreamed to the larger network of associations and contexts surrounding it. This is a movement from the naiveté of the sleeping dreamer to the wariness of the wide-awake interpreter; it is a movement from one kind of reading to another. The allegory, by contrast, includes the clues for the switch within the bounds of the text; but the switch is the same one the dreamer makes. The real difference between dream and allegory is not that the latter is more artful but that it is more self-conscious. While in the dream the need to switch makes understanding more difficult, the allegory makes this difficulty an essential part of the text.

But what about more realistic kinds of literature? If allegory interprets itself, while the dream merely cries out for interpretation, then a realistic text needs no interpretation at all, in the sense that that word has been used here. In a realistic text, there is not such a gap between the manifest and latent meanings; or rather, the latent meaning is less important and has been subdued, and the secondary revision has taken

49. Berger, *The Allegorical Temper*, pp. 33–38.
50. Northrop Frye, *Anatomy of Criticism: Four Essays* (New York: Atheneum, 1966), p. 90.

over. I shall now examine another scene, this time from a realistic novel, and show how the interaction I have described still takes place; but here, rather than shaking up the main story, the interaction is restricted to the verbal level.

The scene takes place toward the end of Henry James's *Portrait of a Lady*, in a room where Gilbert Osmond sits with a folio volume—a sort of numismatic monograph—propped open before him to a page of colored plates.[51] Osmond, husband of the novel's heroine Isabel Archer, is, like Freud, a specimen collector, and he happens to be copying in watercolor the picture of an antique coin. When the scene begins, Isabel has just come in to say that she wants to visit her dying cousin in England. Osmond hears her out coolly, continues painting with his back to her until he reaches a convenient stopping place, and then forbids her to go.

Unlike Freud's dream, this scene completes its meaning on the literal level. Isabel's story is the story of a young woman who wants her freedom; and she seems to have achieved it, until she marries Osmond and falls into a bondage greater than that of any of the stereotyped patterns of life she has refused. This scene with Osmond reveals the essential nature of their marriage: Osmond paints while Ralph dies; he refuses to communicate. The perusal of folio volumes, the meticulous brushwork—these represent in miniature the careful performance which constitutes Osmond's entire existence. Thus the scene *dramatizes* Osmond's sacrifice of life for art. It also *symbolizes* the somewhat more appalling fact that he has sacrificed both life and art for money, for the mere means to art. He has married Isabel for her money, and now, symbolically at least, money has become not only his life—and wife—but his art as well. Osmond may be painting, but what he paints is neither his lovely wife (unlike James, Osmond creates no "portrait of a lady"), nor his beloved bibelots. Instead, he is painting a *copy* of an antique coin, literally making money into art. Something has been short-circuited here.

51. Henry James, *The Portrait of a Lady*, 2 vols., Modern Library (New York: Random House, 1951), vol. 2, pp. 352–58.

The dream, as described by Freud, is neither dramatically nor symbolically meaningful in the way this scene is. But if we move outward from this scene to others in the novel, as Freud moves from the dream to its associations, we find that the paths of movement are really quite similar. First of all, we find an almost mechanical repetition and linking of images, like the ones Freud emphasized in his associations. Just as Freud moved outward in his dream, from "botanical" and "monograph," so we can move outward in *Portrait of a Lady* from "antique coin" and "volume" to patterns of images that seem to have only external connections to the scene and to each other. The physical coin leads us to all the scenes in the novel that concern money and antiques. The particular antique coin reminds us that Osmond has been called an antique coin himself, and for good reason.

Volumes and books are other images that lead us to many associated scenes in this story about the confrontation of fantasy and reality. In *The Portrait of a Lady*, books are opposed to life. They are often associated with Isabel, and her story is in fact rather mechanically structured by three scenes in which she tries to read a book but is interrupted by "life." At the beginning of her story, Isabel is reading in a window seat when her aunt arrives to carry her off to Europe; she is reading again much later when Lord Warburton arrives to propose, and her refusal marks both the end of her innocence and the end of the first part of the novel; finally, she is reading in the last scene of the novel when Warburton arrives once more. But this time he has no offer to make; everything is over between them, and if books offer no possibilities, neither, any longer, does Isabel's life.

Not only does James mechanically repeat the reading scene, as Freud repeats the monograph scenes in his associations; he also creates strangely arbitrary categories, like Freud's category that links flowers, artichokes, and Professor Gärtner. James, like Freud, moves cavalierly from monographs as reading materials to monographs as objects that can be pulled apart like artichokes. Thus we are told that Ralph Touchett reads; but Henrietta Stackpole finds Ralph's li-

brary no more than a collection of valuable leather objects
to sell.

Even more interesting, James's *Portrait of a Lady* moves almost as freely as Freud's associations do between literal and
figurative meanings. Freud moves from the real bookworms
in his herbarium to the realization that *he* is a bookworm, and
James makes a similar movement from literal to figurative
books. In general, James takes books less seriously as props in
his story than as metaphors. Books in this novel are laugh-
able: almost the only ones we read about are bad travel guides
to Italy, or bad novels by lady novelists, or top-heavy volumes
of German philosophy. The true art in this novel is architecture; books are artifices, and they almost always undermine
rather than confer value. Yet James himself is writing what he
calls "the book of life," and he draws on book metaphors to do
so. Thus we may sympathize when Isabel cannot read real
books, but we find it ominous when we discover that she cannot read her husband. Moreover, if relationships in this novel
resemble reading, the characters are like books: Madame
Merle is a "new volume of smooth twaddle" (p. 363), and another is "a sheet of blank paper" (p. 401); Isabel herself is "an
unread book" (p. 13).

The Portrait of a Lady, then, draws on the same kind of indirect and seemingly external associative links that Freud's
dream uses. There is, however, a difference between their use
in the novel and the dream. Whereas Freud's associations
merely repeat monograph scenes, James carefully spaces his
repetitive reading scenes at the beginning, middle, and end of
his novel; and more important, the mere fact of their appearance becomes significant, even apart from their content.
While Freud's associations merely slip from the intellectual to
the physical dimension of books, such a movement in literature is often in itself as important as the two ideas it connects.
Consider Prospero's ethereal magic, inseparable from his
physical book: his renunciation is not complete until he
drowns his book. Or recall the moment when Leopold Bloom
in his outhouse tears a page from the prize-winning story he

has been reading and puts it to more fundamental use. James's switches are not quite so wittily pointed, but they are similar: they are part of what the novel is about.

While Freud's movement from literal to figurative bookworms merely connects two otherwise unrelated ideas (insects and the young Freud), the movement from literal to figurative books in James's novel is more controlled and has become significant in itself. James makes playful use of the similarities between the actual books in his story and the metaphorical ones he invokes in his language; but the whole sense of Isabel's story depends on the difference between these two kinds of books. If real books in *The Portrait of a Lady* are trivial, while metaphorical ones set standards, this is because "reading" and what one reads have been transferred from the mundane sphere of actual events and have become instead the narrator's means for describing something finer and less tangible. James's wordplay is part of a larger exploration of the delicate and paradoxical exchange between imagination and fact in the novel.

And often, through self-conscious comic excess, James makes the two meanings collide head on; that is, he provides within the language itself the shock of reorganization and the double perspective we get from reading allegory properly or from trying to understand a dream once we wake up. Thus he sometimes extends an absurd figurative description and then makes it collide with its literal counterpart. When Isabel is first reading, for example, it is because she does not like the fact that her mind has become a vagabond lately, and she has decided to train it "to a military step," to teach it to advance, to halt, to retreat through a heavy volume of German philosophy; but just then she hears her aunt's entirely *literal* footstep in the next room and promptly forgets about her grand plans (p. 31).

What the analyst shows is that such collisions take place in our thinking all the time, whether or not we are fully conscious of them in the ordinary way. And he describes an openness in reading which allows us to detect the collisions in details that we would otherwise take too much for granted or else think too trivial to examine. Even if these exchanges do not constitute the main interplay in a text—as they do in the work of a self-conscious writer like James—they are still present as part of the body of alternative meanings out of which we carve our final, acceptable readings. We are likely to be better readers of novels, as well as dreams, if we are aware of them—if only to put them aside.

5

Literature as Transference:
Rhetorical Function

> An actor making a gesture is both creating for himself
> out of his deepest need and yet for the other person. . . .
> The actor's work is never for an audience, yet is always
> for one. The onlooker is a partner who must be forgot-
> ten and still constantly kept in mind: a gesture is state-
> ment, expression, communication and a private manifes-
> tation of loneliness—it is always what Artaud calls a
> signal through the flames—yet this implies a sharing of
> experience.
>
> —Peter Brook, *The Empty Space*

> The question the analyst has to ask himself constantly is:
> "Why is the patient now doing what to whom?"
> —Paula Heimann, "Dynamics of
> Transference Interpretation"

The scope of psychoanalytic inquiry has widened since
Freud's first explorations of hysteria in the 1890s. At that
time he was interested in only one part of a person—a repressed part—which he treated as a surgeon treats a ruptured
appendix, removing it as quickly and painlessly as possible,
hypnotizing the patient if necessary. Freud later became interested in more of the person when he studied repressing as
well as repressed forces, and today psychoanalysis has become
established as a phenomenology of the whole person as well
as a study of motives. It has moved away from a study of
wishes only, as we saw in the chapter on fantasy, to a study of
wishes to do something with somebody in a particular kind of

world—a study of a person's whole way of seeing the world and of his relationship to it. Most recently, the scope of psychoanalysis has been widened still further to include a study of the process of study itself. Not only does the patient's fantasy concern relationships with others, but the process of telling his fantasies to the analyst is itself a part of his relationship with the analyst: it is part of a social and rhetorical exchange, not just a transfer of information. This exchange includes both the rational relationship required logically by the treatment situation, and the irrational "transference" relationship generated not so much by present circumstances as by the patient's expectations and biased perceptions. The relationship, in other words, is shaped by the fantasy that is part of the patient's problem in the first place. And this rich exchange, analysts have increasingly realized, matters as much as what the patient actually says.

An increasing number of literary critics in the last few years have used this exchange, which provides the context for the patient's words, as a model for literary texts, just as the patient's words themselves (his dreams and fantasies) were earlier taken as models for texts. Or, to be more precise, the exchanges in the psychoanalytic process were taken as a model for the process of reading, which is seen now as an implied exchange between author and reader through the medium of the text. In this chapter, after elaborating on what I mean by a social and rhetorical exchange, I will examine the psychoanalytic theory of this process. First I will consider the original version of the theory, which Freud formulated partly in discussions of the patient's relation to the analyst, in neurotic transference, and partly in discussions of the joke teller's interaction with his audience; then the more recent extensions of Freud's work, in theories about the nature of transference and in the developmental research inseparable from these theories, will be examined. This research deals with the child's "object relations" and is best represented by Winnicott's theory and later theories about "transitional" objects and spaces, or play spaces. I will also examine some of the suggested ways of applying these theories to literary texts.

Although these theories have been enthusiastically adopted by literary critics as more promising approaches to literature than the old-style fantasy model, they present more problems than the other methods examined in this book. It is still not clear whether these theories can be usefully applied to specific texts, as opposed to the creative process in general. The rhetorical dimension of discourse is much harder to locate in a text than in the psychoanalytic process, and therefore more problematic. It is also difficult to distinguish strictly rhetorical elements from the other dimensions of the text that we have examined in the other psychoanalytic models, especially the revised fantasy model described in chapter 3.

SOCIAL AND RHETORICAL EXCHANGE: TELLING AND MOVING

The need for a listener is especially obvious in the therapeutic situation and in the ritual confessions to which it has often been likened. But we do not have to turn to the psychoanalytic process to find a social and rhetorical exchange. Any effort to shape thought into formal or at least public forms of expression implies a listener, if only an imagined one. The consciousness of having something to say or show implies the existence of someone to say or show it to. Consciousness of being a self with something to express comes about through the ministrations of others recognized as separate from the self. Thus the private experience of self-consciousness is not possible without the public social contexts, structures, and responses that define the individual. These social factors are now being studied from many points of view; the new psychoanalytic awareness of this social dimension is part of a much larger movement which is changing the way we conceive of the individual.

The need for an audience is partly the need to have someone understand and respond to what we are saying. Even if we are merely spouting our desires, as early psychoanalytic theory had it, we want others to know about them and do something about them. Even "pure" desire is desire *for* something; it does not exist without an implied object. But we need an audience in an even more fundamental and less direct way as well. Not only do we need someone to get the message, but we need someone just to hear it, bear witness to it, give it substance and reality.

Freud was primarily interested in the hidden wishes or conflicts in the content of what his patients said; but analysts are now interested also in the more fundamental wishes which seem to be both the ground and the end of communication—the wish for "recognition," as Paul Ricoeur called it,[1] or the wish for "presence,"[2] for relationship. Freud did talk occasionally about the importance of sheer communication, apart from any message—for example, when he described how an idea is changed merely by saying it aloud or by having the analyst say it back.[3] But only recently have the implications of this process been developed. Freud was talking about the meaning of particular symbols when he interpreted a patient's words, but not about the social and dialectical aspects of the symbol or the implications of using a symbolic medium at all.[4] A symbol is a thing that requires interpretation; Ricoeur has even suggested that this is the most appropriate definition of symbol. It may be used to ward off interpreters, but it also acknowledges that interpretation is possible. (To cry, "The listener is baffled!" is no more destructive than to cry "God is dead!")

For the writer, the implicit audience has taken mythological form as the Muse, the one who inspires by being there to listen, who invokes by being invoked. And correspondingly, the fantasies of unproductive writers are haunted by angry

1. Paul Ricoeur, *Freud and Philosophy: An Essay on Interpretation*, trans. Denis Savage (New Haven: Yale University Press, 1970), p. 523.

2. Geoffrey Hartman, "I. A. Richards and the Dream of Communication," in *The Fate of Reading and Other Essays* (Chicago: University of Chicago Press, 1975), p. 37.

3. Sigmund Freud, "The Unconscious" (1915), *SE* 14:202.

4. See Anthony Wilden's comment in Jacques Lacan, *The Language of the Self: The Function of Language in Psychoanalysis*, trans. Anthony Wilden (Baltimore: Johns Hopkins University Press, 1968), p. 230.

muses—the pickers and harpers whose predicted scorn stops speech before it starts, as in the case of the stutterer, who imagines he will be interrupted—or by victimizable muses, who imagined fate scares the speaker into silence lest he destroy them. It is in the context of exchanges such as the one between writer and muse that literature comes into being. The transference model examined here promises to provide a way of showing how that context affects literature in general and how changes in context can influence the shape of particular works.

Still more is going on, however, in this exchange between speaker and listener, or between writer and reader. Not only does the speaker wish to convey a message, not only does he want to be heard and witnessed; he may also want to affect his listener in a way that has very little to do with what he is saying. If the speaker says he has a headache, he is perhaps not just giving us a specific piece of information and not just talking to be heard, without caring if there is a direct reaction to his specific message: he may also be trying to affect us in some other way. I have called this dimension of the psychoanalytic exchange *rhetorical*, because it is defined not only by what is being said but also by the way in which the speaker takes account of and tries to move or otherwise affect his audience. The study of rhetorical strategies belongs to many fields, but psychoanalysis is particularly sensitive to this dimension of discourse. Kenneth Burke once faulted Freud and psychoanalysis for not going beyond seeing the text as a dream to seeing that it is also a "prayer."[5] But Freud knew very well that his patient's words might be prayers—or curses, or invitations, or distractions, or in fact anything at all. Psychoanalysts begin with the assumption that words can mean more than they seem to mean and can do more than they seem to do; they can certainly do more than serve as the bear-

5. Kenneth Burke, "Freud—and the Analysis of Poetry" (1939), reprinted in *The Philosophy of Literary Form: Studies in Symbolic Action*, rev. ed. (New York: Random House/Vintage, 1961), p. 229.

ers of obvious referential statements. Statements are performances.

For one thing, words can be false performances, intended
as lies and designed to mislead, or intended as the only truth
the listener can bear or can grasp. We are now familiar with
the idea that our private personalities are inseparable from
our public masks and are shaped by our public roles, that
there is no self without the presentation of self, as Erving
Goffman's studies argue.[6] In a more extreme but lucidly per-
suasive argument, one woman, who has been through psychosis, compares the asylum's poses to the poses of everyday
life:

> Nobody ever tells the truth anyway, not even in bed. . . .
> At best we offer our pose and our costume for approval
> and kid ourselves that we have caught our partner
> naked. If we have, he fools us and becomes impotent. . . .
> We meet on a perfectly prescribed plain: "Give me a little
> of your lie and I'll return with mine." It is a bargain into
> infinity. We even take our lies to bed with us. Nobody
> makes love for the sake of sexual fulfillment. We make
> love to remind ourselves of our existence. . . . The lover is
> a false god who gives us for a moment a sense of self. . . .
> We give him a posture he never had, and lovingly, vora-
> ciously, steal it, clothe ourselves in his demeanor and
> claim it as our own. A love affair is a series of thefts, and
> we steal what never was. *So, too, the writer and the reader.*
>   [Emphasis added][7]

Even if our performances are not always the designed lies
Cameron describes, their truth or significance may not be totally contained in the literal message they convey: we may tell
others we have a headache because we want sympathy or because we want to make them feel guilty. The significance of

6. Erving Goffman, *The Presentation of Self in Everyday Life* (Woodstock,
N.Y.: Overbock Press, 1974).

7. Martha Cameron, "Why Psychosis?" *Michigan Quarterly Review* 4 (1965):
140.

words may even have nothing to do with what we are saying but only with the *way* we are saying it: an aggressive tone is used to pick a fight; a soft tone may be used to tease by giving information and at the same time making it hard to understand; or we can speak the same words tediously, to bore the listener. The significance of words may even lie in the simple fact that they are words—no matter what words and no matter how presented. Thus, for example, the patient determines to say something, anything, rather than tell the analyst how angry he is about an upcoming summer interruption. Or free association may be used to put on exhibitions for the analyst, who is seen as judgmental parent, as a way of competing with other "sibling" patients.

In recognition of all this, analysts (in France, especially) have shifted the emphasis of their study from the retold dream or fantasy to the process of retelling. Freud presented his "specimen dream" in *The Interpretation of Dreams* as a verbal icon; Jacques Lacan by contrast emphasizes another of the dreams that Freud reports, which is more like an insult than an icon, a patient's dream of "the abandoned supper-party," in which she wanted to give a supper party but could not, because there was nothing in the house but a little smoked salmon, and all the stores were closed. Though we might focus on the symbolic meaning of the dream's content (which does have its own import) in interpreting it, one of the dream's most significant wishes, as Freud shows, lies elsewhere. This is simply the woman's wish to prove Freud's wish fulfillment theory wrong by dreaming about an *un*fulfilled wish. In addition, Freud shows, by thwarting her own wish in the dream, the dreamer was identifying with an envied friend whose charms, she feared, were attracting her husband. The additional significances emerge only when we think about why the dream was dreamed and about the context in which it was told—not when the dream is considered in isolation.[8]

8. Freud, *The Interpretation of Dreams* (1900), *SE* 4:147–51, 154, n. 2; 175; Jacques Lacan, *Ecrits (Paris: Editions du Seuil,* 1966), p. 621.

The single question that dominated early psychoanalytic inquiry was, "What infantile wishes does this material fulfill in the patient?" But analysts now ask a more awkward but more appropriate question: "What is the patient, as who, saying to the analyst, as whom, and from when—and why?"[9] For a long time it was assumed that we knew the answer to the last part of the question: the patient was talking to give the doctor information. But we now know that even plain, "truthful" communication is a complicated process involving not only a referential message (in any of several modes of representation) but a speaker with his own eccentricities and his own attitudes toward what he is saying and the person he is talking to; a listener with his own requirements; and the implicit and explicit assumptions the speaker and listener make about their common language and the current occasion. What the analyst adds is the understanding that not only does communication have several aspects, but it is hard to separate plain, truthful communication from the transference, and that all aspects of an exchange may be influenced by unconscious processes which interact with conscious ones in unpredictable ways.

SOCIAL AND RHETORICAL EXCHANGE: THE PSYCHOANALYTIC PERSPECTIVE

Psychoanalysis has always studied unconscious contributions to social and rhetorical exchange. Nonethless, the way it conceptualizes these has changed. At first, Freud looked only for those unconscious exchanges that resembled the familiar conscious ones, just as when exploring fantasies he initially saw only the ones that resembled our familiar conscious daydreams. And since only relatively mature people engage in social exchanges, the social or rhetorical dimension of a clinical session—the unconscious transference exchanges as well as conscious ones—almost by definition followed the pattern of ordinary social exchanges. Freud contrasted behavior and

---

9. See Paula Heimann's similar questions in "Dynamics of Transference Interpretation," *International Journal of Psychoanalysis* 37 (1956):303–10.

texts that included this dimension to behavior and texts whose primitive quality made them so private that absolutely no exchange with the outside world was involved.

A literary critical model based on Freud's theories must draw primarily on two instances where Freud discusses such exchanges, in both of which he contrasts the material he is studying to asocial and nonrhetorical parallels where there is, he says, no exchange. The first source is Freud's discussion of neurotic transference in psychoanalysis, which he contrasts to the psychotic's total lack of relationship to the analyst (which thus makes the psychotic immune to psychoanalysis and the exchanges it demands). The second source is Freud's discussion of jokes, which require an audience to complete their effect; and he contrasts these to dreams, which are designed to resist an audience, although they make use of many of the same mechanisms jokes do. As we shall see, however, contemporary analysts would not make Freud's distinction between social and asocial processes, public and private symbolic acts. Instead, they see behind the seemingly asocial behavior of the psychotic or the asocial language of the dream a very primitive form of socialization—a socialization that may also underlie our more sophisticated exchanges, although it does not dominate them as it does in dreams and psychosis.

All psychoanalytic rhetorical theories of literary criticism originate, however, from Freud's first discoveries about this rhetorical dimension, in particular from the fact that this dimension is not necessarily explicit or even conscious. In the case of transference, what Freud did was primarily to identify that part of the patient's perception of, feelings about, and treatment of the analyst which is shaped largely by his own fantasies rather than by accurate perception of reality. The patient tries to force or coax the analyst to play out a scene he has in mind, though the patient is not aware of either the coaxing or the scene as such. All he sees is that the analyst is hostile, indifferent, loving, or whatever the scene dictates.[10]

10. See, e.g., Freud, "The Dynamics of Transference" (1912), *SE* 12:97–108.

Although Freud subsequently investigated specific examples of transference exchanges and how they were to be interpreted, in the case of the joke he described the more general conditions of exchange which make the joke possible in the first place.[11] But again, these general conditions are usually neither explicit nor conscious.

They are, however, more obviously related to literary texts than were the transference exchanges and have in fact been taken by both Freud and Ernst Kris as a model for the aesthetic exchange. They deserve closer scrutiny here. The joke, for Freud, is a displaced version of a sexual or aggressive wish, allowing the teller to express his forbidden wish in an acceptable way: instead of raping a woman he tells a dirty joke about raping her. But the joke cannot complete its work of displacement and yield the teller his substitute pleasure unless there is an audience to hear it. Paradoxically, it is often the very presence of a third party that makes the joke's displacement necessary. "There's somebody watching," the teller in effect says to himself, "so I can't have her. But I can get him to share the guilt with me vicariously, by acting out an attack through the joke's characters." This is a quick and clever accommodation to society's inhibitions; the joke teller bribes the observer to join him in a verbal enactment of the crime that civilization prevents him from carrying out. By this means the listener gets the unexpected pleasure of a substitute satisfaction that he has not had to exert any energy contriving, and the teller secures his own pleasure by being reassured that his displacement has worked—that his actions are acceptable and that his guilt is shared. The teller laughs, then, not because the joke produces pleasure in him directly but because he sees the listener laughing and thereby derives pleasure.

Whether or not Freud's account is accurate in detail, its terms are drawn from conscious, adult life, and we recognize

---

11. *Jokes and Their Relation to the Unconscious* (1905), *SE* 8, especially section 5, "Jokes as a Social Process," pp. 140–58, and section 3, "The Purposes of Jokes."

its logic of complicity, sanction, and reassurance. It is, more-over, the kind of adult relationship epitomized in the oedipal triangle, which served so often as a model for Freud. This was the social exchange that interested him most, and it influenced all of his thinking about groups. In talking about the origins of religion, for example, Freud described the group complicity that makes possible the original archetypical patricide: one brother can murder his father because all his brothers take part.[12]

According to Freud, it was out of such transference exchanges that the poet's role evolved.[13] The poet made repetition of the original patricidal crime unnecessary by inventing slaughter on an epic scale and presenting it to the group. And as in the case of the joke teller, the poet who voices the displacement of murder for society then gets a double reward. Not only does he displace his own patricidal wishes, but he receives the secondary rewards of gifts and fame. For some time this theory was the main source for a psychoanalytic audience response theory, most importantly in the writings of Ernst Kris. For Kris, all art is communication, but the process of communication is determined by this secondary, facilitating function.[14] The artist is modeled on the oedipal child, seeking reassurance as he tries to fulfill his displaced desires.

Since Freud, psychoanalytic theory about social and rhetorical exchanges within and outside of the clinical situation has come to include much more than the oedipal model, just as psychoanalytic theories of development have now come to encompass not only the oedipal stage but the entire range of stages from earliest infancy. Analysts have been studying the far more primitive kinds of relationship and the earliest undifferentiated states out of which both mature relation-

12. Freud, "Totem and Taboo" (1913), *SE* 13:125–26 and 141–46; "Group Psychology and the Analysis of the Ego" (1921), *SE* 18:122–28 and 135–37; "Moses and Monotheism" (1939), *SE* 23:81–90.

13. Freud, "Group Psychology," *SE* 18:135–37.

14. Ernst Kris, "Approaches to Art," in *Psychoanalytic Explorations in Art* (New York: Schocken Books, 1964), p. 16.

ships and individuality develop.[15] Instead of seeing psychosis
or dreams as autistic withdrawals from reality and relationship, they see such behavior as a return to primitive narcissistic relationships of infancy. These relationships begin with an
original undifferentiated experience in which the mother is
not separated from the self, fantasy from reality, or wish from
action. The child discovers with surprised delight that the
thumb which randomly appears within sucking range actually
belongs to him and that he can move it about at will, just as he
discovers with rage that the breast (which seemed part of him,
inside him, while he was nursing) is not within his control.

There are many stages in the gradual process of differentiation that has received so much attention since Freud first
described the child's development. At first, the child separates what is inside him from that which is outside, if they can
be called that, largely by what feels good and what feels bad,
but the process becomes more complex as he begins to
coordinate feelings with increased perception of what *inside*
and *outside* really mean. There are stages in which he perceives another person as separate, but only as a mirror of
himself, or a projection of his own feelings, or a substitute for
his frustrated ideal grandiose self. There are stages of magical relationships governed by the child's unrealistic impulses
and perceptions—telepathic and sympathetic unions. There
are also stages in which the child perceives others as separate,
but only as separate objects to be manipulated or as need-
fulfillers for him.

Having explored these stages, modern psychoanalysis
avoids the dichotomy of Freud's original all-or-nothing approach, in which behavior either manifested transference or
did not, and a text either demanded an audience or did not.
Thus the modern analyst would say that the neurotic differs
from the psychotic not in forming a transference relationship
with the analyst but in forming a transference relationship of
a certain, relatively mature kind. The psychotic has retreated

15. See chapter 3, pp. 77–80 and note 53.

not into total isolation but into a stage in which the other is part of himself, or a projection of his own hostile wishes. So, too, the joke and the text are defined not by the fact that they require an audience and are designed for public consumption but rather by the particular kind of adult public for whom they are shaped. While exploring the different forms of public, psychoanalysis simultaneously provides the critic with a new scale of possible discriminations.

In fact, unless we do distinguish between all the possible kinds of implied relations between teller and hearer, studying this dimension of experience tells us much less—if anything —about individual texts than about the general conditions for producing texts. Once we do distinguish between the varieties of teller-listener relations in the analytic situation, identifying the quality of transference relationship can tell us a great deal, apart from the content of the communication. The paraphrasable content may be "I hate you," but the analyst then must ask whether this hate is an adult's scorn or an infant's world-shattering rage. And what does the patient mean by *you*? Is he seeing a real person? An ogre? A magic influencing machine? No matter what the patient happens to be saying, it is significant when he starts talking like a toddler, not bothering to finish sentences or elaborate beyond Tarzan-like exclamations. These attempts at expression suggest the implicit assumption that the analyst, like mother, will understand.

So, too, texts presume a variety of relationships. They may invite complicity or ward off understanding simply by the way the author shapes his communication. The author leaves out too much, perhaps, or trusts the listener to understand his jokes, or uses primitive forms of expression. Consider the very primitive dream text which, according to Freud, allowed for no audience. Despite Freud's claim, the dreamer often chooses to tell his dream to an audience—usually to the person for whom it is intended as a communication, albeit a coded one: for example, it means something to tell someone "I dreamed that you died last night." This telling may be seen as a continuation of a tendency, already at work in the sleeping dreamer, to establish contact with reality.[16] For the dreamer uses recent memories (the day's residue, in Freud's words) to make his dream images, and even the wishes expressed by the dream, though they may be oblique, are often addressed to an audience. The wish in Freud's own specimen dream of "Irma's injection"[17] was a wish to prove to others that he was a worthy doctor, and the wish in his dream of the botanical monograph was a wish to prove his right to take time off for hobbies; surely Freud is not the only one talking in his sleep.

Establishing contact with reality, however, usually takes a more primitive form in dreams, especially the form of looking and fantasy-drenched seeing. To dream is to make the external world into a receptive, bland "dream screen,"[18] that first environment in which the infant dreamed, as he fell asleep staring at the mother whose ministrations blended with his own fantasies and were hardly separate from the feeding he had just had and the dreams he was about to have. This primitive exchange with a "holding environment" is not what we would recognize as an adult relationship of mutuality, but it is a relationship nonetheless.

Even later, after these experiences of falling asleep at the breast, the child does not sleep alone but sleeps with what the analyst would call his fantasied "good object," if not with his transitional blanket or his teddy bear. Later, the adult takes his partner to bed with him, or he substitutes bedtime reading, drinking, or rituals implying company. People often welcome or fear sleep as they welcome or fear the intimate relationships which draw on early experiences of intense union; insomnia often accompanies a distrust of intimacy. Of course, sleep is also related to other forms of fantasy retreats, like un-

---

16. Mark Kanzer, "The Communicative Function of the Dream," *International Journal of Psychoanalysis* 36 (1955): 260.

17. Freud, *The Interpretation of Dreams*, SE 4:118–21.

18. Bertram D. Lewin, "Sleep, the Mouth, and the Dream Screen," *Psychoanalytic Quarterly* 15 (1946): 419–34.

dergoing the sleepy hypnosis of staring up into the big flat face of a movie screen (secure with a tub of buttered popcorn) or curling up with a seductively mindless mystery or adventure story.

TRANSITIONAL PHENOMENA AND LITERARY CRITICISM

One of the most important aspects of the psychoanalytic theories that take account of these exchanges, or "object relations," is their conceptualization of consciousness as inseparable not only from relationship but also from symbolic behavior. The newly popular Winnicottian theories of "transitional objects" and "transitional spaces"—states when the child merges with the outside world, which were described in the preceding section—imply that infants have relationships as well as impulses, and that these are primitive relationships in which the distinction between subject and object is unclear. But perhaps the most striking implication of these theories between the infant's relationship itself and the rest of the infant's perceptions, feelings, speech, and mental representations is unclear.

A discussion of the development of object relations[19] then becomes inseparable from a discussion of the development of symbolic behavior, because the child's first relationships take place in a total "sharing situation" which includes symbolic exchanges.[20] The child who sees his mother offer him a cookie and calls out "ma" (his word for good-things-to-eat) at first does not separate the giver, the cookie, his word for it, his

19. D. W. Winnicott's term, applied to phenomena he discussed in his essay "Transitional Objects and Transitional Phenomena," *International Journal of Psychoanalysis* 34 (1953): 89–97, has recently been taken up by literary critics. Similar phenomena had been discussed under other names by analysts like Melanie Klein and Marion Milner and other analysts, in what has been called the "object relations school"; see chapter 3. See also Phyllis Greenacre's studies of creativity.

20. Heinz Werner and Bernard Kaplan, *Symbol Formation: An Organismic-Developmental Approach to Language and the Expression of Thought* (New York: John Wiley, 1963) pp. 42–44.

feelings about it, and his identification of it. For all he knows, cookies are part of mother's arms, as milk is part of the breast. This is a cookie-experience; there is no clear distinction between self and object; between self and symbol (the exclamation "ma!" is as much a part of the child as hunger is); between self and others; or between the appearance of the cookie and the word for it, which always appears at the same time. Translation of the child's cry would require several sentences: "It's a cookie!" "I want the cookie!" "Give me the cookie, Mommy!" "Mommy is giving me the cookie!" "This sweet thing is called a cookie!"

Object relations theories, then, explore the nature of symbolic action, as they trace the child's evolution from an infant in a presymbolic state into a being who is simultaneously and in closely connected ways becoming a separate self, a member of society, and a user of symbols. It is no wonder that these theories have been so enthusiastically taken up by literary critics. Unlike earlier versions of psychoanalysis, they allow symbolism a space of its own and recognize it as a category of experience rather than as a mere distortion of, or escape from, something else. Freud's map of the mind left no place for symbolic reality; there was only the jungle of the id and the steadily expanding ego, which built its civilization where the id had been. Freud saw fantasy only as a "preserve," a remnant of the old territory left in its natural state. Only once, in talking about the nature of transference, did he discuss anything resembling a space *between* jungle and city, self and society, fantasy and reality.[21]

This, however, is the space that the newer theories begin with; it is taken to be the matrix out of which fantasy and reality later develop. Freud always separated inner phenomena from the outer world in which they manifested themselves. The inner battles over wish and defense were "primary"; what happened at the interface between inner and outer

21. Freud, " Remembering, Repeating and Working Through" (1914), *SE* 12:154.

worlds was "secondary" and incidental—a mere envelope for the joke, facade for the dream.[22] But new theories recognize that symbols are not created in a vacuum; the so-called primary activities are inseparable from the secondary ones, and symbolic action is inseparable from the facade, envelope, or bridge leading outward to reality.

The newer theories show that fantasy is not a retreat into a private world of unreality but a new relationship to the realities of a public world. While the old psychoanalytic theories reinforced misleading and question-begging dichotomies of "art and nature," "fantasy and reality," "self and other," and "word and thing," the newer approach recognizes that the defining quality of human creativity is the suspension of such categories. In the infant's early experience, and later when that undifferentiated state is self-consciously recreated in the transference or the work of art, new relations between the categories are explored, and neither category disappears altogether in favor of the other.

Promising as these developmental theories are, however, their application to literature presents problems, though these have not always been acknowledged. Applications of Winnicott's idea about transitional or play spaces has been somewhat confusing. The term *transitional space* is often loosely used to counter the old dichotomies with new insights about playful, experimental relationships between opposites, such as self and other, fantasy and reality, and symbol and reality. But the very different kinds of "play" implied here are not always distinguished, and the term *transitional* threatens to become a somewhat indefinite mark of approval rather

22. See for example Freud's distinction between primary and secondary gain in neurotic symptoms ("Some General Remarks on Hysterical Attacks" [1909] *SE* 9:231–32); and between primal and secondary repression ("The Unconscious," *SE* 14:202); and between the more primitive aspects of dream work and the dream's less primitive "secondary revision" (*The Interpretation of Dreams, SE* 4:178–83). Freud refers to the joke's envelope in *Jokes and Their Relation to the Unconscious, SE* 8:92, and to the dream's facade in the *Introductory Lectures to Psychoanalysis* (1916–17), *SE* 15:181.

than a precise description. Just what are the things transitions are being made between? And what does this tell us about the literary text? In its general form, this is more a theory of creativity than it is a description of the way any given text works. Art is neither reality itself nor an escape from reality; but what does this tell us about a particular text?

One thing that adds to the looseness of the application of the term *transitional* is the fact that the infant's transitional object, from which all the theorizing begins, is only the first of several developments in which several different dichotomies become apparent to the child. In the earliest stages nothing is separate. The transitional object is both part of the child and a separate entity; the play space is felt to be both made up *and* real, defined by his fantasy *and* his mother's reality. Later, however, the child begins to see his transitional object from a different point of view and starts to venture from his "play space," which is a space in which he merges with his mother. As he begins to leave her and return to her, not only does he begin to experience "separation and individuation"[23] but the union to which he returns becomes more complex: now he sees the physical distinction between him and his mother, though "merging" in other ways. I have suggested in talking about different kinds of object relations implied by, for example, jokes as opposed to dreams, that there are different sorts of transitional accommodations. Only by seeing the different stages and how they affect different texts will critics be able to use Winnicottian theory in practical criticism as well as in general theories of creativity.

A second source of looseness in critics' use of the term *transitional* is the fact that the infant's transitional experiences are transitional only to us, since only we and not he can distinguish between the subjective and objective realities that form the context for his experience. By contrast, however, the work of art is not, as it would sometimes appear in these

23. Margaret Mahler, *On Human Symbiosis and the Vicissitudes of Individuation* (New York: International Universities Press, 1968).

discussions, equivalent to the transference in a psychoanalytic session or to the child's transitional object. The infant's and patient's play spaces are very different from the adult's aesthetic play space in a work of art. The child emerges from his transitional play space; the patient emerges from his unwitting transference relationships; and it is this emergence and its implied self-conscious perspective that provide the model for art. At first, the child's play is not play at all but often all too real (as frightening stories and movies are too real). So, too, with transference behavior in analysis; pop psychologists may refer to such rigid repetitions as "games people play," but these are not games for those involved—not even in child analysis, when a child acts out his fantasies through doll families and a well-stocked doll house. True play begins only when the child realizes the difference between killing a father doll and killing a father, or when the patient recognizes the difference between merely disagreeing with the analyst and having fantasies which turn disagreement into a crushing attack.

But once the child or patient can distance himself from his own behavior, once he can see that there may be a difference between his own version of reality and someone else's version, then "play" begins, and so does the symbolic behavior which is a first version of art. One analyst has even suggested that the mark of successful therapy is the ability to be playful about one's fantasies, rather than denying them altogether or taking them for the truth, and that as an analyst he knows the terminal phase of an analysis has begun when he feels that the patient is sharing a playful approach with him or even initiating one.[24] The subject's attitude toward transitional phenomena and games gives them their special quality and their special role in the whole personality, just as it is the reaction to and integration of fantasies, not the fantasies themselves, that makes a person the person he is and a text the text it is.

24. Harold Searles, "Transference Psychosis in Psychotherapy of Schizophrenia," *International Journal of Psychoanalysis* 44 (1963): 249–81.

This conjunction of transitional phenomena and fantasies brings us to one last source of laxity in the application of these theories. Although they may suggest a more appropriate model for literary texts than the old-style fantasy model, they nonetheless resemble the *newer* fantasy models. As long as we understand that a fantasy depicts action in an external world composed of other people (however primitively this is conceived), and as long as we understand that a fantasy is not a retreat from reality but an alternate version of it, we see that fantasies have always been "transitional spaces," "other stages" of reality. The theories about transitional space are really theories about fantasies, but fantasies now seen as the rich, many-dimensioned phenomena they really are. Object relations theories and theories about transitional phenomena call attention to a new dimension of fantasy life, and they accord fantasy a newly important status in our total mental life; but they do not provide a category for experience or a model for literature that differs from fantasy as we defined it in chapter 3. These theories thus allow us to keep and expand upon all we have learned from long study of fantasy over the years.

RHETORICAL EXCHANGES IN A TEXT

I shall reconsider Dickens's *Old Curiosity Shop* to suggest first what the psychoanalytic theory of rhetorical exchanges can contribute to the understanding of a text and then to suggest how its use is related to the fantasy model. It has already been suggested that the novel's content and structure, as well as the narrator's relation to his material, are influenced by a fantasy about the Ambiguous Seducer and the Pure Maiden. Let us see now what we can find by thinking about the novel in the context of, or as the medium and occasion for, an exchange between the narrator and the reader.

Of course, since *The Old Curiosity Shop* was a serial novel which appeared in segments every week, it was literally just that. Any serial writer is involved in an exchange with his audience, in which both sides give and receive. Dickens was responsive enough to his audience's reactions to make the famous revision of the ending of *Great Expectations*, later on, and had he not been listening to his audience in the case of Nell's story, there would have been no novel at all but only a few short sketches. Dickens had just completed *Nicholas Nickleby* (1838–39) and had no intention of starting another long novel for a while. Instead, he began work on a long-cherished project, a journal on the model of *The Spectator, The Tatler*, and Goldsmith's *Bee. Master Humphrey's Clock* was to contain nonfiction, some whimsical fiction, and a variety of other pieces, including personal reminiscences; all selections were to be short.

Readers, however, did not go along with Dickens's plans, and after rushing to buy the first, much-advertised issue, they ignored its successors. Sales rose again only after the first segments of Nell's story appeared, and Dickens was pressured into extending the story beyond the few installments he had envisioned, into a full-length, unplanned-for novel, which came out in weekly segments, faster than he had ever produced a novel before. This seemed to be the only way to make a financial success of *The Clock*. The pressure Dickens complained about in his letters is echoed in the novel by Codlin, the puppet master, who cannot escape his charge, but has to carry him forever: "Whereas he had been last night accosted by Mr. Punch as 'master,' . . . here he was, now, painfully walking beneath the burden of that same Punch's temple, and bearing it bodily upon his shoulders" (p. 191).[25]

More important than anything Dickens himself might have felt, however, are the details he included in the portrait of the narrator, Master Humphrey, and it is Humphrey we will focus on here, either as himself or as the more anonymous narrative voice that takes over and is only retrospectively identified as his. Actually, Humphrey's fictional presenta-

25. Charles Dickens, *The Old Curiosity Shop*, ed. Angus Easson (Harmondsworth, Middlesex: Penguin Books, 1972).

tion of his story is in some ways just as autobiographical as
Dickens's famous autobiographical fragment about his
humiliating service in the blacking factory as a child. Like
Dickens, who only reluctantly showed the blacking factory description to his friend John Forster, Humphrey is a shy and
defensive narrator, carefully selecting a sympathetic audience. Their differences are revealing too. In the "real" autobiography, Dickens effaced his adult self, except as a means
for conveying facts about his childhood. In Humphrey's
story, we see just the opposite: a writer tells us what it is like to
be a man who tells stories partly as a means of effacing painful childhood memories. Humphrey shares several narrative
traits with Dickens ("love of inanimate objects" as a stimulant
for his imagination, for example), and his treatment of the
quaint curiosity shop tells us much about a trait central to the
man who invented the detective story: curiosity.

An appropriate starting point for an analysis of Humphrey
and his relation to his material and his audience is the fact
that he is remembering. The earliest psychoanalytic interpretations of *The Old Curiosity Shop* merely tried to find out what
Dickens was remembering as he wrote the novel, particularly
as he indulged himself in the sticky sentimentality of Nell's
death. These were attempts to explain Dickens's artistic failure as a descent into the merely personal, usually in the form
of a particular personal memory. It has been suggested that
behind Nell's death is the death of Dickens's young cousin,
Mary Hogarth, whom he had loved unreasonably: Dickens
was so saddened, it is suggested, that he could not be objective
when recreating her death. Going a bit deeper, it has been
suggested that Dickens was in love with the seventeen-year-
old girl, so that the sugarcoating of Nell's death conceals not
only a sadness but a taboo sexual attraction.[26]

Steven Marcus adds complexity to such interpretations
by avoiding literal-minded assumptions about influence. He

26. See my discussion in chapter 3 of the early psychoanalytic interpretations of the novel.

suggests that through Nell's death Dickens may have been mourning his own spiritual death in childhood, during the blacking factory humiliations that he described in his autobiography. Both memories, then—Mary's death and Dickens's own—lay behind Nell's death, and Dickens was both remembering his own experience and identifying with another's. Simply evoking Mary's death is not enough to explain Nell.[27] Marcus's analysis begins to capture the complexity that the background of *The Old Curiosity Shop* must have—a complexity that would almost certainly include the emotional ambivalence which I described earlier. For Nell's death scene not only invites Dickens—or any reader—to take passive pleasure in identifying with Nell (or with Mary, or with one's childhood self who suffered in one of the equivalents to blacking factories, which all childhoods provide); it also seduces the reader into taking a more active pleasure in identifying with the aggressor, in killing Nell, in getting back at the world and replaying the childhood scene so that he can be on the winning side this time. The fluidity of identification contributes to the fantasy quality of the episode and the novel, and Dickens exploits it. At the beginning of the book, we identify with Nell; Grandfather Trent seems to be a selfish ogre, and though he becomes more pitiable during the first part of the story, he is still despicable. We can comfortably feel sorry for and admire ourselves as we sympathize with the dear child who puts up with him. Later on, however, we begin to detect echoes of *King Lear*, and Dickens takes advantage of another form of sentimentality latent in his material, as he gradually transforms Trent into a well-meaning but deluded old man nobly mourning his lost child.

27. Dickens coyly confessed to having been in love with Little Red Riding Hood as a child ("A Christmas Tree" [1850]). Insofar as the confession is true at all, it suggests that Dickens was attracted to victimized little girls long before Mary died in his arms; this early bias—and the fantasies associated with it—may even have helped bring about the overpowering effect her death had on him later. The "merely personal" cannot be explained by the merely biographical.

Searching for Dickens's specific memories, however, explains less about the meaning of the novel than the fact that the story is so intimately connected to the very process of remembering.[28] This process, like the individual memories themselves, is highly ambivalent, and it wavers between the two alternatives that characterize the fantasy about master and victim, which I described earlier and which characterize so many elements in the novel. These opposing versions of remembering charge the process of memory with the same danger that infects all the novel's relationships and activities. The process of remembering can be a leisurely activity in which the narrator has complete mastery and control of what and how much he remembers. But remembering can also turn into a process in which memories get out of control, come alive, and take over; it can even draw one into past experience again, just as the Single Gentleman was drawn into Nell's adventures and Humphrey was drawn into the gigantic clock in London.

For the most part, however, the threat of this kind of memory is never fully realized. It adds excitement to the story, but what we generally feel in the narrative is the triumph of a man subduing memories and taking pleasure in controlling them. For the "pleasures of memory," to quote the famous

28. If we were to consider these memories systematically, I would emphasize Dickens's memory of a brief pastoral period in his life just *before* the move to London and the blacking factory incident. These were his last weeks in Chatham with the beloved schoolmaster who introduced him not only to imaginative works but to the very journals Dickens set out specifically to recreate in *Humphrey's Clock*. Dickens refers lovingly and gratefully to this man, but the scenes in which the schoolboy dies while his schoolmaster sits helplessly by may not be far from Dickens's subjective version of that period. In *The Old Curiosity Shop*, the schoolboy's death marks a transition from Nell's stay with the lively Punch to her stay at the deadly waxworks. It was while Dickens was working on this section that he first hinted that Nell too might die. See his letter to Forster, 7 July 1839, reprinted in *Dickens' Letters*, ed. Madeline House and Graham Storey, Pilgrim edition, vol. 1 (Oxford: Clarendon Press, 1965).

poem to which Dickens alludes in dedicating the novel,[29] include not only the regressive joy of returning to past events but also the miser's joy of telling over his coins. The content of such memories is naturally important, but the process of recovering and remembering provides its own delight, even when the memories are painful and humiliating. Dickens said he cried over Nell's death, but his tears may have been similar to the tears of the Walrus and the Carpenter, who cried over the oysters they devoured.

The delight derived from remembering is strong and, like the Walrus's pleasure, appetitive: there is a devouring memory as well as a devouring curiosity. Whether dwelling on one fixed image, as Humphrey dwells on Nell's, or chasing after it, like the Single Gentleman in his carriage watching the countryside fly by, the process of remembering satisfies a visual hunger. The narrator watches with something like the "infant's omnivorous eye," as I believe some analyst has called it, and presents a search for the "pictorial past,"[30] like the search that took Alex Haley to Africa to look for his roots or the one that takes an analytic patient back to his old neighborhoods rather than to the mere memory of them. The process of narration often takes on this primitive quality of hunger. Some readers feel that Quilp's way of literally gobbling things up, shell and all, is a model for and expression of Dickens's own insatiable appetite for reality in his fiction.

Memory's appetite and its satisfaction also provide the occasion for a social and rhetorical exchange that involves not only the narrator's relation to his created characters and their world but also his relation to his audience. Quilp's appetite is related to the way he teases others by offering and then withdrawing refreshment, and Dickens—or the novel's narrator—is in a way like Quilp in this sense. In the guise of a host, in the

29. "The Pleasures of Memory" was written by Samuel Rogers, who affected the novel in other ways as well. See chapter 3, note 94.

30. Bertram D. Lewin, *The Image and the Past* (New York: International Universities Press, 1969), pp. 22–23.

preface to the first edition of the novel, Dickens invites his readers to a feast and promises them an array of dishes "smok[ing] on the board."

But after tantalizing and rousing his readers' curiosity in the novel, Dickens consistently holds back his promised delights stretching the story out, coyly withholding information and not letting us know what is happening to Little Nell or even whether she is still alive. Quilp made Sampson Brass drool by drinking liquor in front of him, and then he suddenly forced him to drink a cup boiling hot. At the end of the novel, Dickens offers his readers something more like ice cubes, with Nell's snowbound death, but he plays with Nell's death—and with them—in the same way Quilp taunted Brass. The death scene is a juicy morsel, and, having long kept it a secret (Dickens sent a copy of the last chapter to a friend before it was published, asking that he not give the secret away), he teases the reader with it until the very end. Without privileged narrative access, the reader must accompany the Single Gentleman and see only through his eyes, slowly coming closer to the room where Nell lies, approaching from the outside, seeing through the window, not knowing until the very last minute whether she is asleep or dead. As one contemporary reader put it, "Dickens gloats, touches, tastes, smells and handles [the death of Little Nell] as if it were some kind of savory."[31]

In all of these relationships we recognize the same alternatives that characterize the novel's main fantasy: either dominate or be dominated, eat or be eaten. Quilp threatens to devour everyone, but he is eventually swallowed up and drowned in a river; similarly, Samson had imagined "drinking" Quilp from the bottom of his cup, earlier in the novel. These occurrences resemble the narrator's relation both to the memories he draws on and to the audience to which he

---

31. Fitzjames Stephen, *Cambridge Essays* (1855); cited in Kathleen Tillotson's *Novels of the Eighteen-Forties* (Oxford: Clarendon Press, 1954), p. 48.

presents them; to the world he is creating and the people with whom he is sharing it. The narrator either totally subdues his world to his own fantasies, or his world gets out of control and subdues him.

This is why a general theory that equates every text with a transitional object or transitional space only serves here to destroy distinctions. It is true in one sense, of course, that *The Old Curiosity Shop*, like all other fiction, is a "transitional" world that is neither a part of ordinary reality nor a mere falsehood but which has its own provisional truth. Nonetheless, the narrator's limitations give this novel its own particular relation to the extremes of reality and falsehood. For the narrator, it could be said that there *is* no transitional space between his way and the world's way, between fantasy and reality. Instead of playfully suspending the boundaries between fantasy and reality, or between himself and the objective world, the narrator always feels compelled to choose between these alternatives, and he thereby forces readers to choose between them as well. The forced choice has several effects. Most immediately, perhaps, it affects the *things* in the world he creates. The narrator tells us, for example, that he likes inanimate objects better than people; yet he still fears them, because, though safely inanimate, these objects may begin to dominate him if his imagination depends too much on them for stimulation. He sees no third possibility, no relationship *between* imagination and objects in which neither would dominate.

Dickens's famous animated objects, in the world of this novel at least, are either practically alive without the help of imagination, as Humphrey's clock seems to be, or they are merely objects. The animation comes not from real movement but, as in animated cartoons, from rapidly switching back and forth between two possibilities. An example of this is Nell's flickering perceptions the night she spends among the waxworks: the waxworks are first statues and then become "really" alive, but they are never both at once—never alive in the special sense that art makes life come alive.

Humphrey's attitude also affects the fictional status of the whole novel, impelling it either toward pure fantasy or toward hard reality. Quilp and Nell each actually choose one of the two aforementioned alternatives as a description of the narrative in which they appear. For Quilp, his is a true history, and he thinks of himself as Robinson Crusoe, snug in his version of Crusoe's bachelor bower, served by an adolescent Friday. Quilp relives the story of one man's struggle with the everyday details of living, in all their variety and toughness. Nell, by contrast, thinks of her travels as a recreation of *Pilgrim's Progress*, an abstract and allegorical journey toward death that is, finally, a dream. Humphrey, as we have seen, tries to draw a firm line between the opposing stances he assumes. He is *either* a distanced, uninvolved narrator of what might be fiction, or—as he reveals at the end—he is an actor in a true story, drawn into his tale as reluctantly as Oedipus was drawn into his search.

There is only one place in *The Old Curiosity Shop* where anything resembling an imaginative play space is created. There is only one part of the novel in which fantasies meet the real world on a ground midway between them, and creations are known and accepted for what they are: neither real nor false but something different and better. All modern readers have appreciated the breathing space it provides in the novel, and its contrast with the rest of the book points up its difference in imaginative status. This creation appears in the latter part of Dick Swiveller's story. Swiveller begins as a villain and threatens by turn to take up each of the two roles in the fantasy scene of the persecuted child—the possessive parent and the masochistic child. Nell's wicked brother bribes Swiveller to take Nell for his child-wife, along with her supposed inheritance, and to reduce her to an expensive possession; later, Quilp offers to be Swiveller's parent and let him play the part of a persecuted child. But Swiveller refuses both roles and becomes increasingly attractive. He is the only one of the characters who lives in a fiction known and relished as a fiction. He, not the narrator, invents the fairy tale that silently shapes the story: he transforms Sally Brass into a dragon, the small servant into a Marchioness, and his own recovery from fever into an Arabian night.

Only by recognizing the difference between the narrator's and Swiveller's way of telling stories—the difference between their relations to their creations and to their audiences, and the difference between their two kinds of symbolic expression —can we see how the novel works. And these differences are differences both in the nature of their fantasies and in the degree of self-consciousness with which they indulge them. Although it is useful to think about transitional spaces, the critic must distinguish between *kinds* of transitions, as they are elaborated in fantasies and as they are more or less self-consciously integrated into the texture of the story.

6

Literature as Psychoanalytic Process: Surprise and Self-Consciousness

> The roads by which men arrive at their insights into celestial matters seem to me almost as worthy of wonder as those matters themselves.
>
> —Johannes Kepler

> Though everything's astonishment at last,
> Who leaps to heaven at a single bound?
>
> —Theodore Roethke,
> "Four for Sir John Davies"

Each of the models I have described so far emphasizes only one aspect of the material being considered—content, psychic function, means of representation, or rhetorical function. The psychoanalytic process, however, begins with the assumption that communication has many facets, and the analyst must draw on "all the ways by which one human being understands another"[1] as he tries to put his experience into words; the analyst is as interested in why and how something is said as he is in the words that are actually spoken. The psychoanalytic process provides no special or exotic means of reading the unconscious; its strength derives from two simple strategies: first, it insists on paying attention to everything, and second, it mistrusts the seemingly obvious implications of

1. Rudolph M. Loewenstein, "Some Thoughts on Interpretation in the Theory and Practice of Psychoanalysis," *Psychoanalytic Study of the Child* 12 (1957): p. 132.

what it then observes. Freud prescribed "intense but uncritical attention," meaning *uncritical* in the sense of an editorial openness and a suspension of all conclusions. In each
case the analytic listener tries to be open to the sudden
switches and rearrangements that reveal alternate meanings
and expose the dynamic play of meaning behind what may
seem to be a simple surface. The analytic process offers a
more complete model for literary texts than the other methods we have examined; all the ways we understand each other
are the ways we understand texts, too.

The analytic model is a better model for another reason,
too. It is not only more inclusive but also more complex, because it includes, along with a recognition of the separate aspects of discourse, an explicit emphasis on those moments of
insight and self-consciousness that organize and take account
of the rest. Reservations about using psychoanalytic models
for literature usually come from a reluctance to reduce a complex literary text to the model of something much simpler,
like a fantasy or a dream—efforts that, according to Paul de
Man, "apply to less rigorous modes of consciousness than
those at work in literary texts."[2] But the psychoanalytic process is designed to dismantle less rigorous modes of consciousness, to break up the defensively distorted versions of inner
and outer reality that cramp a person's life and his language.
The blindly symptomatic use of fantasy and dream may constitute a less rigorous mode of consciousness than the ordinary text, but when the psychoanalytic process is used cor-
rectly, its elements reflect on one another with the subtlety,
rigor and self-consciousness of a literary text. Ernst Kris's description of "the good hour"[3] in an analysis unwittingly comes
closer to describing the way a poem works than anything he
ever wrote about literature.

2. Paul de Man, *Blindness and Insight* (New York: Oxford University Press,
1971), p. 22.

3. Ernst Kris, "On Some Vicissitudes of Insight in Psychoanalysis," *International Journal of Psychoanalysis* 37 (1956): 445–55.

This resemblance implies that a study of the minute changes which take place during an analytic hour can not only suggest new meanings for texts but can also suggest how *any* meaning is created within and between people. We can thereby gain a renewed appreciation of the way language and literature work, not only in creating fictional scenes but in creating significance apart from any scene at all; in diverting, displacing, or elaborating meanings, expanding an image into a web of associations or condensing a flow of statements into a single focusing insight; in shifting meanings by shifting perspectives or changing the rules for interpretation. Many analysts themselves are coming to see the exchanges in the psychoanalytic process as the most important part of psychoanalysis, whether their interest is expressed in the continental philosophical terms of discourse with the "other" or in terms of the transference and countertransference that Freud first described. And it is in these exchanges, where analysis is most vital, that it is also most suggestive as a model for other disciplines.[4]

PSYCHOANALYTIC PROCESS:
DISORGANIZATION AND REORGANIZATION

The analytic method is a two-part process directed toward the disorganization and reorganization of the ego, as Hans Loewald has described it.[5] Within the bounds of the "thera-

4. Jacques Lacan's emphasis on the role of language and communication with the "other" naturally finds the exchanges in the psychoanalytic situation central to psychoanalysis, but he even goes so far as to take these exchanges as typical of all other human relationships. Not only the French have been placing more importance on the psychoanalytic situation as a source of or even a replacement for psychoanalytic theory or metapsychology, however. See, e.g., George S. Klein, *Psychoanalytic Theory: An Exploration of Essentials* (New York: International Universities Press, 1976); Hans Loewald, "On the Therapeutic Action of Psychoanalysis," *International Journal of Psychoanalysis* 41 (1960): 16–33; Stanley A. Leavy, "Psychoanalytic Interpretation," *Psychoanalytic Study of the Child* 28 (1973): 305–30; Roy Schafer, *A New Language for Psychoanalysis* (New Haven: Yale University Press, 1976), p. 157.

5. Hans Loewald, "On the Therapeutic Action of Psychoanalysis," *International Journal of Psychoanalysis* 41 (1960): p. 17.

peutic frame,"[6] analyst and patient agree to ignore all ordinary rules—not only those of decorum but also of logic, common sense, and taste. This dissolution of rules is neither dissolute nor easy. It does not just provide the patient with an "oasis from the desert of reticence," as Philip Rieff says, but is rather a "forced labor," as Lacan has called it, which "the psychologist (not without humor) and the psychiatrist (not without cunning)" have called *free association*.[7] The labor derives from undoing all the habits and expectations that shape a life in civilization, all the frames of reference and schema we use to organize the deluge of inner and outer sensations into manageable form so that we can communicate with others about them.

These schema shape all the levels of discourse we have discussed in earlier chapters: content, psychic function, representational strategies, and rhetorical strategies. They have become all the more firmly established insofar as they have been drafted into the service of tendentious motives, to construct the prejudices and automisms we use to defend ourselves against the intrusion of unwanted realities. As the patient frees himself from these schema in this laborious free association, the analyst responds with a correspondingly "benign curiosity" or "evenly suspended attention,"[8] which we might call *free listening*.

But psychoanalysis is more than an undoing or loosening of codifications, and while one part of the mind is freely associating, the "observing ego" performs the second part of the process as it tries out new forms of organization. The "observer" (whether internal or external) often draws on the re-

6. M. Masud Khan, "On Freud's Provision of the Therapeutic Frame," in *The Privacy of the Self: Papers on Psychoanalytic Theory and Technique* (New York: International Universities Press, 1974), pp. 129–35.

7. Philip Rieff, *Freud: The Mind of the Moralist* (New York: Doubleday / Anchor, 1961), p. 364; Jacques Lacan, *The Language of the Self: The Function of Language in Psychoanalysis*, trans. Anthony Wilden (Baltimore: Johns Hopkins University Press, 1968), p. 10.

8. Sigmund Freud, "Recommendations for Physicians Practicing Psychoanalysis" (1912), *SE* 12:111.

sources of logic and secondary process thinking discarded by free association, but its role is not to provide authoritative interpretation, in the sense of diagnosing a symptom or filling in a missing memory. Instead, it provides new perspectives, finds new relationships, reorganizes figure and ground, and changes emphasis. Together, finally, the two processes—loosening and reorganization—lead to those moments of surprise that are the characteristic marks of a good analysis.[9] The surprise in psychoanalysis, however, is not the shock of having something brought up from the alien depths, nor the drama of recalling a secret that only the analyst had guessed at before. Rather, it is the quiet realignment, the small shift in perspective, the recognition of what was always there but not seen before, or what was almost there.

For an example of the psychoanalytic looseness and reorganization in which every aspect of the analytic material is subject to doubt and to surprising reversals and displacements, let us examine Freud's analysis of his own "disturbance of memory on the Acropolis."[10] As Freud tells the story, he was seeing Athens before him for the first time, after years of longing to visit the city. Suddenly he found himself saying, much to his surprise, "So it really does exist after all!" Could it be that he had doubted the existence of Athens all along? "Nonsense," Freud said, and not tempted into dismissing the statement as a meaningless social interjection, he set out to discover what it really meant.

9. Such moments of insight have been variously described. Theodore Reik spoke about them in *Surprise and the Psychoanalyst* (New York: E. P. Dutton, 1937). The specifically cognitive aspects have been described by Ernst Kris, in "Vicissitudes of Insight," and Hans Loewald, in "Therapeutic Action." Others have discussed the more emotional, infantile prototypes for insight; see, e.g., Bertram Lewin, "Some Observations on Knowledge, Belief and the Impulse to Know," *International Journal of Psychoanalysis* 20 (1950): 426–31. Jerome Richfields's "An Analysis of the Concept of Insight," *Psychoanalytic Quarterly* 23 (1954): 390–408, gives an introduction to the different aspects of this phenomenon.

10. Freud, "A Disturbance of Memory on the Acropolis" (1936), *SE* 22:239–48.

As he examines the associations he made to the experience, Freud sees that his doubt about Athens was actually an incredulity about his presence there, which, in turn, was based on a sense of guilt at being there. ("It can't be true! [Because] I don't deserve it!") But Freud was not finished. His doubt was "doubly displaced": first, from his presence in the city to the existence of the city itself, and then from the present moment to the past. Why the past? In the past he had never really doubted the existence of Athens, or the fact that he might one day go so far as to visit it. But there *had* been some doubt that he would "go very far" in another sense—in particular, that he would go as far as his father. And yet here he was, in the city his father not only had not seen, but could not appreciate as Freud did.

By the end of the analysis, Freud's expression of doubt about Athens has become an expression of "filial piety." The rearrangement is possible only because he was able to entertain the potential displacements of meaning without holding onto the premature formulations that his exclamation first encouraged. And these displacements affect every aspect of his thinking. The shifts in content are perhaps most familiar from other psychoanalytic anecdotes: Freud's statements float freely from present to past referents (from "I have doubts about myself" to "I have doubts about others"). But all aspects of the psychoanalytic material are subject to shifts, and there are still others, like the shift in the means of representation (from the figurative meaning of "Freud will never go far" to the literal meaning). And finally, there are shifts that draw attention away from one aspect of the material to an entirely new one, at first one and then another of the aspects we looked at in the earlier chapters become important. Thus the seemingly referential judgment about Athens turns out to serve a psychic function as a fear-appeasing offer of filial piety.

Freud's anecdotal report of his detective work makes it sound elementary. But even here, and especially in such a brief example, his sudden shifts of meaning may seem dubiously determined and hard to reproduce. Any example of psychoanalytic reasoning taken out of context is hard to follow, and many of Freud's readers have found his reasoning arbitrary. Even some of Freud's followers have defined the method as "systematic impiet[y]"[11] that belongs to a slightly sinister "school of suspicion,"[12] whose responsibility toward the text is dubious. Their doubts are understandable. There is no denying that the analyst often sounds less like someone who might say something useful about literature than like a hair-splitting pedant, as Freud described himself,[13] a tedious philologist at best, and more often a tone-deaf freshman with a dirty mind. He ignores obvious meanings and disregards the amenities of ordinary conversation ("But I didn't mean that literally, doctor!"); he sees proclivities in Swift's naming a character Master Bates.[14] Like William Empson, he has "erected the ignoring of 'tact' into a point of honour."[15]

In fact, it may sound as if I am invoking Freud to justify the kind of free associational play in interpretation that has recently become familiar in France and elsewhere. When Freud came to America in 1908, with his strange discoveries about sex and about the way the mind works, he warned, "I bring you the plague"; but current literary criticism has plagues of its own, whether caught from Freud or not. Beginning with the recognition of all the nonreferential determinants of meaning, some critics have rejected belief in reference alto-

11. Kenneth Burke, "Freud—and the Analysis of Poetry," in *The Philosophy of Literary Form*, rev. ed. (New York: Random House / Vintage, 1961), p. 248, speaks of the "systematic impieties of the clinic."

12. Paul Ricoeur, *Freud and Philosophy: An Essay on Interpretation*, trans. Denis Savage (New Haven: Yale University Press, 1970), pp. 32ff.

13. Freud, "A Seventeenth-Century Demonological Neurosis" (1923), *SE* 19:83. It is interesting that Freud acknowledges these tendencies in an essay about a pact with the devil and its devilishly pedantic, hair's-breadth loopholes. Such loopholes are also found in pacts with "the unconscious."

14. Phyllis Greenacre analyzes Bates's significance to Jonathan Swift in *Swift and Carroll: A Psychoanalytic Study* (New York: International Universities Press, 1955), p. 99.

15. William Empson makes this claim in the preface to the second edition of *Seven Types of Ambiguity* (New York: Meridian Books, 1955), p. 8.

gether; they regard the name of the father as separate from reference to any particular father and consider all names separate from what they might naively be thought to refer to. Jacques Derrida even goes beyond the *nom de père* to a verbal dadaism and a nihilism, whose current derivatives might seem to infect meaning in the same way Freud seemed to suggest.

Free association and the free play that French theorists describe are not the same, however. In the first place, despite the way the analyst's comments appear out of context, psychoanalytic experience provides evidence that these comments really do express something that is present in what the patient says and are not simply the analyst's own creative reworking of it. The anaylst's "polymorphous perceptiveness," to borrow a term Phyllis Greenacre uses elsewhere to describe the artist,[16] opens the analyst to the polymorphous perversity of "unconscious" expression, so that he can see past the indirections of piety, sophistication, and tact beneath which this perversity, like the Emperor's nakedness, hides. Such social and linguistic clichés are often the means for covering up fantasies and dreamlike expressions and making them respectable ("It was only a joke, doctor!"), just as the agent of secondary revision in a dream takes raw material and hastily constructs a covering story to account for its presence. Free association is not without rules but is governed by rules other than the ones we usually observe.

In fact, while Paul Ricoeur says that "the poem means everything it can mean,"[17] the rules governing the psychoanalytic process strongly suggest that the process can*not* mean everything. The process is indeed unpredictable and sometimes

16. Phyllis Greenacre, speaking of the child, refers to "the inevitable polymorphous character of his perceptiveness" in "Play in Relation to Creative Imagination," in *Emotional Growth, Psychoanalytic Studies of the Gifted and a Great Variety of Other Individuals*, 2 vols. (New York: International Universities Press, 1971), p. 571.

17. Paul Ricoeur, "Metaphor and the Main Problem of Hermeneutics," *New Literary History* 6 (1974): 95–110.

outrageous in its course, but it is neither arbitrary nor always interminable. We can know, in the proper context, when an interpretation has succeeded, just as we know when a line of poetry has worked, although all too often we do not know why. Some of the most exciting discoveries in Freud's case histories—and in analysis in general—have begun with a provocative wrong guess about an interpretation and have emerged through a series of corrections. Anyone who has been on either side of the couch knows that there is less free play in interpretation there than in some literary criticism. The interpretations, even the "right" ones, sound odd; but we know when they have gone wild or stale. "I was going to free associate," said the man as he lay down on the couch, "but I'd better tell you what's on my mind."

This candid patient was judging the rightness of his statements by an intuitive feeling, just as the analyst does. But there are other objectives as well, which can determine how any one statement affects and is supported by the others surrounding it. As even the brief example given above shows, psychoanalytic "truth" comes out of a whole process and not out of any one statement extracted from that process. The movements toward disorganization and reorganization take time; they are neither isolated nor strictly sequential but continuously play against one another. The resemblance between psychoanalysis and literature lies in their dynamic interaction: the interaction between the free-ranging play of mind and the organizing response to it, and the continuing play which they contradict or confirm. Ultimately, the interaction leads to those moments of reorganization when a pattern begins to fit together or a final piece is added; when tentative explorations in different directions suddenly condense into one focused moment, and the random remarks of an hour combine to make a revealing joke, or a list of repeated humiliations is suddenly seen as cover for a deeper ambition. These are the moments of insight and surprise that I have described earlier; they are never isolated moments. They derive from the surrounding play of ideas—or rather, from the surround-

ing process that brings them "close [enough] to consciousness."[18]

The moment of insight is itself a focused moment, but its
power—like the power of an image or a line or a scene in any
literary text—comes from its place in the context of the analysis. The analyst's work, Kris says, is not to make revelations
but to find the conditions for them and to make recall possible by recreating them. The actual insight would not take
place, the surprising idea would not have its effect, if it were
not for the carefully placed—or fortuitously emerging—
anticipatory ideas[19] that establish the terms for interpretation
and set up the appropriate mood. More significant than any
single insight or the recovery of any specific memory in analysis is the whole process of "working through," in which any
idea or memory is less important than its gradually revealed
relationships with all the rest of the patient's ideas, as the idea
or memory appears in new and surprising contexts. Old organizations are exposed and new ones are made possible.

Analysis is effective because of this gradual loosening of
larger patterns and relationships, which makes newer and
freer ones possible. The most important fact about psychoanalysis—and perhaps the most often misunderstood—is
that analysts are not looking for specific things but for *ways of
seeing* things. They are not looking for something hidden but
for new aspects of what was already there; they are not looking for the past but for all the ways in which the past affects
the present, without being recognized as doing so. The analyst does not search for particular sorts of unconscious things,
like sexual fantasies or symbols. There is no predictable specific secret revealed in a switch from manifest to latent meaning; there is no inherently explanatory latent content for a
manifest symptom or symbol ("We cannot assume that this
man must symbolize her father, who's the one she *really*
loves"). Instead, the analyst looks at the play between more

18. Freud, "Wild Psychoanalysis" (1910), *SE* 11:226.
19. Kris, "Vicissitudes," passim.

and less consciously perceived ideas, seeing how the switch from one kind of consciousness to another affects ideas, be they sexual or secular.

When Freud's patient Dora dreamed that her father came to her bedside to rescue her from a fire, Freud—concerned not with some inherently unconscious content ("It must be love for her father") but with the relation between conscious and unconscious ways of seeing the dream—suggested that Dora was using her father to represent another man. The final interpretation depends not on being able to point to the man Dora "really" loves but rather on being able to show how the conscious and unconscious aspects of her love work together (why does she represent the man in terms of her father's being fatherly?).[20]

Just as the analyst looks, not for a particular sort of unconscious content behind the conscious content of his patient's words, but only for the relations between ideas that are revealed by different modes of consciousness, so, too, he does not look for a particular sort of thing that is wish-fulfilling (like sex) behind a particular sort of thing that is defensive (like morality) but rather for the way in which ideas of whatever kind express general psychic conflict. Thoughts have to be judged by their function and context, not by their literal meaning. Wishes can serve as defenses against even more terrifying wishes, and real wish fulfillments are not always attractive. Ideas about oedipal wishes or homosexual wishes are not necessarily the inner-most secrets hidden behind symptoms but may be the symptoms themselves.

One young man, for example, began to fear for his sexual identity when he found himself obsessed by fantasies about homosexual intercourse with his analyst, during the last stages of his analysis.[21] Assuming that he had finally uncov-

20. Freud, "Fragment of an Analysis of a Case of Hysteria" (1905), *SE* 7:72.

21. Hans Loewald, "Comments on Some Instinctual Manifestations of Superego Formation," reported in *The Bulletin of the Philadelphia Association for Psychoanalysis* 12 (1962): 43–45.

ered his darkest secret, he glumly prepared to accept the truth about himself—until further analysis showed that his erotic fantasies expressed his wish to stay in analysis and to continue receiving his analyst's "penetrating" interpretations. Awareness of this wish, it turns out, embarrassed him even more than the idea of homosexuality. Here the supposedly primitive secret actually disguised a more sophisticated wish. In another case, homosexual behavior concealed a still more primitive wish than itself. A seriously disturbed mental patient had been making homosexual advances to his fellow patients, but this no more represented an open wish fulfillment than the case just described; the man was actually searching for a primitive merger with a mirror image of himself.[22]

If wishes are not always wish-fulfilling, neither are defenses always cramping and distorting. One analyst reported a "defense by reality," in which an orphaned girl insisted on facing the facts of her unhappy situation (rather than wishfully distorting them). Her constant reference to her parents' abandonment of her, it turned out, was in the service of her "family romance fantasies" that her real parents were a king and a queen.[23]

In other words, the symptom seldom derives from a simple case of repression, where the trouble is that something is missing and the solution is to replace it. The missing element is almost always present in some relation to the rest of the patient's experience. The analyst, then, is always looking for relationships, not things, and his interpretation takes the form of suggesting a new relationship rather than an answer. Whether the switch he suggests affects the content, the psychic function, the means of representation, or the rhetorical function of the analytic exchange, what he does is reorganize the material rather than produce something new. The exam-

22. Unpublished case report. See also Thomas Freeman et al., *Chronic Schizophrenia* (New York: International Universities Press, 1958), pp. 37ff.

23. Jean Laplanche and J. B. Pontalis, "Fantasy and the Origins of Sexuality," *International Journal of Psychoanalysis* 49 (1968): 2. See also N. Searle, "Flight to Reality," *International Journal of Psychoanalysis* 10 (1929): 280–91.

ples we have just seen refer to a shift in content, but this reorganization also occurs in the less classically Freudian shifts in means of representation and in the assumed rules for interpreting what we hear, as we saw in chapter 4. There the latent meaning is even more clearly present in the material but is just not seen by the patient who is locked into one mode of consciousness.

Sometimes the analyst's contribution is nothing more than a reorientation—a simple change in the truth status of the material already present. This happens in a parapraxis, when the truth slips out, but is taken for an accident. Similarly, dreams "hide" wishes by presenting them as accomplished facts, and Freud's first patients concealed their fantasies by presenting them as memories. There can even be an evasion by too *much* memory, as well as in the supposedly typical case of too much forgetfulness. This occurs in cases of *déjà vu* or *fausse reconnaissance*, where the patient recognizes what he can never have seen; but this unsettling delusion turns out to be a distraction from what the patient is really remembering. He focuses on the scene itself ("I've been in this office before") and removes his attention from the fantasy that is actually familiar ("I've wanted to kill people before, just the way I want to kill this analyst now"). The relationship between cover and truth can become very complicated indeed, and Freud even reports a "supposed parapraxis," where the patient merely *thought* she had committed a parapraxis and left her umbrella at the doctor's office; when she returned to fetch it she realized that she had been carrying it all along.

In suggesting one of these reorganizations, whatever aspects of the analytic material it may affect, the analyst does not have to reach for the ideal of pure scientific truth; he simply takes account of the data in a new way and sees them from a new point of view. His "interpretation" is not a scientific diagnosis but may even make use of "defensive" indirections; it may be metaphorical or ironic, the way symptomatic speech habits can be. Victor Rosen, for example, tells about one patient who hid his meaning in a conversation by breaking it up and taking his own words literally: on the day after getting his monthly bill, the patient filled the hour with general complaints about the price of living, the shrinking value of the dollar, and so on, in such a rambling manner that the patient himself stopped at one point to ask, "But what has all this got to do with the price of lettuce?" Rosen's interpretation consisted of little more than taking the scattered remarks figuratively and reorganizing them. "Yes," he said, "it takes a lot of lettuce to shrink a head," making explicit the unspoken complaint and incidentally providing the first laugh in an otherwise humorless analysis.[24] The interpretation, in fact, may take any form but one—the one fixed by the patient's own chosen, restrictive defenses.[25] Rosen's joke worked for the humorless patient, but elsewhere the analyst might achieve the same end by taking seriously the patient's "joking." The most important thing an interpretation does is change the way the patient views his symptom and free him to see it in a new way. That is why psychoanalysis is different from shamanism, though critics have employed the latter term when viewing the analyst's interpretation as just another fantastic symptom, merely phrased in new language. (Like the medicine man, Lévi-Strauss says, the analyst substitutes a socially acceptable myth for the patient's private myth—childhood trauma for current paranoia.)[26]

Moving from symptom to symptom may well be an endless journey from myth to myth, but moving from symptom to insight is like moving from Ptolemaic to Copernican systems. It is a movement away from insistence on ocular proof and on the letter, away from the focus on a reductively concrete cen-

24. Victor Rosen, "Variants of Comic Caricature and Their Relationship to Obsessive-Compulsive Phenomena," *Journal of the American Psychoanalytic Association* 11 (1963): 719–20.

25. See Rudolph M. Loewenstein, "The Problem of Interpretation," *Psychoanalytic Quarterly* 20 (1951): 9.

26. Claude Lévi-Strauss, *Structural Anthropology*, trans. Claire Jacobson and Brooke Grundfest Schoepf (Garden City, N.J.: Anchor Books, 1967), pp. 191–200.

ter that masks complex forces at work. Moving from symptom to insight is not only a shift from one meaning to another
but a transcendence of the old stale alternatives and an insight into their ground. For instance, this approach does not
involve a switch in the patient's focus from "I don't want to
pay anyone" to "I don't want to pay my analyst" but instead
involves an escape from niggling about payment altogether
and an insight into the more important forces behind such
complaints. The patient does not move from "I fear for my
wife" to "What's really troubling me is that I hated my mother
and was afraid that I'd hurt her," but escapes from needing to
think in terms of hate at all. As Stanley Cavell describes the
therapy:

> The problems are solved only when they disappear,
> and answers are arrived at only when there are no longer
> questions. . . . The more one learns, so to speak, the hang
> of oneself, and mounts one's problems, the less one is
> able to *say* what one has learned; not because you have
> forgotten what it was, but because nothing you said
> would seem like an answer or a solution: there is no
> longer any problem or question which your words would
> match. You have reached conviction but not about a
> proposition; and consistency, but not in a theory. You are
> different, what you recognize as problems are different,
> your world is different. And that is the sense, the only
> sense in which, what a work of art means cannot be
> said.[27]

The one difference between what Cavell describes and the
psychoanalytic process—and this is the final aspect of the
process that I will stress here—is that the latter is more self-
conscious. The patient begins to understand more than just
the one symptom that brought him to analysis; he begins to

---

27. Stanley Cavell, "Aesthetic Problems of Modern Philosophy," in *Must
We Mean What We Say? A Book of Essays* (New York: Charles Scribner's, 1969),
pp. 85–86. This parallel was suggested to me by Henry Abelove.

understand how he has been making his life symptomatic and to recognize the motives and methods he has been using to deal with experience. The psychoanalytic process is more than a means of achieving isolated insights or retrieving isolated memories; it becomes an end in itself. Freud's original goal in psychoanalysis was to fill in the gaps of his patients' memories; more recently, as one analyst has suggested, the goal has become "to show the patient how his mind works."[28] The whole history of psychoanalysis may be summed up as the change in emphasis from one of these two goals to the other; what Kris called the "vicissitudes of insight" have become more interesting than the location of instincts.[29]

The therapeutic value of analysis, in other words—and its aesthetic value, too—does not lie in specific concrete cures for symptoms. And neither do its most characteristic moments. The moment of surprise that I have described is recognized most often by a peculiar sense of rightness, a "clicking," as Otto Fenichel has called it,[30] which brings emotional as well as intellectual recognition. But the emotion does not result from the content of what has been discovered. The moment of insight is often marked by a giggle or by an inner feeling very like one. But this laughter has little to do with what has just been discovered. Painful recognitions about one's family or about one's flaws are no joke; but still the patient laughs. Freud tried to explain this seemingly automatic phenomenon by talking about the economy of energy: according to him, the patient was releasing some of the energy he formerly spent repressing the uncovered idea, so that it escaped in the form of laughter. But the laughter here, like the triumph at a tragic recognition, has nothing to do with what has been recognized; it is a response to the act of recognition itself. That most narcissistic moment in a narcissistic process,

28. Peter L. Giovacchini, "The Influence of Interpretation upon Schizophrenic Patients," *International Journal of Psychoanalysis* 50 (1969): 180.

29. See note 19.

30. Otto Fenichel, *Problems of Psychoanalytic Technique* (New York: Psychoanalytic Quarterly, 1941), p. 8.

the moment of psychoanalytic insight is also—paradoxically—the most objective, when pain and complaints become
building material for a kind of art.

MANIFEST PARALLELS IN LITERATURE

I have suggested that the movement from the psychoanalytic to the aesthetic experience is a natural one. The connection between the psychoanalytic process and the aspect of
poetry that makes it *poetry* (rather than paraphrasable statement) is even closer than the more immediately obvious connection between a dream and a "dreamlike" poem. To compare a work of literature to a fantasy is to isolate that aspect of
the text which returns us to more primitive levels of experience. To compare it to the psychoanalytic process is to discover those aspects that avoid such a return—but this can be
accomplished only by exposing and taking account of the
work's own fantasy and dreamlike elements.

The most obvious literary parallels to the reorganizations in
analysis are found in relatively primitive works where the
switch in how we see things is exaggerated, like the blatantly
"surprising" jokes and the uncanny stories Freud studied,
and these examples provide a good starting place for a closer
look at the relation between the psychoanalytic process and
literary texts. Jokes and uncanny stories depend on a single
surprising moment of reorganization like the moment of insight in analysis, and they have a curiously similar emotional
impact. As Freud suggests, for example, in the following joke,
there is a switch in meaning, which makes us laugh:

First Jew: Have you taken a bath?
Second Jew: No, is one missing?

And in E.T.A. Hoffmann's uncanny tale "The Sand-Man,"
there is a switch that makes us shiver, when the nursery tale
about a sandman coming to take out a boy's eyes suddenly
seems to come true.[31]

31. E. T. A. Hoffmann, *Eight Tales of Hoffmann*, trans. J. M. Cohen

It is significant that jokes and the uncanny are the only genres Freud chose to write about at any length, because they provide the same kind of phenomena that his clinical experience provided. He never connected the two studies, of course; he would not have said that he was using the psychoanalytic process as a model, and he would not have agreed with my analysis of the switch that occurs in both genres.[32] Instead, just as he had defined the goal of analysis as filling in the gaps in memory, he explained the "kinetic" effect of jokes and the uncanny by referring to the specific material which they revealed or "filled in." Freud attributed their power to the simple presence of specific "unconscious" or "wishful" ideas. The joke worked, according to Freud, by making it possible for unconscious material to escape the censor, and our response was not to the joke but to the unconscious material. Normally, we have to suppress the rebelliousness and perversity that makes the second Jew say, in effect, "I'm not listening to you about this civilized business of cleanliness; I'm so far from all of that, I don't even recognize the expression describing it." Similarly, the uncanny story worked, according to Freud, by making it possible for unconscious material—in this case, frightening infantile fantasies about oedipal wishes and the blinding ("castration") that follows as punishment—to escape the censor.

(London: Pan Books, 1952). Freud retells the story in "The Uncanny" (1919), *SE* 17:226–33.

32. Both in his essay on jokes, *Jokes and Their Relation to the Unconscious* (1905), *SE* 8:9–236, and in "The Uncanny," written fourteen years later, Freud tried to reduce the text in question to a simpler energic model of disguised wish fulfillment. Each of these genre essays is a spin-off from one of his major theoretical statements and is implicitly offered as a demonstration of it. This is interesting, because while the two essays themselves offer the same explanation for jokes as for the uncanny, the theoretical claims contradict one another. Freud wrote the essay on jokes while working on his monumental "Three Essays on the Theory of Sexuality" in 1905 (*SE* 7:130–279), which explained behavior solely in terms of the pleasure principle; but he wrote his essay on the uncanny while working on the pivotal essay "Beyond the Pleasure Principle," which suggested that repetition is a motive force for behavior as powerful as wish fulfillment.

Freud denied that comic or uncanny effect could be explained by a conflict between ideas rather than by the presence of an inherently comic or uncanny idea. Theories defining jokes as the product of sense in conflict with nonsense, Freud said, described only an intellectual conflict, just as theories about the uncanny as the product of conflicting interpretations of events depended only on intellectual confusions. Merely intellectual conflicts, Freud insisted, could not produce the powerful effect a joke or an uncanny story has.[33] These effects depend on the fact that a repressed idea from childhood has returned, only incidentally causing confusion.

With the more recent definition of the psychoanalytic process as a switching between two ways of seeing rather than between the absence and presence of a particular element, we can now take advantage of Freud's contribution to make a composite theory. As in the psychoanalytic process, it is not simply the visible presence or absence of some inherently powerful material that makes the joke, but the way the material makes its presence known. The joke depends not on the return of repressed material but on a change in relationship between manifest and latent significance of the same material: the joke begins when our ordinary interpretation gives way to an old, literal-minded one, and an absurd world emerges in the center of an ordinary landscape. Freud saw the innocent beginning of a joke as a mere disguise for or distraction from the really funny punch line; but without the beginning, the joke would not be funny. The humor lies in the movement from the innocent setup to the punch line. Jokes, at least the ones Freud cites, work by switching the grounds for interpretation. We think we are playing one game when we hear the first Jew ask, "Did you take a bath?" But we know we are playing another when the second answers, "No, is one missing?"

---

33. See Freud, "The Uncanny," *SE* 17:230–31, and *Jokes, SE* 8:17–19 and 92–96.

Even Freud, however, recognized implicitly that the joke depends on a general switch in our method of interpretation rather than on the introduction of a particular content. He claimed that what makes the audience laugh is the Jew's taboo motive for switching: the second Jew switches the meaning, not the joke. But even though he tried to locate the power of the joke solely in content and not in a general mode of representation or reading, Freud still felt that he had to take into account the joke's social context. Unlike other fiction, a joke needs an audience, Freud said, and it can only be understood in the rhetorical context of a purposeful exchange between teller and listener. Thus Freud implicitly recognized the joke's switch in narrative and linguistic conventions. Where he said the joke "needs an audience,"[34] we would say that it requires a set of conventional expectations to play with and against.

The same is true in the case of the uncanny. Here, too, Freud attributed a story's power to the mere presence of a forbidden idea, like the idea of castration in Hoffmann's "The Sand-Man"; or to the mere presence of a forbidden "way of thinking," like the fear of magical retaliation in the same story. But in both cases it is the play between two ways of thinking or seeing that causes the effect, as commentators have always noticed. What Freud has added to the understanding of the uncanny, as in the case of the joke, is that the necessary play must be between two different kinds of ideas or two different kinds of thinking, one of which is more primitive than the other. As he pointed out, this is what distinguishes the joke from the merely comic and the uncanny from the merely frightening.

Finally, with the more subtle model of the psychoanalytic process available, we can also use Freud's explanation as a starting point to discriminate between the joke and that which is uncanny. Working with his single-dimensional explanatory

34. Freud, "The Motives of Jokes—Jokes as a Social Process," in *Jokes* (1905), *SE* 8:140–58.

model of repression/openness, Freud wound up with the same explanation for both jokes and the uncanny: what makes a joke funny is the same "return of the repressed" that makes the uncanny story uncanny. We can now be more specific and say that each of these genres is defined by a switch in a different aspect of the material. The success of the joke depends on a switch in content or reference, from "washing in a tub" to "stealing a tub." The uncanny, however, depends on a switch in what is accepted as truth. An old nanny's tale suddenly becomes real when the sandman comes after the grown-up Nathaniel's eyes. The uncanny and its related phenomena—*déjà vu, déjà raconté,* and *fausse reconaissance*—are more unsettling than jokes because they disrupt our sense of ourselves and our orientation in the world; these phenomena are what the analyst calls *ego disturbances*. The joke, on the other hand, merely distorts the message and does not affect us significantly.

The exceptions prove this rule that jokes switch content and the uncanny switches truth status; they illuminate material that falls between the categories of jokes and the uncanny. For example, in a now classic psychoanalytic essay on literature, Norman Holland analyzes a *Playboy* joke that actually works like the uncanny in reverse and falls somewhere between the genres of the joke and the uncanny:

> A young executive had stolen company money and lost it on the stock market, and was about to jump off a bridge when an old crone appeared, said she was a witch, and promised to replace the money for a slight consideration —which turned out to be a night in a nearby motel. Though revolted, the man agreed. In the morning as he was about to escape, the crone asked how old he was. "Forty two," he answered, "Why?" "Ain't you a little old to believe in witches?" she replied.[35]

35. Norman Holland, *The Dynamics of Literary Response* (New York: Oxford University Press, 1968), pp. 3–4. The version given here is only a summary of the original.

Holland explains the joke's effect in fairly strict Freudian terms: we are presented with the desired—but feared—threat of an oedipal encounter between the old hag and the young man, and our laughter follows when we learn, with relief, that we have been saved from it after all. But the joke's effect depends on more than an economy of wishes and fears. It depends on a switch in the joke's status as truth or fictional "truth." We think we are playing one game when the joke begins (a game in which we accept witches as realities), but we realize we are playing another at exactly the moment the executive realizes it. This is the same kind of switch that defines the uncanny. In that case, of course, the switch moves in the opposite direction: in "The Sand-Man," the fantasy sandman turns out to be real, but in the *Playboy* joke, the real witch turns out to be only a fantasy (which is probably why the joke amuses or annoys rather than frightens us). But it affects us in much the same way as the uncanny, challenging us on more levels than Freud's jokes do.

There are moments in his two essays when Freud seems to take all these factors into account and to come around to saying that a joke or an uncanny story is formed not simply by recalled material but also by the way in which this material is brought back. The uncanny, he says, can be generated by the return of even the least uncanny material; and jokes use material that was neither wish-fulfilling nor funny when it was first repressed. The mere resurrection of infantile memories is not enough to explain why we react as we do, even to these primitive forms of literature. One of the most poignant moments in Freud's book on jokes, in fact, is the closing statement, in which he moves away from seeing the joke as a simple return to earlier pleasure and comes closer than he does anywhere else to seeing jokes (and by implication, all the products of our discontented civilization) as something new, designed as a substitute for early experience, perhaps, but not as an imitation of it. Jokes, the comic, and humor, he says, attempt to regain from mental activity a pleasure that has been lost through the development of that activity—a euphoria which is "nothing other than the mood of a period of life . . .

when we were ignorant of the comic, when we were incapable of jokes and when we had no need of humour to make us feel happy in life."[36]

This is not the Freud who saw literature as only a simple escape to a mindlessly literal reproduction of our earliest fantasy worlds. Here Freud sees not simply a return of repressed material but a whole new world that takes account of it. He sees the indirections that move toward new forms of pleasure, the pleasure of insight, the Wordsworthian pleasures of consciousness, and the literary pleasures that escape any simple reflex explanation.

Obviously, the sudden shifts in jokes and uncanny stories move us more crudely than more sophisticated literature does, and their effect has less influence on the way we see the world after we have enjoyed them. The joke and the uncanny story lie at the borders of literature; they are examples of what Stephen Dedalus might call kinetic art, like pornography and propaganda, because, like these two pragmatic genres, they are meant to "move" us, though in a different way. They are in fact defined by the giggle and the *frisson*. Yet all literature moves us the same way these trivial texts do—by the way it presents material and not by its content alone. We recognize poetic touchstones by being "thoroughly penetrated by their power,"[37] and though the punch in a joke's punchline may seem far removed from the finer touch of poetry Matthew Arnold was describing, it belongs in the same category.

The reorganization made suddenly explicit in a joke is related to that which we can find unfolding more slowly and less explosively in every aspect of literary texts—in their content, their function, their language and literary conventions, and their rhetorical dimension. The literary critics who most resemble psychoanalysts are not the ones who talk about fan-

---

36. Freud, *Jokes*, SE 8:236.

37. Matthew Arnold, "The Study of Poetry," *English Literature and Irish Politics*, The Complete Prose Works of Matthew Arnold, ed. R. H. Super, vol. 9 (Ann Arbor: The University of Michigan Press, 1973), p. 170.

tasies but those who talk about ambiguity and who challenge the assumptions integral to ordinary reading processes, like William Empson, Kenneth Burke, and Sigurd Burckhardt. The alternative readings they point out are not always sexual (though Empson's and Burke's often are), but neither are the analyst's; what they share with the analyst is an eye for the tenuous as well as the tendentious and an appreciation of the way supposedly farfetched alternative readings may be much closer to the meaning of a text than we realize, in a context that shapes our final, "acceptable" reading.

In some cases the parallel between the psychoanalytic process and the text is easy to see; the reorganization is quite obviously part of the manifest text and is visible in many separate details. The study of such shifts is in fact one of the most traditional aspects of literary criticism. On the level of individual words and phrases these shifts have been studied as ambiguities of various kinds, the necessary wealth of alternatives that make poetic language. In broader, if vaguer, forms, they have been studied as the "irony" new critics believed to be the necessary condition for poetry. In a very different kind of criticism, Harold Bloom has examined not verbal but rhetorical switches—or "poetic crossings"[38]—in which a poet changes from one to another way of representing and coping with ideas. And more recently, we have begun to hear about a number of more subtly distinguished ways in which a text reveals an interaction between its simultaneous construction and deconstruction of meaning, or in which a text can destroy its own integrity if seen from another perspective.

On a larger scale, traditional critics have studied similar switches and reorganizations. In their studies, the model would no longer be the isolated moment of psychoanalytic insight, which parallels the simple joke or uncanny story; it is instead the entire "good hour" or "good analysis,"[39] as Kris has

38. Harold Bloom, "Poetic Crossing: Rhetoric and Psychology," *The Georgia Review* 30 (1976): 495–526.

39. Kris, "Vicissitudes," p. 452.

called it, which Cavell invoked. This larger unit provides a model for the kind of plot movement Aristotle described when he maintained that tragedy depended on a moment of recognition that reorganized an entire world. This model represents a movement toward revelation not only of a specific fact but of a fact that changes everything, that makes us give up one set of values and the belief that the world conforms to them, and shows us how to find another. This manifest movement toward reorganization can make any story resemble a stylized psychoanalysis, or at least the old-style traumatic revelation analysis.

Not surprisingly, nearly all the texts that Freud chose to analyze at length had this kind of plot. *Oedipus* is the most obvious example (its action "can be likened to the work of a psychoanalysis," Freud said),[40] but Wilhelm Jensen's *Gradiva*, which inspired Freud's monograph on dreams and delusion, is another good example; it tells the story of a man who finds that his current love is a figure from his childhood. Even Hoffmann's "Sand-Man" takes the form of a psychological investigation; the author tries to find out what is the matter with Nathaniel, using outside diagnoses and clinical confession, and exploring the return to childhood. Today, of course, with a newer concept of a more subtle kind of revelation—as in Cavell's description which I have quoted—we might find literary analogues not in the plays about revelations but in the stories about failed revelation. Rather than looking for the caricatural "peak-experience" of old-style analysis, we would look to the analogy of the vision that disappears when Spenser's Calidore tries to capture it on Mount Acidale, or the vision that never materializes for Wordsworth in the Alps.

Whether the plot reorganization is sudden or more subtly interfused, however, the movement of thought in the psychoanalytic process takes more into account than that in the other models. It makes a more suggestive model for Shakespeare's

40. Freud, *The Interpretation of Dreams, SE* 4:262.

plays, for example, than the static character analyses we discussed in chapter 2. What is interesting about Shakespeare's characters is not their diseases but their movement through disease to some kind of curative reorganization. Their proper parallel is not the neurotic but the neurotic in analysis. Freud's patients—neurotics, in general—are caught in stifling, reductive versions of reality, which permit only equally reductive behavior. For example, Frau Cäcilie, whose case was mentioned in chapter 1, was caught in a cliché that was taken literally; she was so obsessed by her facial pains—the only way she acknowledged society's "slap in the face"—that she did not have to cope with anything else or confront any question about her relationships except "Does it make my face hurt or doesn't it?"[41] Every neurotic is caught in a similarly reductive dichotomy, fixated on a question defined by its own terms. Analysis cures by releasing the patient so that he can see the world in new terms.

The parallel between the psychoanalytic process and Shakespeare's plays is easiest to see when a reductive dichotomy affects a character who is trapped in an almost pathologically defensive vision, and the most obvious examples are the several jealous husbands, trapped in obsessive dichotomies that *we* know are beside the point. Othello forgets everything he knows about Desdemona, once he begins his obsessive testing: "Did she or didn't she betray me?" Leontes, in *The Winter's Tale*, hardly bothers to consider the alternatives before he decides that Hermione has betrayed him; and Posthumus Leonatus, in *Cymbeline*, contaminates his marriage the moment he consents even to ask of his wife, "Will she or won't she betray me?" although at first he believes in her. Troilus, who has real cause to feel betrayed, watches Cressida with her new lover and, instead of reacting directly to the situation, is caught up in the terms of a dichotomy as he asks himself, "Is she or isn't she doing this—is this Cressida?" The movement of each of these plays, however, does not simply answer these obsessive questions but changes the terms in which each man sees his beloved. This redefinition of terms is characteristic of many other Shakespearean plays as well. What makes *Antony and Cleopatra* so strange a play, in fact, is the way in which Antony *starts out* by ignoring such reductive dichotomies, although they pose more appropriate questions for him than for the jealous husbands.

Less obvious but much more characteristic of Shakespeare's plays are the similar changes in characters who are not so blatantly disturbed but are nonetheless caught in their own reductive visions. The young aristocrats in *Love's Labour's Lost*, for example, have to be shaken out of their simplistic view of the world. The men have taken sides in the ancient war between discipline and pleasure, and from the moment they announce their withdrawal to a strict academe, they become caught up in a dichotomous view of the world as blinding as Othello's: "Should I devote myself to books or shouldn't I?"—or rather, "Can I devote myself to books or can't I?" Then the Princess arrives with her women, and the men of course all fall in love. But instead of escaping from their dichotomy, the men simply change it slightly and switch sides: the war becomes a struggle between study and love, and they dedicate themselves with equal extravagance to love. What we begin to see is that the categories have become irrelevant. What matters is neither study nor love, but the way in which the young men go about either one. They have rushed into both like brash, self-confident fools, out to conquer; the women are humbler, mellower, more receptive to what love brings and to forces beyond the control of their individual categorizing wills.

Not only characters but entire societies are sometimes caught up in paralyzing dichotomies. In *Romeo and Juliet*, the war between Montague and Capulet demonstrates such a dichotomy; we can see how irrelevant the categories are, how vital the stars that cut across, but the characters cannot see this until it is too late—and perhaps not even then. In *Troilus and Cressida*, we can at least tell the difference between Greeks and Trojans, but the stalemated war their dichotomous outlook generates is again beside the point. We do not care about their obsessive seven-year-old question as to "who will win, Greek or Trojan." What matters is a question that undermines both sides: what does it mean to win? And elsewhere in the plays we hardly have a chance to compare Roman and Goth, reason and love, Caesar and Brutus, before our comparison is out of date. Initially, we may get caught up in deciding who should be king, Richard or Henry, but before the end of the play we are always asking larger questions, like "What *is* a king?" and "Can there be a king?" The terms have changed, and the change is part of what the plays are about.

But in these cases, as the last examples show, the reorganization affects something more fundamental than the character's experience or the plot alone: it affects the audience as well. If Shakespeare's characters sometimes suffer from clichés, so do we as critics. We may avoid Othello's cage; we may escape the empty distinctions between Montagues and Capulets or Trojans and Greeks, which imprison an entire world. But we fall into other pits. We see beyond the distinction between Montague and Capulet, but elsewhere we find distinctions we think are the true ones. We find, for example, dichotomies between artificial and natural; restraint and freedom; wintry rigidity and spring release; and work world and holiday. These dichotomies have been described often, at least in the comedies, and seem to be embodied in the very geography of the plays: we see them in the contrasts between the city and the forest, the men's academy and the park around it where the women stay, the palace and the heath, Venice and Turkish outlands, and Venice and Belmont.

These dichotomies, however, are not the adequate measure of a play; they are the kind of thing cured by psychoanalysis—the wrong set of terms. And the cure is not simply a compromise between these dichotomous terms (Athenian rationality plus a healthy dose of the forest's irrationality), nor a Hegelian synthesis, nor a paradox beyond our common understanding. Rather, it is a complete reorganization, which shows dichotomy to be beside the point. The opening terms in a Shakespearean play slip away from us as the action moves toward a reorganization not only of characters and action but also of the very way in which we see both. The initial questions no longer remain, because the terms in which they have been defined are no longer relevant.

In Shakespearean criticism, the kind of movement characterizing the psychoanalytic process has also recently become the concern of traditional critics. Much of the Shakespearean criticism of the last ten years, though never mentioning psychoanalysis, has traced just such movements in individual plays, though usually implying that the given play is unique in its defiance of categories.[42] It is not in Shakespeare's plays,

42. Kenneth Burke has suggested in the case of several plays that we must stop evaluating characters simply in terms defined by the content or plot and must switch instead to evaluating them in terms defined by their function: the villain Iago (in the plot's literal terms) then becomes a hero, in a way, for if the play is to work at all it needs both hero and villain playing their interlocking roles. ("*Othello*: An Essay to Illustrate a Method," *Hudson Review* 4 [Summer 1951]: 165–203. See also Burke's "*Coriolanus*—and the Delights of Faction," in *Language as Symbolic Action* [Berkeley and Los Angeles: University of California Press, 1966], and "*King Lear*: Its Form and Psychosis," *Shenandoah* 21 [Autumn 1969]: 3–18.) A. D. Nuttall suggests a similar reversal in *Measure for Measure*, where in the *plot's* terms the Duke is a hero coping with Angelo's wickedness, but if we think about the characters' *functions*, Angelo is a scapegoat who takes on the Duke's dirty work; like Judas in Borges's version of the Passion, Angelo is the one who makes the real sacrifice, because only he really loses in the end. ("*Measure for Measure*: Quid Pro Quo?" *Shakespeare Studies* 4 [1968]: 231–51. Nuttall cites Borges's "Three Versions of Judas" in *Ficciones* [Buenos Aires: Emace, 1962]). René Girard has proposed several such rereadings, which for him represent a switch from content terms to structural terms (Girard, "Lévi-Strauss, Frye, Derrida and Shakespearean Criticism," *Diacritics* 3 [Fall 1973]: 34–38). At least two new interpretations of *Hamlet* stress the audience's—and the characters'— uncertainty about not only the facts of the play but the terms in which to measure these facts: Stephen Booth, "On the Value of *Hamlet*," in *Reinterpretations of Elizabethan Drama*, ed. Norman Rabkin (New York: Columbia University Press, 1969); and Howard Felperin, "O'erdoing the Termagant: *Hamlet*," in *Shakespearean Representation: Mimesis and Modernity in Elizabethan Tragedy* (Princeton, N.J.: Princeton University Press, 1977), pp. 44–67. Janet Adelman has proposed a similar uncertainty as the defining quality of *Antony and Cleopatra* (*The Common Liar: An Essay on* Antony and Cleopatra [New Haven: Yale University Press, 1973]). For suggestions that such rever-

however, that the literary parallel to psychoanalytic observation is most common. Critics have most often studied this kind of reorganization in works whose slowly elaborated and repetitive movement is even more like psychoanalysis than the swiftly streamlined movement in a Shakespearean play: a major field of study has been the highly self-conscious epic tradition, which culminates in Wordsworth's self-analysis in *The Prelude*. The readers' response, which Stanley Fish has described in Milton and Paul Alpers has noted in Spenser,[43] is a movement from a cramped, constrictive view of the world to a more open and inclusive, if more confusing, one—just like the movement from symptom to insight. The symptom, as we have seen, is not a raw eruption of conflict but a rigid, unimaginative way of dealing with conflict by reducing it to a "pseudo-concreteness," such as a paralyzed arm, a horse phobia, or an obsession with clean hands.

At the beginning of his quest, Spenser's Red Cross Knight has a similarly unimaginative idea of holiness, as singly reductive as Frau Cäcilie's idea about human relationships and as closely tied to physical manifestations (such as his armor, for example). He thinks that his enemy is the "dragon" and does not realize that the real enemies in his world are not evils like Unholiness and Intemperance but rather the wrong ideas about holiness and temperance—and the lax attitudes that allow us to slip into them. He—and the reader—must slow down enough in the obsessive pursuit of dragons to be able to redefine the world in other terms. Only then can he escape his partial vision and achieve that wholeness which several critics have associated not only with holiness but with health.[44]

sals are characteristic of all Shakespeare's plays, rather than unique qualities defining the nature of a particular play, see Norman Rabkin, "Meaning and Shakespeare," in *Shakespeare 1971*, ed. Clifford Leech and J. M. R. Margeson (Toronto: University of Toronto Press, 1972), and Albert Cook, *Shakespeare's Enactment: The Dynamics of Renaissance Theater* (Chicago: Swallow Press, 1978).

43. Stanley Fish, *Surprised by Sin: The Reader in Paradise Lost* (New York: St. Martin's Press, 1967); Paul J. Alpers, *The Poetry of* The Faerie Queene (Princeton: Princeton University Press, 1967).

44. Stephen Barney discusses this in his chapters on Spenser in *Allegories of History, Allegories of Love* (Hamden, Conn.: Archon Books, 1979), and

This kind of criticism begins with a bias toward the sensitive but tentative reading necessary in a psychoanalysis. Not surprisingly, the starting point for all later Spenserian critics, William Empson's famous description of the Spenserian stanza, is really a description of the kind of attention needed to read it—the kind of "intense but uncritical" scrutiny Freud prescribed for the analyst's "evenly hovering attention."

> The size, the possible variety, and the fixity of this unit give something of the blankness that comes from fixing your eyes on a bright spot; *you have to yield yourself to it very completely* to take in the variety of its movement, *and, at the same time, there is no need to concentrate the elements of the situation into a judgment as if for action.* . . .
>   [Emphasis added][45]

Paul Alpers elaborates on this description, suggesting that "the condition of Spenser's poetry is an abeyance of the will," which on Spenser's part amounts to a failure to maintain a dramatic identity in relation to his poem.[46] But this is very much like the patient's failure—or, I should say, achievement—in the analytic situation. The failure to maintain a dramatic identity is an escape from the ordinary self that maintains a constant relation to what it sees and says and locates itself firmly in the narrative, whether directly, as opinionated narrator, or indirectly, in the person of a specific character. Whether on Spenser's part or on the reader's part, this "abeyance of the will" is one step further from ordinary reality than the "willing suspension of disbelief" we are familiar with. The

---

Isabel MacCaffrey's general remarks on *The Faerie Queene* in *Spenser's Allegory: The Anatomy of Imagination* (Princeton, N.J.: Princeton University Press, 1976).

45. William Empson, *Seven Types of Ambiguity* (New York: Meridian Books, 1955), p. 41.

46. Alpers, *The Poetry of* The Faerie Queene, pp. 95–106. See also Roger Sale's earlier discussion, "Spenser's Undramatic Poetry," in *Elizabethan Poetry: Modern Essays in Criticism*, ed. Paul J. Alpers (New York: Oxford University Press, 1967), pp. 422–46.

latter requires only that we step into a new world, while the Spenserian—or psychoanalytic—stance requires that we give up the idea of any "world" at all, if by that we mean a physical place (however odd) with characters acting within the structure of a plot.

Both in reading and in the psychoanalytic process, the suspension of critical will opens one to moral and perceptual change—to the kind of change occurring in scientific revolutions and in great works of art, which break old schemata or change the way we see them and the way we see the world. Here, again, the analyst and the traditional critic have in common a search for texts that challenge the schemata and rework convention. In particular, they share a sensitivity to all the ways in which a conventional, naturalistic, literal-minded expectation about meaning is defeated; both have become wary of the "referential fallacy,"[47] and they look to other dimensions of a text besides the seemingly obvious literal meaning to which it refers.

Two of the most characteristic concerns of recent criticism, in fact, might be called the defining concerns of modern psychoanalysis: self-consciousness about artistic conventions and fictional status, and a related tendency to see these conventions as ends in themselves—to "find semantic value in formal qualities."[48] In the first case, the critic points to those moments of self-consciousness when we are reminded that "this is only a play"—moments paralleled in analysis by the analyst's habit of calling attention to the patient's defenses and making him self-conscious about them as defenses or fictions. In those moments we see with the eye of the creator, not the audience; means become ends. We experience what

47. Michael Riffaterre's term.

48. Jonathan Culler, *Structuralist Poetics: Structuralism, Linguistics, and the Study of Literature* (Ithaca, N.Y.: Cornell University Press, 1975), p. 183; see also Frank Kermode on the verbal medium's potential to be both a "virtual transparency" and something "technically exploited," so that it is seen in its own right: "Novels: Recognition and Deception," *Critical Inquiry* 1 (1974): 103–21.

George Klein has called a change in mode of consciousness, as we switch from seeing a three-dimensional world on a canvas to seeing a two-dimensional pattern.[49] The power of this change depends of course not only on the way it makes us reexamine artistic conventions of realism (preventing us from accepting, for example, a bare wooden *O* as King Henry's England) but also on the way it calls into question those more insidiously hidden conventions that define "reality." This is precisely what the analyst does when he makes the patient conscious of the conventions he has begun to take for granted in his own role-playing. ("Of course I can't cry in front of my children," the patient may say—a revelation not only about the conventions he has accepted about playing parent but about the ones he may not know he has accepted to define his own feelings.)

In the second case, the critic calls attention to moments in literature that are even more like the reorganization deriving from the suspended will that characterizes analysis. These moments make us self-conscious about convention not simply by naming it but by switching conventions. Shakespeare may call attention to the wooden *O*, diverting us from the thing represented to the means of representation—not England but the barren, wooden boards of the stage. But Samuel Beckett unsettles us in another way when he switches the rules and makes us see the stage as the barren, wooden world. And in Racine's plays, the unities are not mere shapely containers; they become part of the characters' claustrophobic world. Even Shakespeare evokes this queasiness at times, making the audience uncertain about what is a means of representation and what is an end, about what the audience should see and what it is supposed to see through. *The Tempest* observes the unities but is *about* a playwright trying to observe the unities as he presents a drama that spans oceans and stretches from the dark "backward of time" to the future

49. George S. Klein, "The Several Grades of Memory," in his *Perception, Motives and Personality* (New York: Alfred A. Knopf, 1970), p. 303.

brave new world. And the rude mechanicals in *A Midsummer Night's Dream*, instead of asking that we take the wooden *O*, for a forest, enter a forest for their rehearsal and pretend that *it* is a wooden *O*: "This green plot shall be our stage. . . ." (3.1.3–4).

These switches and their significance are part of what these texts are about, and much of the critical commentary has stressed what we can learn from becoming aware of them: the moral maturity not to be surprised by sin and the perceptual alertness not to be fooled by appearances. But besides instruction there is also delight. Poetry's oldest justifications, it turns out, apply to these switches in mode as well as to its content. The analyst sees in the moment of switching the giggle of insight or the more subtle pleasure and release resulting from cure. And like Aristotle, the critics have found this pleasure too—a delight not only in shapeliness but in a change of shape or a switch from chaos to shape. As Stephen Booth has suggested, in explaining how Shakespeare's play of patterns in the sonnets affects us:

> Perhaps the happiest moment the human mind ever knows is the moment when it senses the presence of order and coherence—and before it realizes the particular nature (and so the particular limits) of the perception. At the moment of unparticularized perception the mind is unlimited. It seems capable of grasping and about to grasp a coherence beyond its capacity.[50]

It is in texts where such self-conscious confrontations become part of the literary work, inseparable from the experience portrayed, that the psychoanalytic process finds its closest parallels. In fact, we can now see why *Oedipus Rex* and *Hamlet* have always been inseparable from conceptions of psychoanalysis. Freud said that this was because of their fantasy content—those secrets that he had just discovered but that the

---

50. Stephen Booth, *An Essay on Shakespeare's Sonnets* (New Haven: Yale University Press, 1969), p. 14.

poets had apparently always known. But Freud had discovered the secrets partly by learning to read stories in new ways, and *Oedipus* and *Hamlet* are bound up with the process of discovery as much as with a presentation of facts about the Oedipus complex. They present the reorganizations necessary to incorporate the oedipal fantasy material in a meaningful world. The plays are based on suddenly shifting representations of experience—shifting relations between past and present, fact and fantasy, literal and figurative significance. As in the case of jokes and the uncanny, Freud stressed the importance of certain strong content in these plays, but their effect depends on the way in which that content is presented—on the kind of reorganization of experience that allowed Freud to see in it the secret wishes he was interested in.

The shifts in *Oedipus* in fact make it almost uncanny. Freud locates the play's power in the fact that two desires normally repressed are here presented openly—the wishes for murder and incest. But for anyone seeing the play, the power comes more immediately from the fact that on the literal level the impossible comes true and on another level something which was merely figurative becomes literal. What began as an oracle's pronouncement—which the critic can view as a mere manner of speaking symbolizing our general guilt—comes true. Any attempt to make sense of the events is even more unsettling, particularly if we have just seen Sophocles' play and not merely heard the myth. The play shows a self-confident, ambitious man ruling a city and solving its problems and, after the revelation about what he has done, desperately trying to punish Jocasta and himself. This man and these actions are what the play is about. Behind them we may possibly sense a symbolic murder and an incestuous rape, but only *as* symbols for the onstage drama. They are no more than a projection backward or a reconstruction from Oedipus's current situation, a useful fiction generated solely to explain what is happening on stage. But suddenly the virtual becomes actual, and it is no longer clear what is symbolizing what. The onstage events become symbols for the earlier offstage trespasses. Analysts look at Oedipus confronting the royal couple, Creon and Jocasta, or they look at him breaking into Jocasta's bedroom, waving his sword and crying out on her womb, and they see symbolic displacements of the offstage murder and incest. At first reading, it seems that Oedipus has merely murdered the idea of his father, as we all do; but the second reading shows that in his world the idea is real.

This seamless world generates a confusion that is unlike the simple one in which the past blends imperceptibly into the present (or fantasy blends into reality), as happens in some readings of fantasy material. This is rather a confusion in which the past sometimes seems as if it *were* the present reality; or rather, in which we cannot tell whether the past or the present has priority or whether the fact or the fantasy is "real." The result is a radical doubt about the world that goes beyond moral queasiness—like Hans Castorp's doubt when his doctor on the magic mountain lectures about "love," but uses

> the word love in a somewhat ambiguous sense, so that you were never quite sure where you were with it, or whether he had reference to its sacred or its passionate and fleshly aspect—and this doubt gave one a slightly seasick feeling. . . .[51]

The uncomfortable reorganization in *Hamlet* works differently but has the same effect of challenging not only our images of ourselves but our ability to perceive and interpret the onstage experience. The play is unsettling on every level; the world of Hamlet is a world of unanswered questions and mystery and has lately been seen as one that upsets the audience with its questions as much as it upsets Hamlet. One critic has called this phenomenon "the tragedy of an audience that cannot make up its mind."[52] We initially see the action the same

51. Thomas Mann, *The Magic Mountain*, trans. H. T. Lowe-Porter (New York: Alfred A. Knopf, 1951), p. 126.
52. See Booth, "On the Value of *Hamlet*."

way Hamlet sees it: he thinks he is a revenge play hero, and is caught in a conflict between what he believes he ought to do—murder Claudius—and his own inability to act.[53] But Hamlet's feeling that "one must kill" is no more adequate to the play's world than was the young men's decision that "one must study" in the world of *Love's Labour's Lost*, and we, along with Hamlet, have to reorganize our conception of Hamlet's problem.

Even more unsettling, the simple events of *Hamlet* are hard to sort out. The content here seems to escape its presentation, almost as Tristram Shandy's subject matter escapes his efforts to set it down. We are accustomed to have the dramatist single out important events and devote time to them on stage; we relax in the expectation that he will allocate the scenes and lines in proportion to their importance and that what matters will take place on stage. But time passes unevenly, and events as important as Hamlet's farewell to Ophelia are almost tossed off as incidental reports, leaving us uncertain how to interpret them. Such confusions we are likely to attribute to our own failures rather than to the play, and so we are likely to ignore them as invalid or irrelevant responses. We feel we must have missed something. Still, such confusions leave a trace of Hans Castorp's seasickness.

Both Hamlet and Oedipus, of course, are dealing with material that is as emotionally explosive as Freud said it was, but their power comes as much from a literary and even a perceptual trespass as from a moral one: they violate our assumptions about what things mean as well as our assumptions about heroic natures. The confusion between latent oedipal fantasy and overt action is only one of several confusions; a play's more general instability is what allows the normally discarded fantasy to claim a place—especially in scenes that seem a little odd anyway, like the scene in which Hamlet speaks daggers to his mother in her closet or the one where Oedipus rushes into Jocasta's bedroom with his sword. But effective as

---

53. Booth, *ibid*., and Felperin, "O'erdoing the Termagant."

this primitive material may be, it is not the sole challenge to our ordinary assumptions; these plays challenge us in *all* the ways that the tactless and suspicious psychoanalytic process does.

LESS MANIFEST PARALLELS

What is the difference, then, between the psychoanalytic process and literature—or between what the analyst sees and what the critic sees? The difference is in degree, not in kind, and amounts finally to a matter of tact. The analyst goes further and takes more risks. Even William Empson, despite his program of flouting tact, finally recognized it under another name: every poem has four thousand meanings, he said, but only the "relevant" ones are effective.[54] He did not feel it necessary to explain what he meant by *relevant*. Although by now there are many critics who challenge the limitations of the term *relevant*, the analyst's chief difference from the critic is that he stretches its limits even further.

The critic is willing to question conventions if the text explicitly encourages such questions; but in the end he usually assumes that the governing conventions in the text and in his reading should coincide. The analyst, however, is more interested in the disjunction between the governing conventions and the ones he alternately entertains. He is always ready to see another meaning or a pattern latent in the whole text, which conflicts with the manifest one and which the literary critic would probably ignore because it is so fragile, peripheral, and unelaborated in the ordinary way. The critic filters out these alternative patterns on the basis of convention or on the basis of something like common sense, informed consensus, or an appeal to competence. The analyst trusts none of these.

The analyst is also more likely than the critic to look for primitive material—not only fantasies but primitive levels of

54. Empson, *Seven Types of Ambiguity*, p. 14.

organization. He is likely to question conventions on a much
more basic level than the critic, suspending his belief not only
in morality and decorum, not only in the obvious meaning of
the plot, not only in conventions of genre, but also in conventions of representation and language. Because he is interested
in the remnants of even the most primitive stages of thought,
when the most basic conventions of thinking and representing experience were being internalized and were not yet
taken for granted, the analyst does not automatically take
them for granted. He looks not only for the neurotic patterns
that may have developed later in life and affected a writer's
sophisticated conventions and habits but also for the more
fundamental patterns that, when they go wrong, make people
psychotic. He examines not just certain private symbols but
the more fundamental conventions of symbolism—the ones
that the tactful critics, of necessity, agree to take as their starting point. No wonder the critics have mistrusted the analyst.
It has taken them a long time to learn not to ask the "wrong"
questions about literature, and they are understandably wary
about anyone who systematically sets out to do so.

Two brief illustrations from the visual arts[55] will serve as
convenient models for the difference between critic and analyst and between the sort of analyses I looked at in the last section and the ones I now present for consideration. The first
is Ernst Gombrich's example of misreading.[56] He describes an
Egyptian battle scene in which the figure of Pharaoh is represented much larger than the other figures, not to depict his
actual size but to show his importance. When the Greeks
copied the picture for their own purposes, however, the re-

---

55. It is interesting that so many critical concepts, models, and terms used
in discussions of nonmimetic literature have been taken from the critical vocabulary for the visual arts, where the distinction between naturalistic representation and other conventions is easier to see (though it is still far from
problematic in itself, as Ernst Gombrich has shown).

56. Ernst Gombrich, "Reflections on the Greek Revolution," in *Art and Illusion: A Study in the Psychology of Pictorial Representation* (Princeton, N.J.:
Princeton University Press, 1960), p. 134.

sult was distorted by their misunderstanding: their version showed a gigantic Hercules at battle with Egyptians shown as pygmies, a literal translation of the Egyptian symbols. The Greeks, Gombrich concludes, misunderstood the picture because they used the wrong conventions to read it (they read visually instead of conceptually), and he implies that we should learn a lesson from their mistake. But his example is a specialized one because its two readings derive from different cultures, only one of which has shaped the text.

Walter J. Ong provides us with a second parallel to the difference between critic and analyst in his study of the title page for Thomas Hobbes's *Leviathan*, which he takes to be a typical product of the new *visual* mode of thinking fostered by the spread of printing.[57] The title page consists of a leviathan man made up of tiny figures squeezed into his outlines. Ong laments the disappearance of conceptual realism here, but surely part of the power in this much reprinted emblem is the way it courts both a conceptual and a visual reading, both an "Egyptian" and a "Greek" reading, and plays them against one another. We may have to ignore the Greek reading to understand the first example, but we will miss the visual pun in the second unless we take the Greek reading into account.

The critic reads texts as if they were Egyptian paintings; the analyst, as if they were all emblems like the Leviathan. The question that must be answered is, How far should the analyst take his assumption? How far can he go in trying out new ways of reading? The answer, of course, is that there is no answer, because the question is not complete. It should be rephrased, How far can the analyst go for this particular purpose? The analyst's bias is to include as many purposes as possible within the central one of finding out what the text really means. He suggests that we open ourselves not only to the quite specialized task of "being objective" but also to the far more common state that comes before objectivity, before

57. Walter J. Ong, "From Allegory to Diagram in the Renaissance Mind: A Study in the Significance of the Allegorical Tableau," *Journal of Aesthetics and Art Criticism* 17 (1959): 425–26.

we perceive the pattern in the text and the coincidence between the text at hand and what we have learned about other
texts. His method makes explicit the progress toward an "objective" reading. It makes explicit all the alternate readings
discarded on the way and shows how any reading is the product of destruction and denial as well as creativity and perception. (This denial is not necessarily defensive; it is simply ne-
cessitated by the rules of this "objective" game.)

So at times the analyst sounds like the stereotypical naive
freshman, who regularly approaches highly conventional literature the way the Greeks approached the Egyptian painting, expecting obvious realism and criticizing Dickens's flat
characters or insincere Elizabethan sonnets. The psychoanalytic critic acts as if he had never heard about literary conventions, so he approaches the text with the ragbag of literal-minded reading habits of childhood. He looks for
naturalistic, literal mimesis where there is none, or he takes
what other readers perceive as conventions and interprets
them as literal facts about the fictional world. Thus Kenneth
Muir takes Shakespeare's heroines for transvestites when they
put on their masculine disguises,[58] and Harold Bloom sees
homosexuality in the relation between Sleeping Beauty
and her mother.[59] And Leo Bersani faults George Eliot's
Middlemarch because the narrator claims to be describing a
haphazard world without design yet does so by arranging
neatly paralleled plots and revealing carefully designed coincidences.[60] Other readers would take Shakespeare's disguises
to be externally motivated conventions, and they would interpret George Eliot's coincidences not as literal representations
of simultaneous action but as conventional symbols that indicate more essential connections between events than those
which are spatial and temporal.

58. Kenneth Muir and Sean O'Loughlin, *The Voyage to Illyria: A New Study
of Shakespeare*, (1937; reprint ed., New York: Barnes and Noble, 1970).

59. Harold Bloom, "Driving out Demons," review of Bruno Bettelheim's
The Uses of Enchantment, New York Review of Books, 15 July 1976, pp. 10–12.

60. Leo Bersani, *A Future for Astyanax: Character and Desire in Fiction* (Boston: Little, Brown, 1976), pp. 63–66.

Although we may with some reason feel that these interpretations distort the text, they are nonetheless true to it in a way. The analyst may sound like a freshman, but we are all naive freshmen, even if only for a moment, if only on first confrontation with a new text, in an initial response which we quickly dismiss. These are not just eccentric responses, either, but predictable ones, errors as traditionally associated with a text as the accepted reading is. The *Aeneid* is cumbersome after reading the *Odyssey*; there is too much coincidence in *Oedipus Rex*; and *Paradise Lost* is boring. Our final response may differ from these first reactions, but that response is partly defined by our original reactions. Even if we choose, as mature professional readers, to respect the customary conventions of the work as they were "intended," custom can be dangerous. It can dull the reader to his work as it dulls Elsinore's merry gravediggers to theirs, making it for them "a property of easiness" to sing as they dig (5.1.65–68). A periodic return to the chaos of possibilities emphasizes new details and fosters an openness to new patterns, tones, and nuances. It revitalizes the reader's perceptions of literature and gives him more to work with, even if he does not finally choose to use everything he finds.

The difference between a freshman's ignorance and the analyst's organized innocence—or "applied naiveté" as Brigid Brophy has called it—is important. It is one thing for Thomas Rymer to blunder past all dramatic conventions to support his famous complaint about how improbable *Othello* is. But Stanley Cavell makes a more sophisticated point when he persists, somewhat perversely, it is true, in asking why the audience does not rush onstage when Othello strangles Desdemona.[61] Cavell blames the audience's unfeeling acceptance of a customary distance between themselves and the action onstage and likens this distance to the similar tragic distances that separate the characters on stage, each of which is maintained by convention as well. Why, for example, Cavell asks,

---

61. Stanley Cavell, "The Avoidance of Love: A Reading of *King Lear*," in *Must We Mean What We Say?* pp. 267–356.

does Edgar wait so long in *Lear* to reveal his true identity to his father? By the time he tells old Gloucester who he really is, it is too late, and the old man's heart cracks with the shock. For Cavell, this is an example of people's fear of confronting one another; for other critics, it is a matter of synchronizing plots or of making the physical revelation correspond to the more reluctant spiritual one it symbolizes. Cavell, in other words, has taken what other critics see as dramatic and symbolic conventions and has interpreted them as facts about a character's mind. We may object to his refusal to play the dramatic game; but in *Hamlet*, as we saw, this refusal is what the play is about. Hamlet's whole problem is that he cannot accept certain behavioral conventions; and by the end of Shakespeare's play, we have learned not to accept them either. The question that was "wrong" to ask in *Othello* is the one question we must ask in *Hamlet*.

Using the psychoanalytic process as a model for literary texts does not imply that all conventions, all literal meanings, or all ordinary functions in a text are there only to be questioned. But it does provide a reminder that the questions are always there and that the uncertainty they produce is part of what the text conveys, even if this uncertainty is slight and finally resolved. Texts are more unstable than we might think; they are less fixed than simpler models that merely look for "hidden" material might indicate.

I began this discussion of the psychoanalytic process as literary model by analyzing a joke. Even in that flimsy story about the desperate executive who fell for the old hag's bed trick, it was clear that we had to do more than identify some hidden material before we understood the joke; and we had to use more than one model. Of course, psychoanalyzing the joke's two characters would not work: but neither would any of the more sophisticated models, when taken by themselves. It was not enough to look only at the content or only at the latent fantasy and its psychic function; these had to be seen in the context of the joke's switch in representational and rhetorical strategies, which led to something like a moment of insight and reorganization. I will end this discussion by looking at a much more interesting text, which also happens to be about a bed trick but which is important here primarily because it has proved—partly because of the flimsy dirty-joke device—to be problematic for most critics. I will suggest how psychoanalysis can serve as a way to approach problematic texts like the one at hand, provided that we use *all* the resources of the psychoanalytic process—with its attention to the different aspects of the text; its distrust of literal reference; its lack of tact and its openness to counterintuitive meanings; and its self-consciousness about the process of interpretation. The text referred to is Shakespeare's *Measure for Measure*, a play that has caused more interpretative problems than almost any other.

Measure for Measure is a play about finding—or restoring—lawful order. It gains unexpected complexity as we go on, but a bare statement of the plot does not immediately reveal its problems, just as the patient's first presentation of his case history can conceal neurotic conflicts at work behind the rationalized surface of his life. *Measure* begins with the problem of reestablishing justice in Vienna, where lenient Duke Vincentio has allowed the law to become "more mock'd than fear'd" (1.3.27). The Duke opens the action by ostentatiously retiring and leaving righteous Angelo in his place, to reform the state. Secretly, however, the Duke stays behind disguised as a friar, watching the action, ready to interfere if necessary, to make sure everything goes right. He does not have to wait long: Angelo, in his zeal, not only tries to clean out the Viennese stews but also invokes the old death penalty for premarital sex in the case of Claudio, who has gotten his fiancée pregnant.

Things get even more complicated when Claudio's sister Isabella comes from her convent (she is just about to take her vows) to beg Angelo for mercy; and for the first time in his chaste life that man of ice catches fire and lets his blood govern his reason: he offers to free her brother if she will spend the night with him. This capitulation brings out the worst in everyone: Angelo's own progress into hypocrisy and crime; Isabella's self-righteous elevation of chastity over charity; Claudio's irresponsibility and cowardice. It is at this point that the Duke intercedes to provide Isabella with a substitute (Angelo's own deserted fiancée) for her part of the bargain and then to provide a substitute victim when Angelo breaks his promise and orders Claudio beheaded anyway. Without fully explaining his designs to the characters, the Duke allows each one to continue in his deceptions and self-deceptions and to expose the worst in himself until the final climactic public trial, where he confronts everyone with everything, removes the illusions, extracts Angelo's confession, and brings on the happy ending.

The problem is that the play just does not work. The action is stiff, the characters unpleasant, and the ending contrived. No one believes Angelo's reformation or is content with the Duke's last-minute proposal of marriage to Isabella, who does not even reply. Is this arbitrary device the only way to a happy ending? The play has resisted a sequence of increasingly sophisticated critical approaches to the problem. What I want to suggest is that it invites as well as resists these partial interpretations and that it has thereby encouraged its audience to work through a series of organizations, disorganizations, and reorganizations like the ones in the psychoanalytic process. The working through is difficult, unsettling, even distasteful, just as it is in psychoanalysis.

It may be easy enough for modern audiences to pass beyond the first stage of this series, which is where the first critics stopped. Nearly all the early commentators agreed that this play was *supposed* to be a sort of moral lesson, and then, depending on whether or not they noticed how seriously Shakespeare undermined the moral clichés, they blamed or praised his morality. Many were offended, for example, by Isabella's priggish goodness and blamed Shakespeare for failure to create the right kind of heroine; but Thomas Bowdler was so seduced by her piety that he saw nothing wrong with her at all and would have included the play in his *Family*

Shakespeare if he had not had so much trouble cutting out the "indecencies."

But the next stages of the series which have been offered by modern critics themselves, are somewhat more compelling and harder to work through and beyond. These more recent organizations of the play all begin with the assumption that Shakespeare intended the contradictions, and they go on to try to make sense of them. The commonest critical strategy has been to save the action by seeing it as a vehicle for ideas. This is the strategy behind an older kind of psychoanalysis that sees a psychomachia in *Measure*. Shakespeare has given us what seems to be a Viennese psychoanalyst three hundred years before Freud, conducting his own self-analysis. The Duke steps back from active life to the position of a disinterested "observing ego" and presides over the working out of the psyche's battle between Angelo (who represents the sadistic superego) and the crowd surrounding the clown Pompey Bum in the brothel (who represent the id).

This is also the strategy behind the extraordinary number of allegorical readings, humanist and Christian, which have saved the play for critics who find the action "stiffened by its doctrinaire and impersonal consideration of ethical values."[62] Sometimes the play is read as what Dante would have called a moral allegory: from the beginning, critics have seen it as a "parable" (G. Wilson Knight) of the triumph of mercy over

62. M. C. Bradbrook, "Authority, Truth, and Justice in *Measure for Measure*," *Review of English Studies* 17 (1941): 385–99. G. Wilson Knight's "*Measure for Measure* and the Gospels," in *The Wheel of Fire* (London: Methuen, 1930) is the most well known and frequently answered of the Christian allegories, but there are many others, e.g., Hermann Ulrichi (he called the play "a divine comedy") in *Shakespeare's Dramatic Art* (London: G. Bell and Sons, 1896–1904); C. J. Sisson ("The Mythical Sorrows of Shakespeare," in British Academy, London, *Proceedings*, 1934 [London 1936]); R. W. Chambers ("The Jacobean Shakespeare and *Measure for Measure*" [1937], in *Man's Unconquerable Mind* [London: Jonathan Cape, 1939]). See also the debate between L. C. Knights and F. H. Leavis (1942), well summarized by Rosalind Miles in *The Problem of* Measure for Measure: *A Historical Investigation* (New York: Barnes and Noble, 1976), pp. 60–63.

strict justice (A. W. Schlegel). Sometimes it is read as an "analogical" allegory: the marriage of Isabella and the Duke, for example, becomes the "union of Divine Mercy and Divine Righteousness" (R. W. Chambers).[63] In both cases the argument is that the Duke's actions may seem unnatural if we think of him as a real person, but once we see him as Divine Providence everything makes sense. The characters are ciphers in a formula that really applies to absolutes like "appetite" and "justice," so of course their actions seem unnatural.

But this translation of complex action into simple ideas falls into the same error that the characters make when they formulate the problem in simple terms of liberty and restraint: "whence comes this restraint?" Lucio asks when he sees Claudio being carried off to jail. "From too much liberty, my Lucio, liberty" (1.2.124–25), says the boy gravely—and makes the process sound as automatic and trivial as Freud's energy calculus. Even the Duke's theatrical couplets about tempering justice make an unsatisfactory moral chorus. No easy allegorical formulation is true to the bad taste such lessons leave, or to the "jaggedness"[64] of the action that is smoothed over by such conclusions. There are better ways to make a case for Divine Providence. Criticism at this stage has reached the point of an intellectualized interpretation of the symptom; the psychoanalytic process requires that we work through such premature formulations of the problem, and so does the play.

The real problem in *Measure for Measure* is not so easily formulated, nor is it ever summarized in neat statements by the characters, who always seem to be thinking about the wrong problems. It is not defined by the explicit question posed at the beginning of the play, "How do we make people obey the laws?" Nor is it explained even by the more subtle question we

63. G. Wilson Knight, *The Wheel of Fire: Interpretations of Shakespearean Tragedy* (New York: Barnes and Noble, 1966); A. W. Schlegel, *A Course of Lectures on Dramatic Art and Literature* (1815); Chambers, "The Jacobean Shakespeare and *Measure for Measure*."

64. See A.D. Nuttall's provocative argument in "Quid Pro Quo," cited in note 42, where he uses this term.

are left with at the end of the play: "How can we make sure the laws are administered with mercy?" It is a deeper question about the very nature of law itself—and about the nature of mercy. The real problem in the play has to do with the whole larger human and social context in which such things as laws exist, and it is when the characters ignore this context, rather than when they merely indulge their appetites, that they most need correction. Finally, the problem extends to the nature of the consciousness that creates and perceives these contexts and to the uncertainties and ambivalences which pervade them, once we are open to all the modes of consciousness at work. Part of the play's meaning is the way we must change the terms in which we understand the action and the way we have to question the validity of all terms. In the following sections, I shall trace several stages of working through increasingly more comprehensive and appropriate organizations for the action of the play. Although only the final stages bring up specifically "psychoanalytic" material (infantile and sexual images, structures, and language), the parallel of the literary work to psychoanalysis begins with the whole process of working through to these stages.

The first trouble with the original set of terms is clearest in the all too neatly balanced contrasts at the center of the plot. At first the contrast between upright Angelo and the lowlife in the stews seems to represent the simple opposition between law and appetite. But Angleo's lawfulness is somewhat odd. He enforces the laws not only without feeling (he has never been tempted himself and has no sympathy with sinners) but also without thought. The law for him is an absolute, abstract entity. "It is the law, not I, condemn your brother," he says (2.2.80), really believing that he can separate the law from the human context in which it is applied. He never thinks about the ultimate source and end of laws nor about their effect. Angelo admits that the law may miss some criminals guiltier than the ones caught, but he says that he cannot catch everyone and is satisfied to make do with what he can get. Such morality ends up all too much like the bawd's immorality.

Angelo's sole concern is with catching sinners and Pompey's is with not being caught. Neither thinks of the law as anything but an end in itself, and neither concerns himself with the ultimate values the law is supposed to serve. (Angelo was certainly lax enough in fulfilling his bonds just outside the law when he deserted his fiancée.) Pompey has no values, and Angelo has confused means with ends in whatever values he has.

The same dichotomy between thoughtless obedience and thoughtless disobedience characterizes the brother and sister at the center of the play, those mirror images of one another whose education, along with Angelo's, the action fosters. Isabella's first words are a request for a "more strict restraint" (1.4.4) in the convent she is about to enter, and her absolute dedication to its rules is like Angelo's devotion to his—firm in the letter and altogether uninspired in spirit. Here too the "opposites" meet, for Isabella's sense of duty looks much like Claudio's irresponsibility and self-centeredness. She has to be coaxed into arguing for her brother's life; indifferent to her own physical and emotional existence, she is indifferent to other people's too. Isabella seems oblivious to her brother's suffering and has no sympathy with his very human fears about dying. True, his hope that she will sacrifice her vows to keep him alive is spineless selfishness, but Isabella responds with selfishness of her own. Hers is no ordinary selfishness; her claim that "more than our brother is our chastity" (2.4.185) (and incidentally, more than Mariana's chastity, for she cheerfully leads Mariana to the fate she refused for herself) is based on what she takes to be a holy self-denial. But hers is the selfishness of selflessness: she holds herself back not only from others but from her own fulfillment as well. Like Angelo, she invokes the golden rule, but only in its negative form: she advocates punishing herself as strictly as she punishes her neighbor. How different from Claudio's far more attractively human fiancée, Juliet, who says she loves Claudio as she "love[s] the woman that wrong'd him" (2.3.25)—in other words, as she loves herself.

Isabella avoids the difficulty of puzzling out a paradoxical world by taking up a ready-made law and using its rigors to shape her life; her brother Claudio is guilty of an opposite shallowness. He avoids the same difficulty, but he does it by affably evading the law when it stands in his way, never considering whether laws represent anything but civil agreements. Claudio's crime is his attempt to have things both ways, by postponing his wedding in hopes of a better dowry but refusing to postpone the consummation that lawfully goes with it. For him the wedding is just something society imposes on him, not a ceremony whose significance he recognizes. He seems to have no inner sense of morality, no belief or resolution beyond the pressures of the moment. He is indeed moved by the Duke's sermon about facing death, but the moment he sees a way out of his sentence after all, he forgets the Duke's lesson, and the question of how to die dissolves before the question of whether he can evade the law and live. When he hears about Angelo's disgraceful proposition to his sister, his first response is to say, in effect, "If Angelo can do it, why is it a crime for me?" When the Duke tells Claudio to "be absolute for death" (3.1.5), he finds it as hard to accept being absolute as to accept dying.

It is clear that an obsession with law and appetite distracts from the real problems at hand. The real sin in Vienna is not indulgence of appetite but the detachment from all human feeling which such liberty may lead to—a detachment, however, that can come from too much restraint as well as from too much liberty. Questions of law distract from questions about how well people know themselves and each other, and how well they treat themselves and each other. The real sin is a refusal to participate in human exchange—a failure to recognize what other people are saying and feeling, and also a failure to recognize one's own active role and to take responsibility for one's actions. The real sin, in fact, is economic, not sexual: it is either a holding back—whether represented by Angelo's cold righteousness, Isabella's religion, the neurotic distrust of sexuality[65] that has been hinted at in both charac-

---

65. Hanns Sachs and William Empson, among others, have accused

ters, or even simple modesty like Mariana's—or else the opposite, a sexual exchange that occurs only in a dehumanized
way.[66] What most angers the Duke about Pompey is not his
sexual indulgence but his entrepreneurial *use* of sex detached
from its proper human context. "The evil that thou causest to
be done," the Duke tells the bawd, "That is thy means to live"
(3.2.20–21). Claudio too has detached the sexual act from
the larger social context, where alone it can have its full significance, when he meets Juliet in illegal, hidden "stealth."
He goes on to a more serious kind of detachment when,
begging Isabella to give up her chastity to save his life, he tries
"to take life / From [his] own sister's shame" (3.1.138–39)—a
barter worthy of Pompey himself. Angelo too has dehuman-

Angelo of enjoying a sadistic substitute for the impulses he denies. His
justification for his position is indeed perverse: for example, when Escalus
urges leniency for Claudio because so many others, unknown and unpun-
ished, have committed the same sin, Angelo answers, "The jewel that we
find, we stoop and take 't," (2.1.24). We simply "tread upon" the rest
(2.1.26). This reverses all values by presenting crimes as jewels. For Angelo,
fornication is no better than murder: as well to take a man's life, he says, as to
coin one illegally. Isabella too has made several critics suspect her "rancid
chastity" (Quiller-Couch's phrase, in *Measure for Measure*, ed. A. Quiller-
Couch and J. Dover Wilson, The New Cambridge Shakespeare [Cambridge:
Cambridge University Press, 1922], p. xxx). She shows a suspicious relish for
those whippings; she would "stripe" (or "strip": the meaning is not clear) for,
"as to a bed / That longing have been sick for" (2.4.102–03). In fact, their
markings are *her* jewels: rather than lose her honor, she says, she'd wear their
impression "as rubies" (2.4.101).
    66. Sexual and financial exchanges have always been associated, but this
play emphasizes the connection between "the two usuries" and is in one sense
about the transformation of people into tokens of themselves: "Counter-
feitings and substitutions are the center of action as well as the meaning of
the play" (Robert Ornstein, "The Human Comedy: *Measure for Measure*,"
University of Kansas City Review 24 [1957]: 15–22); "the play is about vicarious
experience" (A. D. Nuttall, "Quid Pro Quo," p. 232). See Marc Shell's study
of economy in literary theory ("The Golden Fleece and the Voice of the Shut-
tle," *Georgia Review* 30 [1976]: 406–29), which explores the relation between
economic and biological creation in *Oedipus Rex*, noting that the Greek *tokos*
means both *interest* and *offspring*. And for a more specifically Shakespearean
study, see E. Pearlman's "Shakespeare, Freud, and the Two Usuries," *English
Literary Renaissance* 2 (1972): 217–36.

ized the sexual exchange: in Mariana's case, no money means no sex (he deserted her when her dowry fell through); and with Isabella he barters sex for her brother's life.

Enter the Duke, like an old-style omniscient psychoanalyst. In one sense, his operations, which counter the other characters' errors, are perfectly satisfactory, even therapeutic, because they force each character to come to terms with his major weakness and not just his offenses against the laws about appetite. Angelo is made to see the power of his own appetite and the limits of law and has to confront the effects of his own actions; Claudio too has to confront responsibility when he thinks he is going to die; and Isabella must participate—at least symbolically—in the sexuality she initially scorned, and later she must publicly admit it. Out of all this somehow comes forgiveness and a happy ending. And indeed, superficially, the Duke seems to be the ideal author of these changes, for he is presented as everything the other characters are not. He is the political and (in disguise) the spiritual authority and brings all the qualities of "a scholar, a statesman, and a soldier" (3.2.237) in a world of extremists, a man "of complete bosom" (1.33) who has "contended especially to know himself" (3.2.232–33) and prides himself on his "skill" in knowing others.

But in another sense the Duke's way of working things out is one of the most problematic parts of the play. The play forces us to notice something odd about itself, if only because the action turns stiff and ritualisitc once the Duke begins his manipulations. For the first three acts, the characters engage in fast-moving, psychologically plausible and realistic exchanges. Suddenly, instead of psychological development we see only ducal machinations, hugger-mugger operations which the provost thinks illegal and critics have found shabby; the Duke treats "his subjects as puppets for the fun of making them twitch."[67] The latter part of the play contains

---

67. William Empson, " 'Sense' in *Measure for Measure*" (1938), in *The Structure of Complex Words* (Ann Arbor: University of Michigan Press, 1967). Mark

conversations that seem to result more from the manipulation of bodies (by both the Duke and Shakespeare) than from any real changes in character.

Neither the Duke's apologists nor his critics, however, have worried about the curious resemblance between his behavior and that of his subjects. The Duke repeats his subjects' crimes, though on another level of action. If there is anyone to blame in this world, it is not a criminal or two, or a few uniquely neurotic citizens, but the therapeutic Duke himself. The very attempt to cure in this way—or to judge, to come to terms with absolutes—is problematic; and the Duke's manipulations are unsatisfactory because they only repeat on an ontological level the ambivalence and ambiguity we saw on the psychological level in his subjects. In other Shakespearean plays where mere human rationality is inadequate to explain the tangled situation on stage, there is often an aura of more-than-human power in the forces that resolve the action. Here it is that power itself which is questioned. Shakespeare invites us to appeal to an absolute authority by embodying it in the Duke; but then he disappoints us. For all that the Duke may seem to be Horatio and Hamlet in one, and the image of authority, he is hardly a model for coping with absolutes like *justice*, or even *death*. His original fault as governor in retreat was not leniency but irresolution. He was ineffective in the case of Barnardine, who was held nine years in prison and is neither freed, nor executed, nor even tried until Angelo takes over. The Duke then moves from paralysis to active manipulation, but again he resorts to compromises and indirections. He reduces the characters to tokens in a private game of chess, which they do not understand or even know exists. The man who told Angelo not to hide his light under a bushel has become the "Duke of dark corners" (4.3.157), dealing in duplici-

Van Doren called the Duke "sluggish in the manipulation of dummies whose predicament he had wantonly created. Our wonderment will only cease when we realize that he is a tall, dark dummy too" (*Shakespeare* [New York: Holt, 1939], p. 218).

ties and arranging for dubious sexual encounters. Even his theology is shaky; he preaches a kind of resignation to Claudio that may frighten the boy but is, as Samuel Johnson saw, not very Christian. He tortures Isabella, letting her think her brother is dead, solely—he says— to "make her heavenly comforts of despair / When it is least expected" (4.3.110–11).

All this high-handedness is perhaps explainable—and has been explained—as the need for indirection to teach people lessons. But there is no way to deny that if the Duke is teaching people like Angelo that the means can't be reduced to the ends, as M. C. Bradbrook explains, then it is odd indeed that he must resort to what Bradbrook herself elsewhere describes as "ruthlessly efficient means."[68] In the Duke's operation not only are means subordinate to ends but structure is more important than the individual, and the symbolic significance of events is more important than their immediate literal impact on the characters (or on us). Once the Duke takes over, people and actions lose their inherent significance and are reduced to parts of his design.

If the raw morality of an eye for an eye, or "measure for measure," is the inhumane law which must be modified, then the pragmatic substitution of a head for a head or a maidenhead for a maidenhead would seem to be equally suspect. "An Angelo for Claudio" (5.1.409) is wrong, but what about a Barnardine for a Claudio?—or a Mariana for an Isabella? The Duke's neat bed-trick and head-tricks take us back to Pompey's economics of "buy[ing] and sell[ing] men and women like beasts" (3.2.2), reducing them to commodities, except of course the Duke would claim that it is not the bad but the good he causes to be done that is his means to live (see 3.2.20–21). (Escalus indeed tells us that the Duke lives this way and would rather see another merry than be merry himself.) The Duke even offers Angelo's money to Mariana at the end; he orders Angelo's death, comforting her, however ironically, with the thought that she can buy herself another hus-

68. See M.C. Bradbrook, "Authority, Truth and Justice," pp. 388 and 387.

band. This is the same parody of true human exchange that
caused problems in the first place. Not only sexual but all human relations threaten to become like the coins that provide
so much of the submerged imagery of the play. The Duke
had warned Angelo that, paradoxically, virtue disappears
when we take it out of circulation and keep it to ourselves;
now we see that it also disappears when it is reduced solely to
its role in circulating, as the Duke's virtue is.

Worse still, all inherent meaning and value disappear. In
the Duke's world, the act of sleeping with a finacée is in
Claudio's case a crime punishable by death and in Angelo's
case a lawful punishment. Even more paradoxically, Angelo's
criminal offer to sleep with Isabella, in exchange for her
brother's life, is matched by the Duke's last words offering to
marry Isabella after he has "restored" her brother to life: the
crime turns into the happiest ending of all.

Nor do the Duke's own explanations for all of this help. In
fact, his original motives are not at all clear. Why *does* he leave
Angelo to do his dirty work? If he wants to clean up Vienna,
as he says, then why put the unreliable Angelo in charge? Perhaps he really only wants to test Angelo; but he cannot logically mean to do both. And as the action progresses, the Duke's
offhand justifications emphasize, even in their wording, the
slippery duplicity that he is making use of. "The doubleness
of the benefit defends the deceit from reproof" (3.1.257–58),
he explains as he substitutes one virgin for another in
Angelo's illicit bed. Or, again, "the justice of your title to
him / Doth flourish the deceit" (4.1.73–74). Say them after
what flourish you will, these words double back on themselves with their *de-*'s and *re-*'s and half-undo what the Duke has
done. Sending Mariana to that problematic bed, he reassures
her that he respects her (4.1.52); but this is a world in which
words have been made wanton: Constable Elbow has by this
point malapropped his way through a series of indignant de-
nials that his wife is a "respected" woman and that he ever respected her before they were married (2.1.162–79). Though
the commonsense reader would have us pass over such pe-

ripheral implications, they "stick," as the character Lucio does, like burrs (4.3.179).

The mere presence of Lucio is in fact one of the stickier problems in the play and generates further doubts about the Duke's integrity. Lucio's role has always seemed odd and gratuitous to critics: there is no parallel to this vulgar busybody in the sources. He is neither part of the Angelo / Claudio plot nor merely a comic parallel.[69] He is less an example of appetite than of a meddling vice. Lucio's liberty does not resemble Claudio's so much as it resembles godlike liberty that the Duke exercises by shuffling people around. Angelo is the Duke's literal deputy, facing the problems the Duke had to face as governor; and Claudio and Isabella can be seen as symbolic deputies facing the same problems the Duke had to face as a human being emerging from immature privacy to the public world. Lucio is the Duke's deputy as manipulator, and in him we see the problems the Duke is only beginning to face. He lies easily and carries out his own manipulations—much to our approval in the first act, when he brings Isabella to Angelo, but less attractively later on, when he arranges an educational arrest of his own by informing on Pompey and then pompously lecturing him about sin. Like the Duke doubling back and forth, Lucio slanders the Duke to the Friar and then slanders the Friar to the Duke; and the parody darkens when he turns on Isabella in order to save his own skin.

If Lucio is seen as the Duke's alter ego, the Duke's excessive anger with him makes more sense, and we can see why Lucio is the last to be forgiven and is given the worst punishment of all. Lucio's ostensible crime is slandering the Duke, which he does with delightful fertility. Though the Duke ought to be above noticing such a crime, it irritates him and provokes one of his two officious soliloquies in the middle of the play (the

69. Lucio is, however, a libertine who has overspent himself both sexually and financially, so that he is now running from creditors in both realms.

other lambasts the opposite form of lying, Angelo's hypocritical pretense of goodness).

To give the Duke credit here, he is in part responding to the act of slander itself, to that blatant bestiality which divides people even as it multiplies "truths," and not to the personal content of Lucio's defamation.[70] Still, Lucio touches a sore spot; one of the reasons the Duke had given for retiring in the first place was the hope that Angelo

> . . . may, in th' ambush of my name, strike home,
> And yet my nature never in the fight
> To do in slander . . .
>
> [1.3.41–43]

In the face of such evidence, we begin to suspect the Duke of either moral stupidity or Machiavellian guile.

The failure of the Duke represents the failure of all authority in the play, official and unofficial. The characters are forced to question both the old laws ("Condemn'd upon the act of fornication / To lose his head" [5.1.70–71]) and old saws ("too much liberty, my Lucio, liberty" [1.2.125]). The whole point of the play is that such things alone cannot ensure the end they are supposed to achieve. Not only do the laws of God conflict with written and unwritten human law ("More than our brother is our chastity" [2.4.185]), but human law itself is a paradoxical business. The Duke is wise enough to know that reestablishing justice means not only getting rid of lawbreakers but also purifying law enforcers:

> He who the sword of heaven will bear
> Should be as holy as severe;
> Pattern in himself to know,
> Grace to stand, and virtue go. . . .
>
> [3.2.261–64]

---

70. Slander here poses the same threat that flattery posed for Richard II and for Julius Caesar (another ruler who tried to separate "name" from "nature"); rumor poses a similar threat in Henry IV's many-tongued world. Lucio is this world's Lucifer—the *diabolos*, or, literally translated from the Greek, the "slanderer." Shakespeare's devils often take the form of Satan the Accuser.

In other words, judge people only if you are perfect yourself. What he does not see is that even this will not be enough. The problem is not with the abuse of justice but with contradictions in the nature of unabused justice and law. Even Angelo gets as far as the Duke's philosophy, but, as he discovers, few of us are "as holy as severe." What then? Judge not lest ye be judged? Shall there be, as the bawd Pompey advises, no judgment at all? And what about the laws themselves, even if administered by perfect judges, if lawful enforcement in one case is a crime in another case? A tricky question.

Nor is it an answer, really, that the Duke teaches "mercy." Mercy is "a bawd" in some cases, as Isabella says when her brother asks for it. It may *seem* as if, even though the absolute power and authority of the Duke fails, there is still the "absolute" love of a Mariana or an Isabella—a mercy beyond all understanding, a power that cuts across all petty categories of justice, an unconditional love that is the only meaning in this shifting world (Sigurd Burckhardt, for example, has suggested something similar when he claims that it is not a feeling but that the absolute *meaning* of the word *love* which is the subject of Shakespeare's sonnet 116: "Love is not love / Which alters when it alteration finds").[71] But I would disagree. Neither "love" nor "mercy" in this play is a mysterious, self-contained, abstract gesture, descending godlike from a position above the rest of the action. When Mariana and Isabella intervene to save Angelo, after the Duke has insisted on justice and condemned him to lose his head, they are being splendidly generous but also healthily selfish. Begging for Angelo's life is, on Mariana's part, an admission—at last—of her own stubborn desire ("I crave no other, nor no better man" [5.1.426]) and, on Isabella's part, an admission of her own role in Angelo's crime—so much so that Johnson called her action mere vanity. This is apparent in Isabella's plea: "I partly think / A due sincerity governed his deeds / 'Til he did look on *me*. Since it is so, / Let him not die" (5.1.445–48; emphasis added).

71. Sigurd Burckhardt, "The Poet as Fool and Priest: A Discourse on Method," in *Shakespearean Meanings* (Princeton, N.J.: Princeton University Press, 1968), pp. 22–46.

Besides, the quality of mercy in this play is very strained indeed. Angelo has been despicable and only gets worse in the final scene of confrontation; we do not *want* Mariana to forgive him. If this is mercy, then mercy is something more—or less—than we had thought. In *The Merchant of Venice*, Portia's speech on the quality of mercy comes at the climax of the action; it presents a truth wrestled from earlier conflicts and is isolated by its poetic authority. In *Measure for Measure*, Isabella, much as she has to learn, already knows enough to give a pretty speech about mercy at the very beginning of the play (she soon retracts it, however, and agrees that it was "slander" against the law, when Angelo's legalism equates mercy with the "foul redemption" [2.4.115] she can offer her brother). *Measure* begins where *Merchant* leaves off: it questions the answers given there and asks us to remeasure those earlier measures taken to ensure a happy ending.

The contradictions in the law make us question Vienna's orderly, rational legal and moral conventions. There is, however, an even more fundamental paradox in Vienna—not a moral but an epistemological one. Just as the Duke thinks to establish law by eliminating its abusers, he thinks to guarantee truth by eliminating liars and slanderers like Lucio. But slander is inevitable in his attempt to bring out the truth. He initially tries to avoid it by letting Angelo act in his name while keeping his own nature out of slander's way. But once he separates name and nature—for however holy a cause—the way is open for all slander. The Duke himself coaches Isabella to "slander" Angelo as part of his grand plan. Of course we might object that he uses false slander instead of true (or "true" instead of "false"? "Falsely" false instead of "truly" false?), but a single lie in the service of truth taints all truths; and by this point we are all a little tired of such distinctions.

The Duke's attempt to reestablish the absolute authority of truth and justice has left us, then, with a license far more threatening than the original sexual license, for it takes away *all* absolutes. The problems in the Duke's world are not incidental—illegal fornication and slander—but essential, inherent in the world itself. The play explores the paradoxes by which our best and most exalted acts can become—with only the slightest change in perspective—our lowest, whether by Lucio's slander or in fact. Nor does it encourage us to exult in the vitality of such a paradox, as we do in the oxymoronic world of *Romeo and Juliet*, where such contradictions strike lightning from Verona's stony walls. In Vienna there is no energizing dichotomy, only a chilling stalemate, an enervating paralysis that makes people withdraw into their private convents, jails, and granges.

There is one final realm in which the Duke mistakes an essential ambiguity for an accidental abuse. Behind the play's world of radical relativity, where best turns to worst and people lose their identities, is a similarly ambiguous vision of sexuality. This vision makes concrete the terrors of ambivalence and shows that the sheer physical acts which laws attempt to curb are no more absolute than the laws themselves. It would appear that the sexual act is the one act in which there can be no confusion, no deception. Sex is the referred of all referents, the source of all metaphor (as indicated by "groping for trouts," "a game of tick-tack," and all the other allusions in this play). It is the truth behind all fantasies, the core that can be symbolized or displaced or sublimated (as Angelo's taboo desire is "sublimated" into civil marriage to Mariana). Elsewhere in Shakespeare, sex is usually all of this, for even though desire is not to be trusted in courtship, when the disguised and fickle lovers dance in and out of their triangles, there is almost always a moment of truth afterward. The deceptions in the forest are clarified by the conception in bed, when the heroine takes off her mask and the lovers get down to "the thing itself."

In *Measure*, however, it is in this ultimate act of self-realization and unmediated desire, the act where one's identity and the identity of the other matter most, that identity dissolves entirely. At the heart of this play—within the mysterious doubly enclosed garden-within-vineyard that Angelo specifies—is an act of sex that is nothing but deception.

Angelo sells his soul for a forbidden encounter, which turns out to be a wedding night with his scorned fiancée; the worst of it is, he cannot tell the difference. As Mariana says, "[He] thinks he knows that he n'er knew my body, / But knows, he thinks that he knows Isabel's" (5.1.203–04). And he knows himself as little as he knows her. "O, death's a great disguiser" (4.2.174), the Duke had said when he substituted one severed head for another. So is sexual intercourse.

Even more important, there is a latent fantasy beneath the surface of the play, which combines these two "disguisers" in a sexual ambiguity as terrifying as the loss of identity—though the Duke dissociates himself from it. He focuses his attention—and his anger—on the verbal slippage in his world, on Lucio's slander. But there are connections between the man who laments, "What king so strong / Can tie the gall up in the slanderous tongue?" (3.2.187–88) and the one who leaves Angelo to tie up the "rebellion of a codpiece" (3.2.115). The Duke was "one that, above all other strifes, contended especially to know himself." Such absolute self-knowledge, however, comes only after passing through the mysterious displacements Angelo undergoes, and after passing through the violence he encounters.

For in the latent fantasy, the two acts of violence that Angelo initiates (at least symbolically) are the same act. The sister is raped, while the brother is beheaded, and the rich, attractive, playful ambiguities inherent in the Elizabethan pun on "dying" are reduced to a bloody, concrete image. "Why, what a ruthless thing is this in him, for the rebellion of a codpiece to take away the life of a man!" (3.2.114–16) Lucio complains. Ruthless but still common in Shakespeare's other plays, where sex and death often furnish forth the same tables, as in *Romeo and Juliet,* where the wedding night ushers in the morning on which Tybalt is killed and Romeo's fate is sealed. (The student whose wit or ignorance led him to give Mercutio's sarcastic dying words to Romeo on his wedding morning—" 'tis not so deep as a well, nor so wide as a church-door, but 'twill do, 'twill serve"—may have been responding to the latent resonance of bloodshed with bloodshed in that play. There, however, death threatened *both* lovers; here Juliet escapes.) What distinguishes this fantasy from the more general Elizabethan equation is that it threatens only the male characters with death; and nearly all males in *Measure* are thus threatened. The women risk losing only their honor (though this may be a soul-death for Isabella, it is not quite the same as physical death). For the man, sex is always a trap. It puts Claudio in prison and endangers his head, and Angelo seals his fate even as he embraces Isabella and thereby gives Mariana the means to marry—and behead—him. This is the brutal measure for measure that the woman always threatens to extract: a head for a maidenhead. The equation lurks not only in the dramatic pun in the siblings' fates[72] but also in Pompey's double role as bawd and hangman—he leads people first to bed and then to the block—and in verbal puns like Lucio's curiously condensed metaphor for Claudio's situation: ". . . thy head stands so tickle on thy shoulders that a milkmaid, if she be in love, may sigh it off" (1.2.176–78). It is the milkmaid whose "head" is usually thought to be in danger, but Lucio's reversal better captures the sense of the fantasy.[73]

Bloody associations are present already in the complex of biblical passages surrounding the two most important allusions in the play: the "measure for measure" passage ("Judge

72. Charles Frey has proposed a most suggestive (though somewhat different) exploration of this pun in "Shakespearean Interpretation: Promising Problems," *Shakespeare Studies* 10 (1977): 1–8. See also the introduction to the Arden Shakespeare edition of *Measure for Measure*, ed. J. W. Lever (London: Methuen, 1965).

73. See also the exchange when Pompey is freed from prison to become hangman:

Provost: Come hither, sirrah; can you cut off a man's head?
Pompey: If the man be a bachelor, sir, I can; but if he be a married man,
he's his wife's head, and I can never cut off a woman's head.
Provost: Come sir, leave me your snatches.
[4.2.1–5]

not, that ye be not judged")[74] and the parable of the candle,[75] underlying the Duke's opening sermon to Angelo:

> Heaven doth with us as we with torches do,
> Not light them for themselves; for if our virtues
> Did not go forth of us, 'twere all alike
> As if we had them not. Spirits are not finely touch'd
> But to fine issues. . . .
>
>   [1.1.32–36]

In both Mark and Luke, these passages appear near the story about another punitive woman, Princess Herodias, who orders John the Baptist beheaded. And we can hear echoes of still another "bloody" biblical passage in the Duke's words to Angelo.[76] This is the story of the "woman with an issue of blood," who came up secretly behind Jesus to touch his garment because she believed it would make her whole; and Jesus knew she was there because "he felt the virtue go out of him." The Duke of course makes the "issue" of virtue positive, but its going forth echoes Jesus' loss when the unclean woman's touch made the virtue go out of him. *Issue* in Shakespeare nearly always refers to blood and sometimes to offspring. Here, where the Duke means something more abstract, both of these meanings lurk in the background. This is part of the violent sexual fantasy; this is the issue feared in

74. "Judge not, that ye be not judged. For with what judgment ye judge, ye shall be judged: and with what measure ye mete, it shall be measured to you again" (Matthew 7:1; see also Luke 6:36–38).

75. "No man, when he hath lighted a candle, covereth it with a vessel, or putteth it under a bed; but setteth it on a candlestick, that they which enter in may see the light. For nothing is secret, that shall not be made manifest; neither anything hid, that shall not be known abroad" (Luke 8:16–17; see also Mark 4:21–25 and Matthew 5:15).

76. Matthew 9:20; Mark 5:25–34; Luke 8:43–48. Sir Walter Whiter first printed out this allusion (*A Specimen Commentary on Shakespeare* [1794; reprint ed., London: Methuen, 1967], pp. 203–04), and although it has been questioned (e.g., by the Arden edition editor) as the sole determining force in the passage, its contribution is elsewhere examined with interest (e.g., by Kenneth Muir in his *Shakespeare's Sources* [London: Methuen, 1957]).

creating issue: bloody on the woman's side, depleting on the man's. This is what comes from "the dribbling dart of love" (3.3.2), the form by which the Duke scorns love—a form entirely different from "Cupid's rich golden shaft," which Orsino dreams about in *Twelfth Night*, or from "Cupid's butt-shaft," as Armado calls it in *Love's Labour's Lost*. Such associations are latent in the raw material behind the play.

It is precisely when this deadly side of sexuality manifests itself that the Duke loses control of the action. The Duke, the man who counseled Claudio to "be absolute for death" and then with irritation went off to persuade Claudio's substitute Barnardine "willingly to die," cannot handle death. Like the thirteenth fairy in "Sleeping Beauty," or like the disguises of a repressive consciousness, he can displace the curse even though he cannot eliminate it—so long as the curse is merely sexual. He can prevent Angelo's sexual crime from having bad ends by displacing it to Mariana, turning the criminal fantasy into lawful marriage; but the beheading is harder to displace. What escapes the Duke's neat "web" is the way sex moves to death; the bed-trick necessitates a head-trick when Angelo orders Claudio killed anyway. The process of finding a scapegoat for the boy who was intended by Angelo to serve as scapegoat for the whole corrupt city is not as smooth as the Duke would like it to be. The Duke, still in his disguise, is forced to show his hand when the Provost refuses to substitute heads until the Duke / Friar brings a letter from the "absent" Duke: "Here is the hand and seal of the Duke; you know the character, I doubt not, and the signet is not strange to you" [4.2.191–93].

Even then, once the Provost agrees, Barnardine himself refuses the role, and a scapegoat for the scapegoat must be found. There is no displacing death; the Duke is powerless to create a symbol for Claudio's death by his own authority alone. What saves the whole structure is something that comes from outside the Duke's closed system altogether—the head of Ragozine the pirate, dead of natural causes ("O, 'tis an accident that heaven provides!" [4.3.77]): not a symbol, but death itself—a given.

The Duke's powerlessness here is indeed sign of a general inadequacy in his manipulations; its exposure is Shakespeare's counterpart to the Duke's education of Angelo. (Angelo has once refused to bed a fiancée, and when he takes another woman, he discovers that it is his fiancée after all, come to claim her rights. Similarly, the Duke has refused to sentence Barnardine during the old order, and later when he needs someone beheaded, it turns out to be Barnardine come to claim his due. Both men must face the responsibilities they have avoided in the past.) But surely the Duke's powerlessness also comes out of his more specific failure to come to terms with the underlying sexual ambiguity and this general inadequacy. The Duke, who thinks that he knows himself and that he has a "complete bosom," needs to have Lucio throw back his friar's cowl disguise to make sure that he does after all have his own head on his shoulders (and that the rest of his anatomy is intact?). He also needs to admit that he possesses an incomplete bosom after all, with all the vulnerability which that implies, when he proposes to Isabella.

I have suggested that *Measure* is a play about order that challenges the attempt to find order or establish absolutes—even absolutes like "mercy." What it substitutes instead is a human context of mutuality in which the process of working together to find or invent authority is as important as the lost absolutes themselves, whether they be ducal seals or sentimental abstractions. The primary subject of the play, I would suggest, is the difficulty of growing up—the problem of learning how to move away from self to other; from adolescent ideal to adult, compromised human realities; from a "life removed" without issue to some more fruitful exchange. It is about the problem of moving from the realm of fantasy to the social realm of language, a realm disciplined not so much by the hard realities of fact as by the hard realities of the way *others* see facts—their schemata, their conventions, even their fearful fantasies.

What then does the analyst add when he points to the sexual fantasy hovering behind the action? Having shown how

Angelo sees through Claudio's summary of the action, how the Duke sees through Angelo's summary, and how the audience sees through the Duke's version, the analyst then adds one more turn of the screw by suggesting that even the primary subject which an educated audience sees in the play depends ambiguously on other grounds. It depends on sexual grounds. In one sense, of course, this is a play about sex that is *not* about sex. We would all feel cheated if we felt that Shakespeare were merely writing about sexual experience and not about something higher, more complex, and more psychologically interesting. Sex is only a symbol; the ancient law about chastity is itself a scapegoat, a mere example of law in general. The play, as I have suggested, is really about growing up. Nonetheless, the very action that curbs sexuality generates a cluster of latent sexual fantasies. Although these may never literally take over the plot, they are manifested, as we have seen, in the play's action and language, teasingly close to the actual content of the play.

But these fantaises do not always work in the same way, and it is the switch in their role that is one of the most powerful factors in the last scene of the play. In the near-tragic world at the beginning of the action the fantasy is all but literally true, but by the time we reach the comic ending, it is subdued, inaccurate, denied, and even replaced by a countering fantasy. In the opening scenes, the fantasy's bloody expectations have found a way to infiltrate Vienna. Not only does it come through in the links we have seen between sex and death, but it determines that Claudio must die—or must be "cut off," as Angelo says. Claudio is "condemned by Angelo upon the act of fornication to lose his head"—condemned, that is, not only by Angelo the character but by Angelo the representation of the Duke's dark fantasies—in other words, by a point of view that sees sex as deadly.

So long as this view holds, the fornicator of course must die. Although this is not necessarily "his" view (I do not want to raise questions about either the Duke's or Angelo's unconscious thoughts), Angelo, the Duke's deputy in the play, is a walking representative of this view, and his resultant behavior is one of the weak spots that has made Vienna vulnerable to the fantasy's power. Angelo treats women precisely as women treat men in the fantasy. He couples only for selfish reasons; he is twice guilty of "promise breach" in the exchange; and so long as he is in power, he has no scruples. No wonder that he should fear what the woman would do if she ever got power over him.

As soon as this view is countered, however, the fornicator may live; Claudio may return to life. And in that last awkward, unrealistic scene, where rational explanations fail and supernatural explanations ring false, the fantasy *is* countered when Mariana and Isabella beg for Angelo's life. Of course the women's petition changes everything on the manifest level, too, but there it is a gratuitous gesture, something new in the world of the play. On the latent level their action is not only a good act but a direct denial of the fantasied bad act; it exactly undoes the threat's potential in Viennese sexuality at the beginning of the play.

The new version of the fantasy shows that sex and death are *not* the same. The image of the fatal female prison is replaced by the image of Mariana in her mysterious enclosed garden. She may have trapped Angelo into marriage there, but what matters is that she now releases him from the trap of death. In spite of everything, she still wants him—and wants him alive. Angelo is "safe." Instead of a woman who cuts him off, we find one who saves him unconditionally: in her two manifestations as Isabella and Mariana she forgives him *both* for raping her and for running from her. This turnabout forces everyone to recognize the distinction between marriage and death; only the unregenerate Lucio continues to combine them, as he goes offstage squawking at his sentence to marry Kate Keepdown: "Marrying a punk, my lord, is pressing to death, whipping, and hanging" (5.1.522–23).

The sudden change is attractive. But it is not easy to undo a powerful—and in its own way perversely attractive—fantasy. Such welcome and unwelcome things at once are hard to reconcile, as a character in *Macbeth* says when he learns that Malcolm, the Crown Prince, had been lying about his own criminal bent.

This play about sex that is not about sex, then, is about sex after all. As the fantasy flickers in and out of the surface action, we shift from fornication as a literal act to fornication as a symbol for something more important, and then back to a new version of the literal act. The uncertainties produced when sex becomes a symbol for sex are extensions of the uncertainties we examined earlier, and they are part of what the play is about. The biblical parable of the candle is the ostensible starting point for this play which purports to deal with the problems of virtue, but the parable of the candle is not *only* a parable about virtue. In Luke, at least, it is also a parable about parables; it is about how to disseminate not only our goodness but also our good news. And both are problematic.

The characters may not realize how thoroughly the moral— and especially the epistemological—foundations of their world have been shaken. But we do. My point in invoking a psychoanalytic reading is to suggest that the foundations for our world are a little cracked as well, though we may be too blinded by habit and convention to notice.

There is one last group of literary critics, who defend the Duke. These critics, not yet mentioned, try to save the play by invoking conventions whose rules would ostensibly explain away my objections to the action of the play. Thus, for example, they invoke the historical conventions the reader needs to know, before he can react properly to the seeming identity between Claudio's "crime" and Angelo's punishment. An Elizabethan audience would realize, the argument goes, that Claudio was bound to Juliet by a *de praesenti* contract and that Angelo was bound to Mariana by a *de futuro* contract, which legally became a marriage contract if the parties consummated the relationship.[77] The difference between the two, ap-

77. Ernest Schanzer, "The Marriage Contracts in *Measure for Measure*,"

parently, lies in whether the partners say "I take thee" or "I will take thee." Such precision, however, is worthy of Angelo himself, and if it is the only explanation we can find, surely we are worse off than before. Or more interestingly, some critics invoke not historical but literary and dramatic conventions. We may suspect the Duke's motivations if we see him as a real person, but once we realize that he is the traditional Disguised Ruler we can see his shady manipulations as motivated by the genre to which his type belongs. Similarly, we moderns may be offended by the kiss of a Substitute Bed Mate, but Elizabethans treated such substitutions like folktale episodes, not to be judged in moral psychological terms.[78]

Nonetheless, as the most recent scholarship suggests, Shakespeare turned the bed-trick with a difference and did everything he could to provoke "inappropriate" and "modern" responses. There is simply no indication that his audience felt any easier than we do about Mariana's fate.[79] There is no

Shakespeare Survey 13 (1960):81–89; see also the Arden edition, Introduction to Measure for Measure, pp. 13–22.

78. These conventions are invoked especially by W. W. Lawrence in Shakespeare's Problem Comedies (New York: Macmillan, 1931). See also Mark Van Doren, Shakespeare; E. M. W. Tillyard, Shakespeare's Problem Plays (London: Chatto and Windus, 1950); and Ernest Schanzer, The Problem Plays of Shakespeare (London: Routledge and Kegan Paul, 1963).

79. See G. K. Hunter, "Italian Tragicomedy on the English Stage," Renaissance Drama n.s.6 (1973): 123–48. Rosalind Miles, in her historical investigation The Problem of Measure for Measure (London: Vision, 1976), finds that "Isabella displays virtually no correspondence with other characters of the drama of the period" (p. 266). However, see Joycelin Powell's essay "Theatrical 'trompe l'oeil' in Measure for Measure," in Shakespearean Comedy, ed. D. J. Palmer and Malcolm Bradbury, Stratford-upon-Avon Studies 14 (New York: Crane, Russak, 1972), pp. 181–209. This is the most sensitive and convincing defense of the awkwardness in Measure for Measure that I know of; in the process of arguing his case, Powell refers to the timeless generic conventions of drama (rather than to specific historical conventions). This focus allows audiences to see the "awkwardnesses" in the play as "natural" representations of human experience, because of the nature of dramatic presentation: according to Powell, the play sounds odd if we read it, but not if we see it performed. Fine as Powell's interpretation is, it nonetheless requires more contributions from critic and audience than from the play itself. It requires too

disputing the fact that conventions remain as separate from the experience in the rest of the play as Isabella's convent remains separate from it. No amount of scholarship can explain away the fact that, for whatever reason, the second half of the play presents experience in a different way; people no longer matter so much as individuals. Nor can we ignore the fact that, whatever our intellectual, competently conventional interpretation of the ending, we were able to get along fine without conventions earlier in the play; and the effort to invoke them in the second half of the play simply does not feel right. Shakespeare plays the conventions against one another as he forces us to switch them, and he thereby calls attention to them, instead of letting us comfortably take them for granted.

Our uncertainty about foundations begins as soon as we begin to question the conventional ground rules. To feel it requires no more than a slight reorganization of the things we hear and see. It requires only an ear for puns (head / head) or for cultural allusions ("issue of blood" in "finer issues"); or an eye for shifty literary conventions (which smoothly substitute a Mariana for an Isabella and, even worse, substitute an automatic intellectual response for our more spontaneous emotional response to the bed-trick). This uncertainty requires no more than a slight change in perspective (as when villain becomes martyr-hero) and a willingness to move from the sublime to the ridiculous and back again. Thus Mariana, veiled, speaks in riddles, saying that she is neither wife nor maid nor widow, and Lucio decides she is a "punk": for him the mysterious virgin birth (Mary was, strictly speaking, neither wife nor maid) is an all too common south bank reality in London's brothels.[80] This is the kind of ambiguity—like the ambiguity in the analyst's office—in which miracles are mistaken for dirty jokes, because they are indeed like the maid Lucio de-

much translation on our part in order to get from the play to its meaning; Powell provides a brilliant defense of the play's subject, but not of its method.

80. See Hunter, "Italian Tragicomedy," p. 148.

scribed, so "tickle on their shoulders" that they can be stood on their head at any moment. But as in the analyst's office, where mutual reorganizations rather than divine revelations are the cure, it is only out of such radical doubt that a new kind of certainty can develop, a certainty based on human exchanges rather than on absolute truths.

7

Critic as Psychoanalyst and Psychoanalyst as Critic: Some Conclusions

What, then, can the critic learn from the psychoanalyst? The discussion of these models should have suggested, I think, that to a degree critic and analyst are doing the same things already, although they may not see it that way. Naturally there are similarities: psychoanalysis and criticism are both interpretive arts that have come of age during the same century and have been influenced by the same intellectual currents; they have gone through similar stages on their way to their current positions. The analyst began by simply asking his patients for a report of what really happened, and as I have suggested, he worked out the several models for interpretation in the process of becoming increasingly interested in *other* aspects of what the patient was saying. This drift away from the "referential fallacy" and simple mimetic concerns has characterized literary criticism as well; and there is an intriguing if imperfect parallel between the sequence of psychoanalytic models described here and the critic's movement away from realistic character analysis, first to an examination of mythic structures, later to the study of modes of representation in nonmimetic texts like emblems and allegories, and finally, today, to an examination of the rhetorical context and functions implied by a text. Even the analyst's latest focus, on the psychoanalytic process as a self-conscious end in itself, has its parallel in the critic's recent self-consciousness about the act of interpretive reading.

Even more obvious to the critics and analysts themselves are the similarities that have developed because the two have gradually begun to adopt popular versions of one anothers' techniques and terminology, sometimes purposefully and sometimes almost without noticing that they have done so. A context of literary interpretation has nudged psychoanalysis toward the humane disciplines and away from Freud's admired physical models ever since Freud cast his first case histories in the form of short stories; and analysts have benefited as critics have perfected techniques of close reading and have refined their understanding of narrative structures. Similarly, popular versions of psychoanalytic techniques are now common property of all interpreters, and it is standard procedure for a critic to mention fantasies or acknowledge the punning wit of the unconscious in a text, if only to dismiss them. Gestures toward psychoanalysis are also nearly inevitable in current biographies.

Nonetheless, no matter how close their parallel paths, critic and analyst have seldom met with much mutual satisfaction. Although the real similarities between the two fields have made them especially promising resources for one another, the superficial familiarity is misleading and has served more to keep them apart than to bring them together. Familiarity, if it has not bred actual contempt, has certainly dampened curiosity and encouraged complacency. The critic and the analyst both seem to feel that they understand what each other does and can do it better—at least for their own purposes. Freud was not the last analyst to classify the artist's contribution to fantasy as an admirable but irrelevant "aesthetic bonus"; and critics often admit the presence of fantasy in a text only so that they can get beyond it to more important things. To the degree that the real difference between analyst and critic has been recognized, the critic finds most of the analyst's insights beside the point. The critic trying to get to the center of a work has little use for the analyst working in the margins or on the other side of the page. What I have tried to suggest in the preceding chapters is that on the contrary, the analyst's work can indeed be both different and relevant, provided that it is not taken as a substitute for the critic's investigations but rather as a separate investigation that can supplement the critic's work in various ways.

Before going on to review these here, though, I should stress that the analyst's primary contribution is much less a matter of new psychoanalytic meanings than it is a bias or a set of expectations about meaning. This is the bias Freud prescribed when he told analysts to listen to *everything* the patient said with the same evenly hovering attention. Though such a bias gives analysis many things in common with other kinds of interpretation, nonetheless the differences are significant. First of all analysis goes further. It is simply less discriminating, at least at first. The analytic stance fosters openness and encourages the reader (just as it literally gives the patient courage) to look at details that have not traditionally been given a role in interpretation—not only those details which are too embarrassing but also those that have seemed too obvious to deserve attention or too trivial to bear the weight of interpretation.

Partly as a result of this openness, the analyst is particularly sensitive to the presence of primitive material and structures that the critic is less likely to see or find of interest. By primitive, I mean on the one hand that the material is shaped by primitive drives and conflicts rather than by cooler and more objective aims, and on the other that it has primitive form. The analyst is alert to the ways in which a text may serve a wishful, subjective function as well as an objective one; to the ways in which the text's mode of representation may work in a private and illogical fashion as well as in a public and logical fashion; to the ways in which a text's rhetorical function may be something other than objective, public communication; and to the way in which even the most sophisticated and self-conscious interpretive act has its own primitive dimensions and has roots in infantile curiosity, physical penetrations, and fantasies of omniscience. In other words, the analyst reminds us that there is always more in a text than we normally see, and much that would surprise us. These unnoticed elements are not unconscious secrets but merely the details and patterns that become available only if we are willing to be flexible in the sort of consciousness we bring to bear on texts. The analytic stance gives the critic more to work with, even if he decides not to use everything it enables him to see.

Once the analytic stance has revealed the primitive material in the text, the awareness of its presence can be extremely helpful to the critic, so long as he does not use it reductively. It can explain and unify otherwise disparate details in a text or point out new connections between a group of texts. But even more important, once the primitive material is identified the very effort to define its limited role and to distinguish between the whole text and, for example, the fantasy embodied in it, can help the critic understand the way literature works. In literature the fantasy is never presented nakedly but is seen in the light of sophisticated, adult ways of thinking; and it is the interplay between surface sophistication and primitive fantasy that matters. *Oedipus Rex* is in part, as Freud said, "the imagination's reaction" to oedipal fantasies; and there is much to be learned about the quality of the literary imagination from comparing its reactions to the stereotyped and desperately conventional ones that conceal the fantasies in daydreams or produce rationalized facades for dreams.

Ultimately, however, psychoanalysis provides not only a tool for practical criticism but also a basis for understanding how literature works. The strategies employed in the psychoanalytic process reveal more than the secret meaning of one patient's symptoms. They provide the techniques, the categories, and the vocabulary for examining the conditions of meaning and for studying the way we make sense of things—or fail to do so. The psychoanalytic process begins to show what happens when we create a fantasy or a memory, or tell a story. Up to now, analysis has been most useful in simply pointing out that creativity has primitive dimensions. Analysts have investigated the fantasies that accompany the creative act and transform it into a joyous oral merger with the world or into an act of restitution after a fit of infantile, world-destroying rage. More recently and more provocatively, they have begun to understand the more general conditions for creativity and have begun to describe the "transitional" space that characterizes the infant's first creative acts, in which no clear distinction is made between fantasy and reality or between self and other. But in addition to helping us understand the primitive sources for such experience, psychoanalysis can provide a model for the more sophisticated aspects of experience as well, in the play of insight during the psychoanalytic process. In fact, psychoanalysis may ultimately have more to contribute on this general level than on the level of interpreting individual texts, just as structuralism may, as Jonathan Culler has suggested, be more useful as a poetics than as a way of finding new meanings in old texts. We are yet a long way from this general understanding, and we can come closer to it—and to the individual insights psychoanalysis can afford—only if critic and analyst each understand—really understand—what the other is doing.

Index